SIR HALLEY STEWART TRUST: PUBLICATIONS

Volume 5

BETWEEN
GOD AND HISTORY

BETWEEN GOD AND HISTORY

The Human Situation Exemplified in Quaker Thought and Practice

RICHARD K. ULLMANN

LONDON AND NEW YORK

First published in 1959 by George Allen & Unwin, Ltd.
This edition first published in 2025
by Routledge
4 Park Square, Milton Park, Abingdon, Oxon OX14 4RN
and by Routledge
605 Third Avenue, New York, NY 10158

Routledge is an imprint of the Taylor & Francis Group, an informa business

© 1959 George Allen & Unwin Ltd.

All rights reserved. No part of this book may be reprinted or reproduced or utilised in any form or by any electronic, mechanical, or other means, now known or hereafter invented, including photocopying and recording, or in any information storage or retrieval system, without permission in writing from the publishers.

Trademark notice: Product or corporate names may be trademarks or registered trademarks, and are used only for identification and explanation without intent to infringe.

British Library Cataloguing in Publication Data
A catalogue record for this book is available from the British Library

ISBN: 978-1-032-88962-7 (Set)
ISBN: 978-1-032-88214-7 (Volume 5) (hbk)
ISBN: 978-1-032-88434-9 (Volume 5) (pbk)
ISBN: 978-1-003-53773-1 (Volume 5) (ebk)

DOI: 10.4324/9781003537731

Publisher's Note
The publisher has gone to great lengths to ensure the quality of this reprint but points out that some imperfections in the original copies may be apparent.

Disclaimer
The publisher has made every effort to trace copyright holders and would welcome correspondence from those they have been unable to trace.

This book is a re-issue originally published in 1959. The language used and views portrayed are a reflection of its era and no offence is meant by the Publishers to any reader by this re-publication.

RICHARD K. ULLMANN

BETWEEN GOD AND HISTORY

THE HUMAN SITUATION EXEMPLIFIED
IN QUAKER THOUGHT AND PRACTICE

Ruskin House
GEORGE ALLEN & UNWIN LTD
MUSEUM STREET LONDON

First published 1959

This book is copyright under the Berne Convention. Apart from any fair dealing for the purpose of private study, research, criticism or review, as permitted under the Copyright Act, 1956, no portion may be reproduced by any process without written permission. Enquiry should be made to the publisher.

© *George Allen & Unwin Ltd. 1959*

*Printed in Great Britain
in 11 on 12 Pilgrim type
by
East Midland Printing Company Limited
Bury St. Edmunds, Peterborough, Kettering
and elsewhere*

TO WOODBROOKE

PREFACE

This book was planned as a second contribution towards critique and apologetics of Quakerism, the first being a booklet called *Friends and Truth* which was published by the Friends Home Service Committee, London, 1956. While the author has not lost sight of his original intention, the scope of the book has widened in the writing. It is hoped that it will make a contribution, from the Quaker point of view, to the study of the predicament of Western man.

The author is deeply indebted to his friends and colleagues of Woodbrooke College, Birmingham, especially to the Director of Studies, Maurice A. Creasey, who read the whole typescript and offered most valuable advice throughout, and to L. Hugh Doncaster, who has checked especially the chapters three and four on Quakerism. Edward H. Milligan, Librarian of the Society of Friends in Friends House, London, has had the great kindness of reading the proofs. The responsibility for the whole and all details, however, rests exclusively with the author.

I have to thank the Sir Halley Stewart Trustees for their generosity in making the publication of this book possible, and the Publishers for having ensured this valuable assistance.

R.K.U.

February, 1959

CONTENTS

PREFACE 7

PART ONE

IN THE WORLD AND OF THE WORLD

1. Man in Suspense 13
2. World and Time After Christ 24
3. The Quaker Attitude to History 42
4. The Quaker Attitude in History 71

PART TWO

DOING THE WILL OF GOD

5. Outline of the Main Argument 99
6. God's Will for Man 104
7. The Conditions of Action (I):
   Action Between Intention and Result 130
8. The Conditions of Action (II): Involvement 161
9. God Through History 193

INDEX 206

ABBREVIATIONS

Journal: The Journal of George Fox edited by John L. Nickalls (Cambridge University Press, 1952).

B.Q.: The Beginnings of Quakerism by William C. Braithwaite (London: Macmillan and Co. Ltd., 1912).

S.P.Q.: The Second Period of Quakerism by William C. Braithwaite (London: Macmillan and Co. Ltd., 1921).

L.P.Q.: The Later Periods of Quakerism by Rufus M. Jones (London: Macmillan and Co. Ltd., 1921).

Q.A.C. The Quakers in the American Colonies by Rufus M. Jones and Others (London: Macmillan and Co. Ltd., 1923).

Q.P.W. The Quakers in Peace and War by M. E. Hirst (London: The Swarthmore Press Ltd., 1923).

F.Q.: Friends' Quarterly

PART I

IN THE WORLD AND
OF THE WORLD

I

MAN IN SUSPENSE

Limitations of the Dialectical Method
There are many ways of circumscribing the human situation which has been specified here as that 'between God and history'. We could instead speak of trying to be 'in the world but not of the world', of having 'no abiding city' but hoping 'for that which is to come', of belonging to nature as 'body' but to God as 'soul', and so on. In whatever way we express it, the fundamental human experience underlying such descriptions is that of an ambiguity, a tension, a suspense. The materialist, so called because he thinks that he is exclusively concerned with the material foundations of reality, and even the cynic who denies all values, material ones as well as non-material ones, can all the same not help being in suspense between making their rational judgments on the world on the one hand, and harbouring sub-conscious or semi-conscious aspirations of altering it, if only for their own convenience, on the other.

This tension in our human situation is not parallel with, or due to, an actual division of man into different components such as mind and matter. As Gabriel Marcel has shown most clearly among modern thinkers: I am not divided into body and soul, flesh and spirit, I am a person who not only *has* my body but also *is* my body, and whose body has and is *me*. If the materialist derives everything from the physical aspects of life, the spiritualist is no less one-sided if he neglects the physical side of creation. Body, or flesh, is created by God as really as mind or spirit. It is, in Johannine terms, the very flesh or *carnis* of the incarnation, while in Pauline terms 'flesh' seems to indicate not a regrettable physical fact, as later interpreters would have it, but rather the negative pole of an inner tension, hence something at least as spiritual as physical. We cannot think or speak of tension without visualizing and naming some poles; but when doing so, the real thing is the tension felt, which exists not so much *between* two poles as *within* one person. Exactly so I am one incarnate being, an ego embodied, but in this oneness I am a multiple unit, according to the aspects which I happen to regard as relevant at any particular moment.

For centuries past Western thinking, strongly influenced by Greek philosophy, has been based on an often very radical division of man into compartments. Philosophical Idealism, especially since Descartes, is more responsible for this unnatural partition than Materialism which reacted against it. This partition, however, has been given up as meaningless by some recent schools of thought, together with other things which they declare meaningless because they are too logical to understand anything greater than logic, and too positive to understand anything deeper than positivism. In this particular case, however, they have, much against their intentions, restored to us the freedom of returning to the Hebrew and early Christian concept of the inherent unity of man. Psycho-somatic medicine and the advance of spiritual healing symbolize this return to man's oneness. Theologically it used to be expressed in the phrase of the 'resurrection of the body', since body and soul were conceived as one unit, though body may have been understood as a transfigured body. In contrast to this formula, Greek and Hellenistic thought emphasized the 'immortality of the soul', a phrase which implies not only the separateness of body and soul, but which is prone to reduce the body to mere flesh in a derogatory sense, and to the source of all evil.

This is not the place for discussing in detail the implications of these two phrases.[1] All I want to stress from the outset is that the subsequent usage of words like body, flesh, soul, mind, spirit, or any other dialectical pair of words is due largely to the way of human thinking in contrasts and of expressing thought in conceptual language. Language acquires more lucid-

---

[1] Bultmann, among modern theologians, has given special attention to this problem in his *New Testament Theology*, I, 190 ff. (London: S.C.M. Press, 1952). Cf. Macquarrie, *An Existentialist Theology*, pp. 44 ff. (London: S.C.M. Press, 1956).

ity in contradistinctions while at the same time moving away from the reality it tries to describe. Of course, I do not wish to decry the different spheres or fields of reality, that is, their structural being in the whole of Being, but I wish to emphasize that they become dialectical and even antagonistic essentially through our human way of experiencing them, looking at them, thinking and speaking about them. Thus misled by our very capacity to think and to speak, we tend to treat concepts as though they were the real thing. This, I believe, is the weakness of all dialectics, philosophical and theological alike; not least of the present effort. It is in particular the besetting sin of neo-orthodox theology, which gives us many a fine analysis of the paradoxa of religious experience, but states them as though it described objective facts and the real, literal self-revelation of God. God's revelations, however, come to us only in the forms grasped and interpreted by men, be they Peter, Paul, John or any other inspired agent. Even if we admit that whatever the apostles say, Christ himself is God's 'objective revelation', his mighty act: the connection of Christ with the person of Jesus introduces human interpretations and opens the question whether and in what way this revelation can be of a kind different to any other witness that God has left of himself among the nations. There is no revelation without a human agent to whom it is revealed. All revelation is at the same time human experience, or it is not at all.

A fashionable phrase in neo-orthodox usage is 'God's yes and no' to man. It may be an adequate exposition of the Biblical texts (which, I repeat, are not God's own revelation but the human, if apostolic, interpretations and understandings of such revelation in the mysterious phenomenon, Jesus Christ). Certainly, the phrase of 'God's yes and no' is an excellent description of the experience of being rejected and yet accepted, unworthy and yet forgiven, a failure and yet somehow enabled to make good. That phrase, however, becomes presumptuous when it goes beyond the sphere of interpreted experience and claims to render in human language God's actual treatment of man, his divine saying of 'yes' and 'no' to us. 'Yes and no' is no real or objective dialectic, but merely a human expression of the human experience of suspense, of 'being-between'. It speaks, not of God, but of the human experience of God, analysed by thought and expressed in dialectical terms. It is, of course, very difficult to circumscribe any revelation without using dialectical terms: they just cannot be avoided; but it is *our* language and *our* concepts which are dialectical, not the divine-human situation, which in the last resort is inexpressible, being the nonsense of a dialectical oneness, an I-Thou relationship where I am in Christ and Christ is in me and yet Christ and I are two.

In the same way the division of God and history, used in the present study, is no actual antithesis. History is *God's* history, in the sense that God is revealed in and through it. But being the Lord of history, he is not confined in and by it. Man, on the other hand, is thus confined, and it is for this reason that history may appear to him the very antithesis to God. It is in his encounters with God Transcendent that he feels his bondage most strongly, but also in them that he feels release from it, though in fact he is never truly released this side of death.

The word 'history' is, then, used here to circumscribe man's contingency in time and place, his 'historicity'. Later in this study the word will occur also in the more usual sense, namely for the development of human affairs in time, the trend of events of which man is both subject and object. Only in so far as man is able to assess the trends of development and has a grasp of human affairs in time will he be able to respond creatively in and to his own situation. His historicity, therefore, includes an understanding of the past's leading up to the present, so that he can intervene constructively in the present towards the future.

Man is not always conscious of his historicity; and when conscious of it, he may either try to deny the existence of anything that is trans-historical, or, on the contrary, may yearn to leave history behind for the sake of the Trans-Historical. Neither, however, is possible, because man is inherently man-in-history, subject and object of events in time, and yet always trying to 'overstep history'[1] because though bound in history, he feels almost a stranger in it.

[1] Jaspers, *Origin and Goal of History*, 272 (London: Routledge & Kegan Paul Ltd., 1953).

At all times and in all civilizations human beings have thus felt estranged: estranged from the divine and eager to be reconciled; estranged from themselves and struggling for peace of mind; estranged from heritage and environment and trying to become re-adjusted to them, or to adjust them to man. True, man has, in his highest moments, the experience of his inherent oneness with God; he therefore knows about oneness in spite of all dialectics and, in his knowledge, never gives up yearning for it. But this yearning is itself a feeling of discrepancy between what *is* and what *ought* to be, between the actual and the possible, possible at least in thought and desire, however impossible in fact; it is a sense of fundamental dissatisfaction.

That discrepancy is not a division into components or compartments like that between flesh and spirit: it is rather like a separation of the whole unit, of body *and* mind *and* soul, from its ground and from its ultimate destiny. Such separation, however, feels like a crack within: it causes an inward pain like the separation from a loved one. We therefore experience separateness as division within ourselves, as discord, disharmony, dilemma, difficulty, division, dialectic. The prefix 'di', 'dis' and 'dia', words such as 'ambiguity', 'duplicity', 'doubt', and particularly the telling preposition 'be-tween', all referring to the numeral 'two', describe vividly the feeling of one person hanging between two poles: they express tension, predicament, suspense. These tensions are the reality of human existence, far more so than the poles which, while also reality, may be turned by man-in-suspense into abstract or emotional constructions to rationalize his experience of tension. It seemed right to specify here that suspense or tension as one between God and history since this book is engaged on the study of the historical in its religious and ethical aspects.

Man's Historicity

Our generation is inclined to think of tension and suspense as an essentially modern, even recent experience, little known in previous ages. However, when surveying the fears and superstitions of primitive societies and the artistic and philosophical utterances of more sophisticated ones, we find sufficient evidence for the fact that that experience is a basic element of human existence and is not due to the invention of *angst* by some extentialists. It would not be difficult to show that even the apparent equanimity of stoic and saint is achieved as a superstructure over a basic tension. The emphasis, however, and the forms of expression change from era to era and are, for us today, tied up with the situation of Western man in the mid-twentieth century.

Men live, at all times, with some desire for change, some urge for improvement, whatever this may mean in their individual day-dreams or in those of their societies. We may describe that desire as man's direction towards the future, and in so far as it may never become a presence, a direction even beyond the future. On the other hand, man's direction towards the future is impaired by the anxiety whether the future may not bring him loss rather than gain. At the end of his foreseeable future he knows, rationally for certain, that he will undergo an entirely unimaginable experience: dying. While in no way drawing the pessimistic conclusions which Heidegger has drawn from the fact that man is being-unto-death, I would still regard as exceptional, rather than normal, a state of mind which does not fear death at all, but even welcomes it wholeheartedly as the gate to paradise, or to nothingness. I cannot appreciate in the least the death-wish glorified by German romanticists, and probably overstressed by certain psychologists, but believe profoundly that life wants to live and, normally, to live on this side of the grave. Put in Christian terms: to lay down one's life seems to me a sacrifice rather than a 'gain';[1] otherwise it would lose all moral meaning and would become its own reward.

There is, then, in man an urge towards the future intermingled with anxiety about the future's uncertainties and the certainty of death. Hence the urge towards the future is held back by a clinging to the present and even a nostalgic bent towards the past. The relentless progress of time and the transitoriness of every phase of life and experience, stand in sharp contrast to man's calling out for 'the beautiful moment to abide' (Goethe) and to his seeking 'the snow of yesteryear' (Villon). This contrast is another experience of tension in man's existence. His desire for the past, however, is not

---

[1] *Philippians I*, 21.

directed towards the real past, for man's memory is a dangerous trickster: it forgets the ugliness of former times, or transforms it into grand adventures of which he is, if not the unconquerable hero, at least the successful survivor. In a similar way memory twists the beauty of past happiness into the sadness of sentimental reminiscing on what has been lost. The real past continues less in man's conscious memories which he holds as a possession than in that subconscious layer by which he is more possessed than he is possessing it.

This applies similarly to the memory of mankind, including historiography. If it is true that 'memory represents man's capacity to rise above, even while he is within, the temporary flux',[1] it is equally true that it reflects more faithfully the moment of remembering than the fact remembered, and allows only for a relative detachment from the temporal flux. The paradox that, on the one hand, we are aware of ourselves as being-in-history, but that, on the other, history is available to us only in our momentary memory and our momentary expectations and projects, underlines the paramouncy of the Now over the two other dimensions of time. Not only for spiritual experience but also for temporal judgment, the Now, the Present, the Instant, takes the centre of human existence.

Even where a man seems to be set altogether for change, that is, towards the future, the past is present in every situation: as his natural inheritance in body and mind, his acquired heritage of traditions and the succession of environments in which he has lived. Man, the product of the past in its manifold shapes, lives in the present towards the future: he is fully absorbed in the progress of time. This absorption, however, does not make him a mere object of events, nor does it deprive him of his freedom. He is not simply ruled by past and present towards a pre-ordained future, but reacts and responds—now —by action to past and present-just-past. He is both object and subject within time's progress: he is formed by events in time, but he also helps to form them by his decisions and his indecisions, and in forming them, forms himself. Man is in history, is conditioned by history, and creates, both for good and ill, new historical conditions by which he is then again con-

---

[1] Niebuhr, *Faith and History*, 20 (London: Nisbet & Co. Ltd., 1949).

ditioned.[1] His freedom is very real: it is not confined to the willy-nilly acceptance of inevitable conditions, as Determinism has it; his freedom lies in his creativeness, that is, his power of directing himself towards the future and thus to shape new conditions out of the inevitable ones which are given to him as working material. Indeed, he himself is given to himself as working material, in freedom to work it. The more creative his responsive decisions in the given conditions, for instance by selecting and re-shaping certain trends within the conditions and neglecting others, the greater his growth in selfhood and hence his power over the given conditions. This situation of being conditioned and yet a free agent is another experience of tension: man is suspended between the inescapable past and present, and the will for personal creative decisions made at present towards the future.

The Basis of All Philosophy of History[2]

Inescapably bound into the progress of time, we have no way of knowing, theoretically or scientifically, anything that is beyond time. All our human knowledge happens to us in world and time, and what seems to go beyond them, in moments of great spiritual experience, we do not know clearly but see as in a glass darkly. We have merely a feeling of something that transcends our grasp, that is, at the other side of 'knowledge' in the more common sense of the word. True, some will say that it is not there at all, that it is sheer wishful thinking and illusion. But how can a sound person deny the possibilities of the eternally unknowable?[3] From this logical necessity others will argue, often with some hidden truculence, that since we cannot know anything about the eternally unknowable, we should not bother about it. But the unknowable, the unimaginable, the transcendent is still there; its lure is inescapable, yet it always escapes us because it is outside world and time. Once

[1] Cf. Tillich, *The Protestant Era*, 183 (London: James Nisbet & Co. Ltd., 1957).
[2] For the following refer to Collingwood, *The Idea of History* (Oxford University Press, 1946), and Bultmann, *History and Eschatology* (Edinburgh University Press, 1957).
[3] Sartre's 'proof' that God cannot exist, is logically untenable. Cf. Copleston, *Contemporary Philosophy*, 211 ff. (London: Burns & Oates Ltd., 1956). The same applies to earlier attempts, especially Feuerbach's.

more we are in suspense, namely between the world in which the known or possibly knowable happens, and all that which transcends it and yet is its ground, its alpha and omega. That suspense is very real, however consistently some human intellects may wish to denigrate it as a 'universal obsessional neurosis' (Freud). In that suspense, world and time are envisaged as one pole; the other is somewhere in the indefinite, and we give it different names such as God, the Eternal, the Beyond, the Transcendent, the Absolute, Ultimate Reality, and so on. For him who accepts it in faith it gives, not indeed knowledge, but a certitude beyond all knowledge, the basis of all his being. He therefore proclaims it in the form of the most certain knowledge.

And yet, even such experience as seems to take a man completely away from world and time in mystical ecstasy, happens to that man in space and time, at least in the eyes of the beholder. It is still connected with an embodied ego which remembers and reports its experience, however inadequately and darkly, or just senses it vaguely at the off-side of thought. With this we touch our real difficulty when speaking about God as the Lord and Maker of history or, perhaps less concretely, about the anonymous Purpose inherent in history. This difficulty is two-fold:

(1) With regard to history we want to find some meaning which, however, we might see clearly only if we could take our position outside it. We then could look at history as though it were a concrete and definable object. Being inside, and not knowing beginning, middle and end, we have no real vantage point for our judgments.

(2) With regard to God we take up a position as though we could have knowledge of what in itself is not within world and time. But even our most direct experience of God, or at least our assessment of such experience, as his 'word' or his 'revelation', happens to us in time and hence is temporal, not eternal. And yet, the experience that the Divine outside and beyond history breaks into it, reaching from outside down to us who are in history, is the only vantage point we can assume if we are to find any meaning at all in history.[1]

[1] Cf. Dodd, *History and the Gospels*, 166 ff. (London: James Nisbet & Co. Ltd., 1938).

In short, without faith in the experience of, and the encounter with, the Transcendent, in the reality of what really transcends world and time, we have no possibility of discovering meaning in history. This assertion will be strongly denied by non-religious thinkers whose philosophy of history seems capable of dispensing with concepts such as faith and revelation, and even with all metaphysics. Whether they know it or not, they hold on to some, let us call it *'a priori'*, which does the trick for them. Whosoever finds meaning in life or history cannot but base it on certain 'assumptions'. They may seem to be thought out, or inducted by strictly scientific methods, but actually they appear in the personality of the thinker like Athena from the head of Zeus. They are signals of an underlying, though unadmitted faith. They result from a man's confrontation with the Transcendent which he may wish to deny because he cannot grasp it; indeed, that denial may become an 'obsessional neurosis' with him.

In this way, 'atheistic', 'scientific' Marxism lives by the faith in an inexorable goddess: History, who reveals herself in dialectics analysed by the priests and theologians of the Communist Party. Spengler's civilizations, it is true, are born by 'chance', whatever this may mean; but once they have been born, they are ruled by goddess Fate who reveals herself in the laws of all organic life: birth, adolescence, prime, senility and death. For the Christian all revelation of God is centred in Jesus Christ; he therefore finds the meaning of history in the incarnation, life, death, resurrection and second coming of Christ. The Old Testament Jews see God revealed in his covenants with his people; the meaning of history is found in man's obedience to God's covenanted law, and God's blessing as reward. For the scientific humanist the content of revelation lies in 'evolution'; consequently the meaning of history in human progress; the divinity behind this revelation is either not named or may be called Life Force, Inherent Purpose or some other abstract.

Where revelation is seen primarily in the mystical experience itself, history is likely to lose much of its meaning; for in this experience world and time are left behind as largely meaningless, all meaning being found in Ultimate Reality and Pure Being. Consequently this world of ours and its history become either unreal illusions of no value, and as such possibly evil, in the way Oriental mystics have mostly seen it; or this world consists only of transitory phenomena symbolizing eternal Being in divers forms and shapes, and history consists only in repetitive occurrences returning in eternal circles, as for instance Platonism propounds.

This relative meaninglessness of history has been the philosophy prevailing in most civilizations at most periods. Our modern quest for meaning, on the other hand, is part of the Judaeo-Christian heritage which has imparted itself to Western civilization and its different philosophies. Where in Western civilization only little importance is attributed to history, this is due either to Platonic and mystical influences, or to a radical cynicism which denies all meaning of life and universe and for which history is therefore nothing but trying 'to give meaning to the meaningless' (Th. Lessing), 'a tale told by an idiot, full of sound and fury, signifying nothing'.

We must realize, however, that the different philosophies of history mentioned, and others which could be adduced, are not clear cut and cleanly separated as they appear in this enumeration. In the New Testament, for instance, we find some fusion of Judaic, Platonic-Hellenistic and Christian elements. In Christian mysticism the Greek element has somewhat moved to the fore, in Puritanism the Judaic element has gained ground, and in the last two centuries scientific humanism has taken over many Christian strongholds. Quakerism, too, has appropriated aspects of several of these philosophies, a fact that may be behind some of the puzzles which our Quaker faith offers to ourselves and others.

2

WORLD AND TIME
AFTER CHRIST

Histories of Salvation

The Jews count their years from the creation of the world; the Egyptians and Chinese after dynasties and rulers; the Greeks from the first of their religious sports festivals, which were celebrated at Olympia every four years; the Romans from the foundation of their city; the Mohammedans from the flight of their prophet from Mecca to Medina; the Christians from the birth of Christ. This enumeration of usages, chosen quite haphazardly, shows that Christian reckoning is not the only one connected with a religious event in time. Indeed, if we look at the more decisive spiritual happenings in human history, much is to be said for speaking with Jaspers of 'the creative climacteric around 500 BC'[1] or of an 'axial period between 800 and 200 BC',[2] namely the period of Laotse and Confucius, the Upanishads and Buddha, Zarathustra, Amos, Hosea and Isaiah and the great Greek philosophers.

There is a different reason why Christ can be considered the pivotal event: Christianity seems the only religion in which the believer sees in the central event at the same time the most important incident *of* history and the clue *to* history itself, that is, history's one vantage point. Christ is for the believer more than an outstanding historic fact which divides the temporal flux, more than a tradition cherished through the ages, or a pious reminder to remain faithful as, for instance, the Exodus from Egypt for the Jews. True, Yahweh has confirmed the Exodus through his providential concern for his people and the nations of the world, revealing himself in ever

[1] *Reason and Anti-Reason in Our Time*, 30 (London: S.C.M. Press, 1952).
[2] *Origin and Goal of History*, passim.

new acts of justice and mercy. The messianic expectation of later Judaism—an expectation not unknown in Hellenistic and Oriental religions—goes still further and visualizes the eventual fulfilment of history, thus adumbrating the Christian idea of history as a 'history of salvation' (*Heilsgeschichte*). Christ, however, introduces an entirely new dimension in that in him there is not only beginning and end, but also the *middle* of history. He is a definite event of the past, and yet beyond all events; he is the historically vouched fulfilment of a primary promise of God, and yet himself a promise of another future. In this respect the Christian claim stands unique among historical religions.

This 'uniqueness', however, requires further consideration. All religions, even those which would not normally be called historical, such as the nature cults, are still historical in so far as they appear in history. Not all of them, however, are historical in that they enter history through a traceable founder like Jesus, Mohammed or Gautama, or that they have been clearly developed by a succession of great leaders like Moses and the Hebrew prophets. They may have grown through social custom; and not only priests and medicine-men, but also laymen and especially lay-women, may have added, probably without realizing it, to an edifice of beliefs which tries to express the awfulness of the Transcendent both in devotional grandeur and the rituals of superstition.

Again, not all historical religions are historical in that they direct part of their attention to 'temporal' matters such as political and social affairs and to all those aspects of life which, in common parlance, make the raw-material of historiography. Indeed, it may be argued that such this-worldliness is rather a feature of Judaism and Zoroastrianism than of Christianity. Not a few Christian theologians have held that Christ is little, or not at all, concerned for the affairs of this world, but takes us away from it and its political and social concerns, into a better world, so that time remains no more than an unpleasant transitory phase.

Such denigration of world and time does not necessarily exclude the recognition of Christ as the clue to history, but it limits the historic to its other-worldly aspects. In this reading the only history deserving that name is a world drama with a metaphysical plot: Adam, created in the image of God, is fallen, and with him all his kind. God intervenes by sending his son, the second Adam, who brings salvation to the believer of these facts and condemnation to the disbeliever. No aspects of the manifold happenings in time really matter apart from personal believing and disbelieving. Even the question how far personal faith should influence public affairs is not tackled with full earnestness because public action seems divorced from personal conduct like this world from the other, this aeon from the coming aeon.

I wonder, however, whether Christianity may, in this otherworldly interpretation, still claim uniqueness, and whether we were not moving the Christian plot close to the Buddhist 'history of salvation'. It is true, the plot of the Buddhist history of salvation is different; it is connected with Buddha's vow, prompted by pity, not to enter Nirvana himself before every other soul can enter with him. Buddha's concern is salvation *from* history rather than one *through* and *in* history. It is salvation from existence, not from sin.[1] Similarly the otherworldly interpretation of Christianity seems to describe a salvation *from* history and *from* time. This interpretation, however, is incompatible with the facts. The historical event called Christ cannot be taken out of history nor redeem us *from* it, because the act of redemption happened itself in history, 'under Pontius Pilate', through cross and resurrection. There is no continued waiting for Nirvana right to the end of time, but a quite definite series of events which as such are concluded and past. Hence Christianity, unlike Buddhism, does not tend towards the effacement, but towards the validation, of history.

This does not imply that every single event in time, every human action, is truly meaningful: meaningful are those events which happen at the ordained hour, in God's own good time, in moments of historic crisis, in the 'fulness of time', for which, since Paul Tillich, the Greek word *kairos* has been widely used.[2]

[1] Söderblom, *The Living God*, Chapter V, especially pp. 144 ff. and 159 ff. (London: Oxford University Press, Humphrey Milford, 1935). Cf. Kraemer, *Religion and the Christian Faith*, 85 (London: Lutterworth Press Ltd., 1956).
[2] *Kairos*, 1926. English translation in *The Interpretation of History* (New York: Charles Scribner's Sons, 1936).

I daresay that the Christian history of salvation, rightly understood, is unique in exactly this: that it follows Judaism in accepting time and world as the handiwork of the Creator and as the stage where man is called to act in response to his will, but that it adds to all this the fact that redemption has already happened in a clearly historical event.

True, the world is 'fallen', but God, caring for it in its fallenness, is not only the Alpha and the Omega, the world's end and beginning, but has also become its middle in Christ. The historicity of the fact of redemption marks an important difference between the Christian and the Zoroastrian history of salvation. According to the Avesta, world and time are not held together in the hand of God: eternity itself is already divided between Good Thought and Evil Thought. Outwardly the Zoroastrian plot has many features in common with Christianity and Judaism: man is called upon to join on earth the battle between Good Thought and Evil Thought; he will be rewarded according to the part he has chosen, either after death, or on judgment day when the good and the evil ones will be sorted out by molten metal. Ultimately, Evil Thought himself will be defeated. The Zoroastrian work of salvation is called *frashokereti* or 'working forward', an expression which indicates clearly that salvation has its history.[1] But here the likeness with Christianity ends. Zarathustra himself is called saviour (*saoshyant*), but he performs no unique saving act like Buddha or Christ; any other human being who joins the battle on the side of Good Thought is equally called a saviour and the final Saviour will be born, from Zarathustra's seed, only at the very end of time. This last feature comes close to the Messianic expectation of Judaism, and to all interpretations of Christianity which over-emphasize the futurity of the Kingdom at the end of time.

In a less futuristic interpretation of Christianity, salvation is an act of divine intervention in time and revealed as already accomplished, at least partially, in one decisive event: it will not only happen in the end, it has actually happened in the work of Christ 'under Pontius Pilate'. For this reason it is of both temporal (historical) and trans-temporal (metaphysical)

[1] Söderblom, *op. cit.* Chapter VI, 211 ff.

significance that we are now living in the Christian era, in the new aeon of which Jews and Greeks and Orientals had only dreamed; in the time between Christ's Ascension and his Second Coming; in the Kingdom of God which has already come with Christ, but which paradoxically is still to come; or according to Oscar Cullmann's reading,[1] in the Kingdom of *Christ* which is connected with time, and precedes the Kingdom of *God* which is beyond the end of time.

The Paradox of the Kingdom of God

It is exactly this paradox of the Kingdom which has already come and yet is still to come, which has opened the way to different interpretations of history. Some readers of the New Testament prefer to stress the futurity of the Kingdom as the end of history, as the 'last' or 'ultimate' events with which time ceases to be. This 'eschatological' interpretation[2] leads easily to a denigration of time and history, because these are important only as this-worldly events and make it possible for a 'temporal' *realpolitik* or business method to exist alongside, but apart from, the final Christian hope. In this reading, the world, though 'after Christ', is still fallen and, as some insist, completely depraved. Christ has realized the Kingdom only in and for himself; for the period after Christ he has inaugurated no more than its eventual possibility, revealing a promise which is warranted by the fact of his resurrection, but postponing its actual implementation until his second coming. While we can partake in eschatological expectations, we are still debarred from participating in the actual Kingdom inaugurated by Christ's resurrection. In the phrase of Reinhold Niebuhr, who re-interprets here a word of Albert Schweitzer's, we live now in an 'interim', 'between disclosure and fulfilment' of the meaning of history.[3] Only the meaning may become clear to us, but nothing of the fulfilment can be with us because, stricken by original sin, we destroy any fulfilment that may be close to us, through human self-aggrandisment and self-interest. Christian hope is therefore directed towards

[1] The Kingdom of Christ and the Church in the New Testament. In *The Early Church* (London: S.C.M. Press Ltd., 1956).
[2] From Greek *eschaton*, 'ultimate'.
[3] *Nature and Destiny of Man*, II, 50 ff. and 298 (London: James Nisbet & Co. Ltd., 1943).

the end of time, while there is little or no hope for the things *before* the 'last', the 'penultimate things',[1] for the interim 'after Christ' in which we live. Only rarely does Niebuhr recognize proximate possibilities in spite of limitation and corruption[2] however much he tries to re-introduce *relative* values within human affairs.

Generally speaking, in this reading of the New Testament there prevails a profound pessimism for all affairs in world and time, in spite of that ultimate Christian hope. Niebuhr is right in stressing that there is no fulfilment before and without judgment. But as the word says, judgment applies in both directions, not only in that of damnation but also in that of grace and fulfilment. Niebuhr, and the many theologians who share his view, have distorted the balance of Christian eschatology: the word 'judgment' is applied to the interim in the one-sided sense of condemnation instead of in that pictured in the story of the Last Judgment which knows also grace and fulfilment. Clearly, either both damnation and fulfiment (grace) can enter time, or neither can. If we are under judgment here and now, we are also in a world into which fulfilment can break, at least in some measure, and where the Holy Spirit can work miracles.

Oscar Cullmann[3] seems to come nearer the truth when comparing Christ's first and second comings with D-Day and V-Day; and John Marsh goes still further towards an optimistic eschatology when he compares our situation 'after Christ' to that of 'men in an occupied territory who, in spite of its having been liberated, live, for lack of news, or lack of belief in the news received, as though their country were still under the dominion of the occupying power.[4] The liberation is an accomplished fact in time.

With this we turn to the other emphasis in the teaching on the Kingdom of God, namely its potential realisation 'on earth as it is in heaven'. In this reading the Kingdom has, through the grace of God, entered history once for all and can, through

---

[1] Bonhoeffer, *Ethics*, 79 ff. (London: S.C.M. Press, 1955).
[2] For instance, *op. cit.*, 218/9.
[3] *Christ and Time* (London: S.C.M. Press, 1951).
[4] *The Fulness of Time*, 177/8 and 155/6 (London: Nisbet & Co. Ltd., 1952). Marsh's critical Appendix on Cullmann is important.

God's grace and his Holy Spirit, permeate history itself. Though originating from outside time, the Kingdom is already in time, it is 'within' or 'amongst' us or at least 'at hand', that is, available if we avail ourselves of it; it is, or at least may, become a temporal reality.

If this temporal reality is seen as material reality, if, in other words, the meaning of the word Kingdom (*basileia*) is shifted from the rule or *kingship* of God to that of God's *territory*, we must, with Niebuhr, call this a 'utopian' interpretation because it tends to reverse his distortion of balance and to over-weigh the other side of the scales. It tends to neglect the condemnation inherent in all human fulfilments and to put human fulfilments into the place of God's fulfilment; it overlooks the continued imperfections in all temporal perfection. Thus it leads again to a denigration of time and history, though from the opposite end. If the Kingdom is already realized, worldly affairs can either be completely neglected as has happened with chiliastic sects[1] whose faith led to social dissolution. Or else it awaits, and works for, the establishment of God's territorial Kingdom in time which is, as it were, only a matter of days or months: in this case all previous history has no value of its own but receives its worth exclusively from being the preparation for the coming of the Kingdom. This means that the most glorious temporal achievements and the most wonderful spiritual events of the past, apart from Christ himself, are devalued to stepping stones, as though they had not happened immediately under God.

On the other hand, the will towards greater perfection, towards the realization of the brotherhood of men under the fatherhood of God is, as hope, a valid hope: it is hope for Christ *in* the world, not only a hope for Christ at the end of the world. It believes in the potential redemption or transfiguration of all things that are under judgment, by the grace of God. The Kingdom of God is no futurity, but 'at hand'.

The paradox of the Kingdom which is come and yet to come is the most profound philosophy of history ever invented. The presence of the Kingdom validates every moment of time, puts every epoch into 'immediate relation to God' (Ranke)

---

[1] 'Chiliastic', believing in the Millenium.

and thus avoids its devaluation to a mere means to a futurist end. And yet, the Kingdom is still to come; and every moment of time, while a moment validated by the Presence, is also significant for the whole pattern and thus enjoys an inherent power of direction and purpose, though neither direction nor purpose are clearly apprehended. Every moment has significance both in itself and towards an end.

These two aspects of the paradox, when compared, seem to exclude each other logically, but they can be held and believed together by the same person. It depends largely on background, situation and temperament which of the two predominates in his mind and feeling at one moment or the other. The paradox of the Kingdom is one form in which Christian man expresses his awareness of being suspended between time and timelessness.

Meanings of Eternity

With the word timelessness we touch another term which may help to elucidate the paradox of the Kingdom which has already come and yet is still to come, namely the different meanings of 'eternity'. The more common understanding of 'eternity' is either 'immortality' or 'temporal infinity'. Immortality has, in the Christian world, adopted a strangely lopsided meaning: we would not easily speak of God as immortal, in the way the Greeks did of their gods. God is the eternal rather than immortal because not only can he not die but, unlike the Olympians, he was never born. Nowadays we connect this word with human individuality and its future after death, without giving much thought as to whether individuality may have existed before birth, a problem with which the Oriental teaching of the transmigration of the soul is much occupied. Immortality is, as the word says, eternity without a past, and thus not truly eternal. It is different from the meaning of temporal infinity or endlessly continued time which has always been and will always be.

Eternity, however, can denote a dimension quite different from time plus time plus time *ad infinitum*, namely a realm completely outside, above and beyond time. It then has no past or future at all, no 'as it was in the beginning, is now and ever shall be'. If understood in this way, eternity may mean one of two things which are easily confused: it can be either 'timelessness', or 'continuous or continually available presence'.

Timelessness, being altogether outside time, is a characteristic feature of the Platonic Ideas: they are unchangeable, static and fixed in a heavenly place, as 'eternal' prototypes. Many religious concepts, even God, have been changed by human thought into nothing more than eternal and immovable Ideas: Goodness, Love, Beauty, Truth. The root of the Quaker aversion to notions lies in the fear of comprehending unchangeable Ideas instead of meeting with the living God. This fear is also, in the interpretation of Jaspers, the profound meaning of the second commandment, which forbids fixations, that is static images of God.

'Continuous presence', on the other hand, describes eternity which is that from beyond time breaking into every passing moment of time and thus validating it beyond any value it may acquire as part of the temporal flux. Presence has here no truly temporal, but an existential meaning, that is, a meaning connected with live experience of God and actual encounter with him.

The New Testament writers, and many Christian thinkers ever since, have struggled with the task of putting religious insights into our temporal and spatial terms. For instance, we use, when speaking of the Kingdom, the adverbs 'now' and 'then' to indicate, not 'now' and 'then', but 'earth' and 'heaven'; or vice-versa, we use 'here' and 'beyond' to indicate 'time' and 'eternity'. The Christian saints, thus vacillating between temporal and spatial terms, did not perchance anticipate imaginatively the continuum of the modern physicist, his space-time universe! All they tried was to move outside those four dimensions which could not contain their experience. They seem to waver between temporal and spatial language because they feel the limitations of both. Spatial terms may lose the dynamic actuality of experience and lead to the creation of static dogmatism; temporal terms may lose the dynamic actuality of experience to some event of the past of which only empty tradition is retained, or to some other-worldly futurity which may be wishful thinking without present experience. The very word 'presence' uniting temporal and spatial associations, may still be misunderstood or misused for a static (Platonic) eternity.

Nor am I sure that Berdyaev has been more successful with his brilliant attempt at distinguishing three kinds of time: cosmic, historical, and existential time. On this distinction he erects his own utopia: man's divine creativity will bring about a complete change of structure of his consciousness, away from objectification in historical time and towards existential subjectivity. This change of human consciousness (or what I would prefer to call this transfiguration of man) will, according to Berdyaev, inaugurate 'meta-history' in which the Kingdom of God will be a *real* Kingdom.[1]

What Berdyaev and what, with different words, the writers of the New Testament try to convey, are man's dynamic experiences of God. As such they escape of necessity the spatiotemporal formulation of human language. The derivation of manifold dogmas from merely tentative and approximate linguistic utterances could not but lead to error and division. The mere ambiguity of 'kingdom' as 'reign' and as 'realm', and the varied meanings of reign (rule), open endless possibilities for interpretation and misunderstanding. If, however, the words of the New Testament are taken less as communication of objective contents and more as expression of spiritual experience, a phrase such as 'life eternal' may have neither a temporal nor a trans-temporal meaning, but may hint at a different quality of living, namely living the 'more abundant life'. It may indicate the capacity of living in eternity, or better, in the presence of eternity, while still alive in time, and without much reference to the situation after individual death or at the end of history. This 'eternal life in time' may come close to the meaning formulated by C. H. Dodd as 'realized eschatology'. It emphasizes the quality of a life in God, and vice-versa, of God's entering history in a human life, as he had entered it in Jesus Christ.

The decisive aspect of 'the more abundant life' is that it is

[1] *Slavery and Freedom*, concluding chapter (London: Geoffrey Bles Ltd., 1943). The use of 'meta-history' for the time of utopia is more adequate than Marx's attempt at calling the time of his utopian classless society 'the true history of mankind', while dubbing 'pre-history' all ages before it. Is it for this reason that Marxists cherish so many 'pre-historic' methods of thought and action?

in man that time meets eternity; or put differently, eternity is met by a man in time. Eternity, experienced in some moments of time as from beyond, is potentially present in any moment because it is always available. The God-centred life is lived in history as from outside history; but for making this possible it must be lived in history. Eternity, in the sense here described, is more a mystical, existential than a temporal concept and therefore, in its Johannine version, very congenial to Friends. But it must be clearly understood that this mysticism does not take us so far outside as to make us forget time in eternity, but that it meets eternity *in time*. Jaspers calls this 'the fundamental paradox of our existence, the fact that it is only within the world that we can live above and beyond he world' and that 'historical consciousness . . . rises above history'. He adds: 'There is no way round the world, no way round history, but only a way through history'.[1] It is this, on the one hand, which some mystics are inclined to overlook, when 'leaving time' in mystical ecstasy, and which, on the other, some neo-orthodox theologians wish to deny outright when they speak about God's totally unilateral activity of salvation and the complete separateness of man from God. Humanity could not live human lives but for that tension between time and eternity: it is its spiritual atmosphere, the very air which it breathes.

World and Worldliness

The word 'world' gives us a third approach to elucidating the different meanings connected with the Kingdom of God. 'World' is used, most obviously again in John's gospel,[2] in two almost contradictory ways. On the one hand, the world is God's creation, loved so much by him that he gave for it his only begotten son. It is like the flesh into which the word has been embodied and which has been saved and sanctified through this incarnation. On the other hand, 'world' stands almost for evil itself. It is the location where people are unfortunately bound to live while on earth, but with which the true

---

[1] *Origin and Goal of History*, 275.
[2] For the world as God's creation and object of his love see John I, 10/11; I, 29; III, 16/17; IV, 42; VI, 33; VIII, 12; XII, 47. For the world as evil and hostile see John I, 10/11 (again); VII, 7; XIV, 17; XV, 18; XVI, 20, 33; XVII, 9, 14. Refer also to I John on many places.

IN THE WORLD AND OF THE WORLD 35

disciples of Christ have no inner community, to which they cannot conform. They are called out of the world, are 'chosen' or 'elected' as a 'New Israel', are set apart as a 'remnant', 'a peculiar people', 'the people of the New Covenant', 'the Church of Christ'.

The Greek word for church, which means normally 'public meeting' of a military or civic kind, has been reduced by some theologians to its root: *ekklesia*, they say, are those who are 'called out' of the world. True, ekklesia does originally mean those who are 'called out', not altogether dissimilar to our use of 'call up' for national service. One may doubt, however, whether the etymological composition of the word was still felt after centuries in which the word meant 'assembly' pure and simple, and whether it was used by the first Christians with more deliberation than that habitual among non-conformists and Friends when they speak of their 'meetings'.

It is noteworthy, however, that the Quaker theologian Robert Barclay, using the same etymological deduction, has argued that *ekklesia* or Catholic Church comprehends

'all and as many, of whatsoever nation, kindred, tongue or people they be, though outwardly strangers and remote from those who profess Christ and Christianity in words and have the benefit of the Scriptures, as become obedient to the holy Light and testimony of God in their hearts, so as to become sanctified by it, and cleansed from the evils of their ways'.[1]

Only for 'the outward profession' it is

'necessary to be a member of a particular gathered church, but not to the being a member of the Catholic Church; yet it is absolutely necessary, where God affords the opportunity of knowing it . . .'[2]

Thus Church is for Barclay a strange blending of universal and yet select membership of those who—whether Christian or non-Christian by background—respond to the Inward Light. By allowing for possible response in every man, separation in the strict sense of the word is avoided. All the same, the idea that the word 'Church' means 'those who are called out of the world' seems far-fetched and proves too much. The Church is, in the words of Bishop Newbigin, 'not a segregation, but a congregation', namely the 'congregation of God'.[3]

[1] *Apology*, Prop. X, II.
[2] *Ibid.* X, IV, cf. S.P.Q., 344/5.
[3] *The Household of God*, 29 (London: S.C.M. Press, 1953).

There is, however, no denying that the emphasis on being *in* the world, created and so loved by God, but not *of* it in its ungodliness, confronts us with the question what the relation of Church and individual Christian to the world ought to be: should they withdraw from it while being merely spatially in it, bearing a witness to Christ *against* the evil world? This is the position adopted for instance by monasticism and anabaptism, a position which found favour with Friends particularly in the period of their own withdrawal from the world. Certain sections of American Quakerism and individual Friends in other parts are still inclined that way, especially since the history of recent decades has shown up the ambiguity of all human activity in a way which the over-optimistic generation preceding ours would have hardly thought possible.

The danger of that position lies in the intentional abandonment of the world as the stage of Christian service. Leaving the world to the world and turning away from it shows a definite lack of concern for the total work of salvation. True, the Society of Friends as a body has, even in the period of most radical seclusion, thrown up Friends such as John Woolman, Dr Fothergill and Elizabeth Fry, who reached out to the world and helped their suffering fellow-men not only as individuals but as social groups. That very contact with the world, however, as an object of charitable Christian service, has often enough increased, among certain Quakers, the sense of being different—'in all humility', of course. Whenever this phrase is used by a Friend, or any other good Christian, I tremble with apprehension as to what extraordinary claim, denying all humility, may follow in the next clause. Friends have certainly not escaped the sin of pride, the off-shoot of outer or inner separateness. The spirit which two and a half centuries ago turned the live witness of plain speech and dress into marks of desirable peculiarity has not ceased with the termination of the outward symbols. The consciousness of being different and, consequently, of being on the sure road, of being truly guided by the Light by which others, too, could be guided (but so obviously are not!)—all this denies redemption not only to the world, the others, but also to the person who separates himself from it, perhaps less by open conduct than by secret conviction. Tolerance itself has frequently become a symbol of smugness and aloof superiority.

Moreover, as we shall see in more detail later, for modern man it is practically impossible to contract out of the wider, the evil world: no longer can you be in the world without being of it. Nor, indeed, was this as easy in the past as is often assumed. The hermits may have succeeded but with this they became guilty of separateness and the sin of caring more for their personal salvation than for God's witness outside themselves. The monks, however, in spite of their withdrawal, and just through it, turned out to be the preservers of worldly knowledge in agriculture, building, literature and all fields of higher culture at the very time when they withdrew from civilization's wickedness and let it go to its doom. They separated themselves from the world of sin, not from the world of men. Being the torch-bearers of civilization, they fulfilled their historic mission by becoming willy-nilly involved with the world, eventually to such an extent that they became very worldly indeed. In this way the promise that the meek shall inherit the earth has often been foiled by the fact that once they have entered their inheritance, they lose their meekness. They become 'the victims of their virtues', as Arnold Toynbee has put it in describing this tendency in Quaker history.[1]

Perhaps the most ironical example of the impossibility of being in the world but not of it, in a spiritual sense, have been those evangelists who, ardently convinced of the complete depravity of the world, went out to preach with special enthusiasm the gospel of Christ to a world which, in their view, could do little more about its own redemption than waiting passively for an act of God's grace. Their sermons did not separate them, but took them right into the world to which they appealed with fire and fury and which, against their innermost theories, must therefore harbour some capacity for redemption.

With this we come to the alternative of a witness *against* the world, namely the recognition that the world, however fallen, has not turned unredeemably evil. If it is seen as the stage,

---

[1] *A Study of History*, Abridged Version, 393 (Oxford University Press, 1946).

not only of God's action, but also of man's reaction to God, it shows some of the original divine features through all fallenness. It is no longer the place to which we are bound while turning morally away from it, but with which we are so deeply concerned that we get inevitably involved in it. Just as we feel the divine image within us, so we see it all round us, if sadly distorted in either case. Church and individual Christian are called, not only to strengthen the power of the divine in themselves, but to appeal to it in all human beings, even the 'most unlikely ones'. This is really the missionary command we have received: that we should respond to the light that shines in everyman.

This is, for example, the attitude of the different schools of 'natural theology' which assure us that man, in whatever place and at whatever time, is aware of divinity within and outside himself, through the *logos spermatikos*, 'the seedling word', that is, merely by his nature of being man; though they do not deny that factual knowledge of the historical Christ might, or would, facilitate for him a truer insight into the divine will. The recognition of the divine power in the world makes the world not only acceptable, but seems to vouchsafe its eventual redemption—the redemption of all.

Recent history, however, has shown up the danger of too great an involvement with the world: Christians who turn to 'that of God' in all people may overlook their darker sides, not only in others but in themselves. They may come to see the source of sin rather in social conditions and outward situations than in human imperfection. Resolved to organize away those bad conditions, they lose increasingly the sense of that true religious command which has sent them forth into the world in the first place: they see the fruit of the spirit as fruit of material betterment.

There are grave dangers both in turning against the world and in trying to win it over. In fact, the contrast of being in, but not of, the world seems not to demand any theoretical solution at all. It seems just another example of the way in which the words of the New Testament are taken too literally, that is too much as principles and laws and not enough as expression of a live situation, as the description of another tension which is existentially inevitable. There is always a spiritual need for withdrawal before you can sally forth into the world, and always a spiritual need to withdraw again after having become involved: the retreat of Jesus into the wilderness and his drinking wine with the publicans, his fight with the scribes and his withdrawal to Gethsemane—they are all essential messages to us. Nor are these alternations necessarily bound to different periods of life: they can interchange very rapidly, within seconds. Once I am born into flesh, I am of necessity *of* the world, not only *in* it, if only through my physical needs. So was Jesus—what else is the meaning of 'Incarnation'. 'In' and 'of' cannot but co-incide for all of us to a certain extent. The only question is where we have to draw the line, and this depends on the situation to which we have to respond by choice and decision.

Choice and decision, however, are not just clear, conscious processes; they may go much further back in the human mind than that. Perhaps we can shed some more light on our problem if, with existentialist philosophy, we recognize that *my* world, that is, the world of my 'being-in-the-world', is already a world of my own selection, of my innermost occupations and concerns, not the objective environment surrounding me, of which only a small part has ever any relationship to me. In a word, it depends on myself, on the ultimate decisions of my self, what my world is to be. If I 'mind what is pure' my world will be pure, but it will be evil if my concerns are evil. In the words of Angelus Silesius:

> Thou wilt be changed, o man, into the things thou lovest:
> Thou wilt be God, if God, and earth, if earth thou lovest.

On the other hand, if we accept that 'world' in our present consideration is not merely a subjective, but also an objective term, the fact remains that separation from it is certainly nothing we should undertake on principle, for instance by abusing functional or terminological distinctions such as Church and State, elect and reprobate, saint and sinner, as though they divided 'in the world' from 'of the world'. Separation is rather something that happens to us when the world begins to 'hate' us and to separate itself from us because we are obedient to God. Separation, in brief, is an attitude of the world, not a Christian attitude, and the Christian who applies it has himself become of the world. While the world may wish to separate itself from us, for us all wilful seclusion can only be a preparation for the re-entry into the world and for thus becoming again more part of it. It is therefore never a real withdrawal.

To put this in Quaker terms: the teaching of the universality of the light implies acceptance of every human being, but he who testifies to it consistently in his life, will by this fact alone become suspect to the world and be set apart by it. His is therefore a separateness tending to include all, just as the Light of the World could not lighten the world if it was not separate and thus enabled to shine, that is to participate, in every corner. If, on the other hand, we consciously aim at seclusion for the sake of discrimination, be it even in the name of one of our 'historic testimonies', it will inevitably end in the sin of pride. William Penn's words are still valid:
'A recluse life, the boasted righteousness of some is not recommendable . . . The Christian convent and monastery are within, where the soul is encloistered from sin . . . True godliness doesn't turn men out of the world but enables them to live better in it, and excites their endeavour to mend it; not hide their candle under a bushel, but set it upon a table in a candlestick'.[1]

The task of the candle, however, is to give light, not to set on fire. We must bear our testimony quietly and leave the reactions to the world. Even reactions may become another cause of pride for us. True, we are not *primarily* responsible if the world withdraws from us because it is scandalized about some fruit of the spirit we show forth by the grace of God. We may not, and probably should not, even know of those fruit or what that scandal is about, and should certainly avoid seeking any merit in it; for this is our *secondary* responsibility: it is exactly this scandalized world which must be sought out again and again, must be reconciled to us for the sake of God, as part of God's work of redemption—of redemption both for ourselves and the hostile world, both of whom are far more members one of another than either side is inclined to admit: fellows equally in sin and in salvation.

There is, then, no being-in-the-world which does not tend to become a being-of-the-world; just through our withdrawal

[1] *No Cross, No Crown*, quoted after *Christian Life, Faith and Thought in the Society of Friends*, 110 (1942).

and our exaggerated concern for personal purity we may show how much we are of it. But there is also no being-of-the-world which does not tend to become a being-in-the-world-of-God; just through the fact that its being happens in the world, it participates in what is, and remains, God's creation and bears his image however distorted. It is still true that while being in the world there is a very great danger of losing that image or at least its finer features. Wherever we go and whatever we do, we have to find our position between the *in* and the *of*, under ever new guidance of the Spirit, in every new situation. 'He plucks the world out of our hearts, loosening the chains of attachment. And He hurls the world into our hearts, where we and He together carry it in infinitely tender love'.[1] In this sense we live between the Kingdom which has come and is available, and the Kingdom which is to come and towards which to seek is commanded to us by inner commitment. We live thus suspended between the two aspects of the Kingdom: in its Presence, and towards its futurity.

[1] Kelly, *A Testament of Devotion*, 43/44 (London: Hodder & Stoughton, 1957).

3

THE QUAKER ATTITUDE TO HISTORY

Suspense is the inescapable situation of man, the inherent condition of his being. He is free, in thinking and feeling, to move towards one or the other of the poles between which he experiences himself as suspended. He may even imagine that he has reached the pole on the one side or has been hurled to the pole opposite; that, in our context, he has attained to live fully in the Kingdom of God here and now, or that he is fully excluded from it until Judgment Day. Such an imaginative one-sidedness, though itself rooted in some special experience, will change his way of experiencing God, world and himself; it will influence his actions, will colour his views and utterances and define his philosophical and theological locus. With all this he remains man-between, and the tension which seems overcome at one moment, is still structurally present and will soon enough re-assert itself in some different form; and whatever seems neglected by one-sided emphasis, returns, sometimes with a vengeance, in the actuality of living the life of man.

It was a tremendous and overwhelming experience for early Friends to re-discover the direct communication between God and man, the immediate guidance through the Holy Spirit, the awareness of the divine Presence within them and amongst them. This discovery is the key-note of innumerable pronouncements. For our present purpose it may suffice to quote one of them, both to remind ourselves of the impact of that discovery on the minds of early Friends and to lead us on in our considerations. Francis Howgill says in a well-known passage:

'The Lord of heaven and earth we found to be near at hand, and, as we waited upon him in pure silence, our minds out of all things, his heavenly presence appeared in our assemblies, when there was no language, tongue nor speech from any creature. The Kingdom of Heaven did gather us and catch us all, as in a net, and his heavenly power at one time drew many hundreds to land. We came to know a place to stand in and what to wait in; and the Lord appeared daily to us, to our astonishment, amazement and great admiration, insomuch that we often said one unto another, with great joy of heart: "What, is the Kingdom of God come to be with men? And will he take up his tabernacle among the sons of men, as he did of old? And what? Shall we, that were reckoned as the outcasts of Israel, have this honour of glory communicated amongst us, which were but men of small parts and of little abilities, in respect of many others, as amongst men?" ' [1]

The Mystic and the World

Let us begin our examination of this passage with the clause: 'our minds out of all things'. We must understand at the outset that any form of immediate religious experience, any mystical communion with God, tends to reduce world and time to a secondary place. Mystics try 'to find God at first hand, experimentally, in the soul herself, independently of all historical and philosophical pre-suppositions' (Von Hügel). Divine Presence, the Here and Now of God felt so clearly within, devalues all other, all outward, experiences of life. This leads, in extreme cases, not only to the complete neglect of matters temporal, but even to the self-effacement of personality. For instance, the pantheistic mystic has the one wish to lose the identity of his self in the universe, to be swallowed up in what Spinoza has called 'God or Nature',[2] thus speaking of a God very different from the Father of Jesus Christ or the God of Abraham, Isaac and Jacob, who is not himself Nature but Creator. In characteristic inversion the mystic may express this not as himself being identified with God, but as God being identified with him; he may turn a monist for whom there is no God apart from his own self in isolation.[3] All significance of life consists, then, in attempts at, and progress towards, that identification of man and God, either as self-deification or as

[1] Testimony for Edward Burrough, at the beginning of the latter's *Works*, quoted here after *Christian Life, Faith and Thought in the Society of Friends*.
[2] *Deus sive Natura*.
[3] This is called *pan-en-henism* by Zaehner, *Mysticism Sacred and Profane*, *passim* (Oxford: The Clarendon Press, 1957).

self-effacement. All other aspects of world and time become irrelevant, indeed they are disturbing influences trying to slow down or reverse that merger, and may therefore appear to the mystic as the radical evil which desires to deprive him of perfect unconscious bliss in perfect self-effacement or perfect isolation.

This experience determines the monistic mystic's relationship to his fellow-men. In world and time they may disturb his ascendency; it is only in his Universal Self that all other selves can be united with him, not in a this-worldly fellowship with God. True, because of that ultimate unification of all in All, some monistic or pantheistic mystics will recognize them as brothers even on earth, indeed, form brotherhoods with them for a deeper appreciation of the ultimate goal, but these efforts are usually accompanied by the introduction of a more theistic view of God. All the same, their fellowship will be often a detached kind of brotherliness, no live relationship between personalities recognizing and furthering one another in the development of full temporal selfhood; for it is exactly selfhood which is to be lost in the ultimate merger. This kind of detached brotherliness consists in an anticipation of the annihilation of all selfhood in the One. The monistic mystic, therefore, knows neither a truly individual immortality, nor is he very much concerned, in a practical way, with the material furtherance and welfare of other human beings, that is, the things which are the content of history; on the other hand, the more he is inclined towards pantheism, the easier he finds it to recognize the present and future oneness of all life without distinction, that is, including non-human life, because human selfhood is for him no ultimate value and has no greater significance than any other existent things.

Monistic mysticism is more an oriental than an occidental experience, though it can be found in the West, too, just as theistic mysticism is far from unknown in the East, though usually considered as a lower stage. The fact, however, that there exists a variety of mysticisms according to time, place, tradition and personality is very relevant: it disproves in the most striking way the assumption, shared by some modern Friends, that mysticism is the common and uniting faith of mankind, its 'perennial philosophy', which leaves behind all

IN THE WORLD AND OF THE WORLD 45

other religions as mere stepping stones. Mysticism is neither a faith nor a philosophy: it is a psychological and spiritual phenomenon discoverable in quite different religions, namely the possibility of, and tendency towards, direct religious or semi-religious experience. While the phenomenon is common or at least outwardly comparable, the forms of experience, and the spiritual knowledge it conveys, remain very different, even contradictory. Not only religious symbols, but also religious contents and the goals of mystical search, are clearly conditioned by the historical environment; and even where the symbols and the very words such as 'God' and 'Self' seem the same, the underlying realities may be incompatible. Contrary to what Aldous Huxley and others assert, the Universal Self, seen with or without the help of drugs, is certainly not the 'God of Abraham, Isaac and Jacob, God of Jesus Christ' who was seen by Pascal in his great vision. Yet the common fact, that is, the possibility of, and tendency towards, direct religious experience, remains.[1]

Apart from this common fact there is nothing more characteristic of mysticism in different environments than its claim to universality while in practice being rather more exclusive than inclusive, rather more aristocratic and high-brow than democratic and low-brow. It rightly affirms the oneness of God; though, as indicated, this one God may look very different to different mystics. It also affirms (and again rightly in the belief of the present writer) that the human ability of mystical experience is universal, though not everybody may be aware of his ability, and it may be experienced in quite different ways: as encounter of I and Thou, as identification of God with myself or myself with God, as present closeness (embracing and being embraced), or in some other form, all forms being conditioned by the historical environment, the personality and, not least, the momentary spiritual situation of the mystic.

It is a mistake to conclude from the affirmation of the oneness of God, and of the universal ability of direct mystical experience, that the actual experience is basically the same whenever and wherever it happens and that the content of

---

[1] Cf. My *Friends and Truth*, 48 ff. Refer also to Otto, *Mysticism East and West* (London: Macmillan & Co. Ltd., 1932), and Zaehner, *op. cit.*

experience is independent of time and place. An essential part of all mystical experience belongs to this world and its history and is therefore temporally conditioned. In the words of von Hügel:
'Religion deals, indeed, centrally, with God, and He is not successive, but Simultaneous; but then, Religion is man's apprehension and experience of God, and man can as little apprehend Eternity, the All-Present, out of Time and Succession, as he can vividly apprehend Spirit out of all relation to Body. But, if History and the records of History are important in Religion, we cannot simply eliminate learning, tradition, Doctors, Rabbis. These may have their abuses, and may require check, supplementation, renovation by intuition, inspiration, Prophets; but they cannot simply be supplanted by the latter'.[1]

The universal fact, independent of time and place, is merely man's ability of experiencing the Super-Human, Super-Temporal, Other-Worldly and of doing so without apparent mediator. But he is himself a medium as a human being in time and place, he mediates his immediacy to himself, and he uses, as his own medium, other media in his world and time, or with Jaspers, other cyphers and other myths, which suddenly open up to him and then yield an apparently 'immediate' religious insight.

Due to the environmental influences of Christendom, Western mysticism has, with some exceptions, been less inclined than its Eastern counterpart to try and lose all connection with time and world. For that it would have to lose touch with the historic event of Christ and would have to whittle down even the meaning of symbols such as Light and Seed which in Western feeling are closely associated with New Testament usage. Of course, such loss of touch with Christian tradition has happened at times, not least in Quaker history, and right to our own days. Some of our Unitarian and our Gandhian Friends believe that they have dispensed with the narrowness of Christian mythology. Their belief may be based either on true spiritual experience or else, as in some cases, only on vague reasoning, so characteristic of many fine men of goodwill in

[1] "On the Place and Function, within Religion, of the Body, of History and of Institutions". In *Essays and Addresses*, II, 66 (London: J. M. Dent & Sons Ltd., 1924). This lecture, given in 1913, is still one of the most profound critiques of George Fox and Quakerism and worth pondering upon even where we disagree.

the contemporary world. One thing is certain, their belief, their underlying faith, does not turn them away from this world; on the contrary, it increases their sense of the reality of brotherliness between real personalities, and of responsibility for human affairs in world and time, often more so than with those whose beliefs have kept closer to the New Testament mythology. Willy-nilly Western mystics have, with few exceptions, remained executors of their Hebrew-Christian heritage and are turned back, through their religious insights, to working in this world, to action in history.

Peculiar Universalists

Wherever the immediate communication with God is experienced as communication through or with Christ, the mystical drift away from world and time is halted and reversed into a drift towards loving God's loved world and acting in it responsibly, that is in response to God's will for his creation. This does not mean that the Christian mystic is never tempted when, in Howgill's words, his mind is 'out of all things', to try and stay as far outside as possible. Not only individuals, but whole groups of Christian mystics may, in quietist aloofness, seek a peace such as the world cannot give. But the experience of a loving community in Christ, of a pentecostal oneness similar to that described by Howgill, cannot but bring them back to the world, if perhaps not the whole group, at least those among them who have truly felt what communication with God through Christ involves. They experience relationship between brothers in Christ as one between true selves trying through mutual care to help one another to still greater selfhood in God. The self-identification they seek is not with God, but with Christ, and through him with their fellow-men. This implies active concern for the real welfare of real persons in God's real world, hence practical arrangements for the sake of Christ, not only as relief of all kinds of suffering, but also by political and social measures. The mystical experience issues in prophetic commission concerning world and time, in action in history, though it is bound to repudiate forms of action which are incompatible with its religious insights.

This happens because the content of Christian mystical experience is of necessity shaped after the life and ministry of

Jesus: guidance by the Inner Christ cannot easily be kept apart from imitation of the Historic Christ, that is, self-identification with him as the first-born brother, which is entirely different from an attempted self-identification with the Father, not to mention the Universalf Self.[1] We can observe, throughout Quaker history, a tidal movement between the Inner and the Historic Christ, sometimes emphasizing one, sometimes the other; but we also observe that for the great Quaker saints the identification of the two was not really difficult, though perhaps expressed less clearly in thought than in practice.[2]

Already the early formulation by Fox of his great discovery indicates that the inner experience is addressed to all humanity: the ability to have immediate communication with God, 'that of God', is at once filled with universalist content: it is 'that of God *in everyman*' to which we are to respond. The universalist tendency in Christian mysticism is directed towards the fulfilment of all human personalities in communion with God here on earth, in a Kingdom which has come; whereas in monistic mysticism, as we have seen, universalism is directed towards the disappearance of all human personality through merger with God, in a great yearning for states as far removed from this world as possible.

The integration of spiritual insight experienced as personal salvation, on the one hand, and of embracing mankind and the whole creation in the love of Christ and thus living on earth as in God's Kingdom on earth, on the other—this integration is, according to Dr Schweitzer, the historic portent of Paul's genius: Paul gathered into one 'Redemption by Christ' as personal event, and the living in the spiritual society of the Kingdom of God on earth.[3] Maurice Creasey, who calls these two aspects the 'intensive' and the 'extensive' interpretations of Christ, has shown that the same integration, overcoming

---

[1] Schweitzer, *The Mysticism of Paul the Apostle*, 378/9 (London: A. & C. Black Ltd., 1953), and Underhill, *The Mystic Way*, 63/4 (London: J. M. Dent & Sons Ltd., 1913).

[2] For a recent Quaker statement on this problem cf. Hobling, *The Concrete and the Universal*. especially pp. 16 ff. (London: George Allen & Unwin Ltd., 1958).

[3] *Op. cit.* 380 ff.

the tension between the Inner and the Historic Christ, was the true significance of early Quakerism.[1]

The universalist or 'extensive' drive of the Quaker mystic, however, is bound to clash in history with other men, in the very attempt at joining with them in communion with God. He is foiled in this attempt by those who have not, or not yet, made use of their innate ability for direct communication with God through purity and love; by those who have not, or not yet, entered the Kingdom. Faithful to his insight into God's unending, suffering and forgiving love, he is, after every frustration, even more exercised to testify to his knowledge and to use many peculiar ways for convincing the unconvinced. But his peculiarities separate him even more from those who have not accepted their inner guide, or mediate the inner experience to themselves in a way different from that of Friends. Such peculiarity has nothing to do with withdrawal or willed seclusion; on the contrary, it is an even greater exertion of his universalist drive. The true grandeur of peculiarity is the joyful acceptance and use of his own sufferings, due to persecution by those who reject him, as his final universal appeal to all men, particularly his enemies.[2] Thus he repeats, in measure, the event of Calvary where the Cross was established once and for all as the symbol of man suspended between God and history, between the will in time to work the redemption of all, and the opposite will of those who would reject him.

This, however, is only one aspect of his peculiarity. The Christian mystic, rebuffed and thus set apart by his enemies, may easily succumb to the temptation of condemning them and, in the case of George Fox, of even rejoicing at their misfortune. T. Canby Jones has been driven to the conclusion that 'when we remember the great vehemence with which Fox promises eternal destruction for the unrepentant wicked, it is not possible to make him a universalist'.[3] But Canby Jones himself quotes statements from Fox which do not only protest

[1] *Early Quaker Christology* (unpublished), Section 6, particularly pp. 355-359.
[2] Cf. Nuttall, "The Church's Ministry of Suffering" (London: Independent Press, 1954). In: *Studies in Christian Social Commitment*, ed. by Ferguson.
[3] 'George Fox's Understanding of Last Things', *F.Q.*, 1954, 204. My following considerations owe much to this penetrating study.

D

against the Calvinist idea that God could have 'ordained the greatest part of mankind for hell',[1] but also Fox's approval, 'rather inconsistently', of such passages in Acts and Epistles as stress, the restoration of all things to the Father through Christ.[2] Earlier on, Jones summarizes 'Fox's understanding of the development of history' like this:
'It is now only a matter of time until all churches, all governments and all men shall come to this Light of Christ and be subject to him and then he shall restore all things to God the Father'.[3]
This contradiction in Fox, and in many earlier Quaker writings, can be traced to the New Testament, indeed, if we believe our records, to Jesus himself. In his earlier ministry Jesus appealed to all men to avail themselves of God's grace whereas in his later period, having been rejected by many, he speaks much more of the condemnation of the unrepentent.[4] We may perhaps say that the Christian mystic, and prophet in history, is by insight and character a universalist, but through his struggles in history he becomes emotionally, and perhaps sometimes even in thought, a separatist. He lives truly in the tension between God and history, and thus appears as what I would like to call a peculiar universalist.

In the history of the Society of Friends we can find a few pantheistic mystics, we can find unitarians, quietists and separatists, and indeed non-mystical Protestants of different outlooks, and evangelicals; but it seems to me that, truly understood, Quakers are inherently peculiar universalists, peculiar because their mystical drive towards God and his universal Kingdom is hemmed in by negative experiences encountered in their prophetic drive for the realization of the Kingdom on earth.

The Second Coming of Christ

Let us now return to, and re-read, the passage from Francis Howgill quoted at the beginning of this chapter.[5] What he

---

[1] *Ibid.*, 203. For a significant example of Fox's view see *Journal*, 550: '. . . God would have all men to be saved, mark, all men . . . he that believes is saved and he that believes not is condemned already.'
[2] *Ibid.*, 204.
[3] *Ibid.*, 198.
[4] Cf. Cadoux, *The Life of Jesus*, passim (Pelican, 1948).
[5] Above, pp. 42/43.

describes with beautful enthusiasm may be called a pentecostal experience. It is pentecostal in the original sense if we identify that 'heavenly presence' with the Holy Spirit of Acts or the Comforter of John's gospel. We may do better, however, by thinking rather in Pauline terms, since with Friends as with Paul the two divine 'persons', Christ and the Spirit, are not clearly distinguished, but describe almost without discrimination a mystical relationship with God through Christ. If, finally, we remember some other utterances of early Friends, and especially of George Fox, we begin to wonder whether the phrase that 'the Lord appeared daily to us' does not refer exclusively to the 'person' of Christ; and whether the interrogative clause: 'Is the Kingdom of God come to be with men?' may convey a meaning far more concrete than joyful amazement, namely a theological affirmation in form of a rhetorical question: early Friends were certain that their experience was evidence for the actual Second Coming of Christ and the actual arrival of the Kingdom of God on earth. It was therefore not only a mystical experience, but in and with this experience also a historical event to which they bore witness. Just as Christ was born under Cyrenius and had been crucified and risen under Pontius Pilate and then ascended to heaven, so 'he hath now again the second time appeared and is appearing in ten thousands of his saints', 'in our day', under the Rump Parliament, Cromwell and the later Stuarts.[1]

Early Friends were not alone in this belief: the rule of the Saints and the expectations and rising of the Fifth Monarchists show clearly that the idea of the Messianic Kingdom being at hand permeated the thinking of those restive years. As we shall see in the next chapter, early Friends were greatly tempted to participate in utopian movements which misunderstood the word Kingdom as meaning, not the spiritual Kingship of God, but the establishment of a divine territory on earth. Friends were saved from this error (then as again in later periods) by their deeper spirituality and their mysticism. They had no need to fight for Christ's coming for they knew for certain that 'Christ *is* come and *doth* dwell in the hearts of his people

[1] Barclay, 'Truth Triumphant', 210, quoted here from Doncaster, 'Early Quaker Thought on that State in which Adam was before he fell', *Journal of Friends Historical Society*, 1949, 15.

and reigns there'.[1] For Friends, Christ's re-entry into history had happened without a millenial revolution, the Kingdom of God had come not as a political but as a spiritual reality, as Christ's Second Coming, a coming into the hearts of his people.

It is important to understand that for early Friends this was a new event, not a continuing situation 'after Christ' which had begun under Pontius Pilate and had lasted already for sixteen hundred years.[2] Like the continental Anabaptists of the sixteenth century, early Friends regarded the period between the Primitive Church in the first century and their own experience in the seventeenth as that of a great defection when the church lived 'in the wilderness'[3] and only a few scattered people held to the truth. Fox speaks of 'the *beginning* of the spreading of the Gospel after *so long night of apostasy since the Apostles' days,* that now Christ reigns as he did in the hearts of his people'.[4] And Penington says of some Old Testament prophecies:

'These scriptures and many more are sweetly and preciously fulfilled . . . *in this our day*. They were once (*in a degree*) fulfilled in the day of the appearance of the Word of Life in the prepared Body of Flesh. They were again *more generally fulfilled*, in the day of the pouring out of his Spirit, and gathering people to him, both from among the Jews and Gentiles . . . and they are *again* fulfilled in the hearts of many, *after the long night of Darkness and great and large apostasy from the spirit and power of the apostles*'.[5]

The reality of Christ's second coming was felt so deeply that Fox could argue with I Corinthians, 11, 26, that the time of an outward celebration of the Last Supper 'till he come' was past and they celebrated now the 'inward and heavenly supper' of Revelation, 3, 20. In the certainty of the second

[1] Fox, *Journal*, 261. (My italics.)
[2] They would not have appreciated Rosenstock-Huessy in *Heilkraft und Wahrheit*, 38: 'The incarnation is a process put in motion for nineteen hundred years'. (My translation.)
[3] Lewis Benson, 'George Fox's Conception of the Church' in *F.Q.* (1956), 144 ff.
[4] B.Q. IV. (My italics.)
[5] *Works II*, 211. (My italics.) I owe this quotation to Creasey, *op. cit.*, 270/1.
[6] 'A Distinction Between the Two Suppers of Christ'. In *Works II*, 935 ff., here quoted after Creasey, *op. cit.*, 132/3. Quoted also in *Christian Life, Faith and Thought in the Society of Friends*, 114/115.

IN THE WORLD AND OF THE WORLD 53

coming he and his friends went up and down the country, 'sounding the Day of the Lord', as though now, for the first time since the Baptist and Jesus, the Kingdom of God was again at hand and could be entered here and now by those who received Christ into their hearts. Here and now the true church was restored by gathering in those who were convinced of the truth that Christ is present again.

The frequent use of the expression 'Day of the Lord' includes an eschatological association and, in the usage of Fox, a denigration of time and world. As Canby Jones points out, for Fox 'time is a characteristic of fleshly, earthly existence from which we shall be ultimately delivered'.[1] His admonition to Friends to 'be faithful and live in that which doth not think the time long'[2] contains something of that intense expectation of the end of all things which we know so well from the first generation of Christians. It contains, in fact, a tendency to deny the historicity of man, at least at that juncture of Quaker history.

We must therefore qualify our statement that the Second Coming is understood as an event *in history* by emphasizing that Fox did not necessarily wish to validate time and world in general. His view of history is largely confined to a history of salvation as he understood it. 'For early Friends history was divided into three phases: before the Fall, in the Fall, and in the restoration by Christ'.[3] After the discovery that Christ is come, they were not greatly concerned for anything other than the 'restoration by Christ', which for them was rather connected with Christ's Second Coming to which they testified, than with his first coming of which the Gospels speak.

In early Quaker writings there is almost more emphasis on the fact that Christ was before the world was than that he became flesh and died under Pontius Pilate. Though in no way denying the full reality of that life and death in history, they saw in them 'outward' events which had little relevance apart from their 'inward' mystical dying and living with Christ.[4] Worldly history of what we call the 'Christian era', that period of 'apostasy', did not interest them, nor did the temporal

---

[1] *Loc. cit.*, 196.
[2] *Journal*, 575.
[3] Doncaster, *loc. cit.*, 16.
[4] Cf. Creasey, *op. cit.*, Section 2, D, on 'Christ as Incarnate'.

future, the 'time' which will not be 'long', but merely an interim.

Their 'sounding the Day of the Lord' points therefore to an event in history only in so far as God uses a moment of time for his final work of salvation. The present or near-present contains all relevant history: it is the fulfilment of time, the *kairos*: 'Christ *is* come . . . in *our* day'. But as not all are already saved, the 'interim' gives them another chance. This interim is admitted by a curious use of tenses and prepositions:

'. . . but he is risen and come in his Saints who *is* Lord and King, who *will* reign over all the World, and bear the government upon his shoulders, and so farewell World, for ever adieu: for the Lord *is* King in his Saints: he guards them and guides them with his mighty power, and *doth preserve* his seed and children from the seed of evil doers, *into* his kingdom of glory and eternal rest . . .'[1]

Obviously Fox wrestles here with the paradox of the Kingdom. He puts it even more clearly in another passage of the same pamphlet where he says: 'The Lord Jesus Christ . . . he *is come* and *coming* to rule all Nations with a rod of Iron'.[2] Samuel Fisher tries even harder when he refers to Christ as him 'that before then was come, and then came, and is come, and comes, and is to come, from the beginning to the end, the first and last . . .'[3] Early Friends, however, do not conceive this paradox as a tension within individual human experience, they try to solve the tension in a simple and direct way. The Kingdom, they hold, is altogether present and fulfilled for those who know that Christ is come into their hearts as their immediate teacher; whereas it is still in the future for those who have not yet been convinced.

Corresponding the Day of the Lord proclaimed by Fox has two aspects: it is 'great and terrible'[4] or 'mighty'[5] for those for whom it is meant as a call to repentance, and leaves them just a time-not-long, a short interim; for those who are already convinced of the truth, the Day of the Lord is both

---

[1] Quoted after T. Canby Jones, *loc. cit.*, 201, from *Newes out of the North, 1654*. (My italics.).
[2] Quoted *ibid.*, *196*. (My italics.)
[3] *Rusticus ad Academicos*, 618/9, quoted here after Creasey, *op. cit.*, 70.
[4] *Journal*, 38.
[5] *Journal*, 121. Many other Friends used this phrase, e.g. William Dewsbury, *B.Q.*, 74, and Mary Weatherhead, *Q.A.C.*, 220.

IN THE WORLD AND OF THE WORLD 55

present and joyful. As Fox writes again: 'We witness the happy day of the Lord *is* come, *the good and happy day*, and glad tidings to souls, the day of Christ; praises, praises to him for ever'.[1] Canby Jones sums up this position when he says that in Fox's view 'the Day of the Lord has fully come for the righteous. . . . As far as the wicked are concerned the day of vengeance is already dawning, but most of its fiery judgment is yet to burst forth.' Jones makes the important addition that 'Fox strikes a minor note about final fulfilment, but he puts the emphasis on the present realisation of the kingdom of Christ in His Saints'.[2]

This emphasis on the Presence is the corollary of their present communion with God as described in our quotation from Howgill; it has remained the principal emphasis in nearly all periods of Quaker history. But the word 'presence' itself has changed its meaning since the days of George Fox. Soon after the first generation of Friends the interpretation of mystical experience as Christ's Second Coming in history and near its end, evaporated. This does not mean, however, that Friends repeated the development of the second and third generations of Christians, who pushed the Second Coming from an immediate expectation to one further ahead in history or to its very end. The Second Coming was no *expectation* for early Friends, however immediate, but an immediate *reality*. Since that identification of the Second Coming with their own experience had been lost, the whole idea of a return of Christ has never again taken much room in Quaker thinking, and eschatological concepts were replaced, if at all, by utopian hopes and designs. Still, the mystical insight of Friends into spiritual Presence has led them again and again to the prophetic task of trying to realise the Kingdom at least piecemeal, if not as a divine territory, at least as a spiritual realm of universal brotherhood. Thus history, while neglected by their mystical life in Presence, took hold of them whenever they tried to translate it into political and social practice.

This, however, is very different from the belief that the Kingdom has actually come, as *given* by God, and that they live in

---

[1] Quoted after T. Canby Jones, *loc. cit.*, *201*. (My italics.)
[2] *Loc. cit.*, 202.

the Kingdom. It means men's *working* for a Kingdom which is in the future, and in order to do so, to live 'as though the Kingdom of God had come'. This 'as though' has a long tradition in Quaker and in Christian thinking; we find it also with Fox when he admonishes his Friends: 'Let him that buys or sells or possesses or uses this world be *as if* he did not'.[1] The 'as though' or 'as if' does not indicate a moral duplicity though it can easily lead to pretence and even hypocrisy. Its inherent ambiguity elucidates man's situation as suspended between God and history. It may therefore well exist alongside the experience of Presence: that is, Presence not of the Second Coming, but Presence as mystical experience of the Holy Spirit, or of the Christ who is with those who are gathered in his name. Sometimes even this Presence is understood less as that of the Spirit of which we read also in the New Testament, than as a divine function of man. Such an interpretation, found not infrequently among modern Friends, has taken the last step towards the obliteration of any belief in a history of salvation, for spirit is here no longer a self-revelation of God in time, but an anthropological fact, a part of human nature, identifying itself with God.

With this we touch one more aspect of Fox's belief in the Second Coming of Christ: it underlines the small understanding of history, not only of history in general, as was normal at that time, but in particular of the history of salvation, that is, of the significance of Christ's first coming. Of course, we must never overlook the frequent references to the life, ministry and death of the historic Christ in the writings of early Friends; above all, not the severe suffering of early Friends for the sake of Christ, for the Christ who had come 'in our day', under Cromwell and Charles II. In this way they identified themselves with the life of the Historic Christ, whose pattern they re-lived, more faithfully than many before and after them, sometimes unto death. All the same, their present experience of the Inner Christ, his Second Coming, made it less essential for them to try and grasp the meaning of the Historic Christ, his First Coming. They 'found it natural to speak of Christ in

[1] B.Q., 516/7. (My italics.)

the present tense rather than in the past';[1] and Penington argued that 'to know and own Christ outwardly, as he appeared in the body', was no longer proof of a Christian spirit: 'The distinguishing Knowledge and owning of Christ is to know and own him inwardly'.[2]

The Inner Christ is universal; he was before the world was; he inspired already the good pagans long 'before Christ', and he might speak to the Great Turk, to whom Fox sent an epistle quoting the Koran. There could be no clear conception among early Friends what it amounted to to live in Christendom 'after Christ' if, on the one hand, 'after Christ' meant for them after about 1647 A.D. or whenever one or them was convinced of the truth, and if, on the other, Socrates and Plato could be called, with Justin Martyr, 'Christians before Christ'.

Socrates' refusal to take fees for teaching and his condemnation of the Sophists for money-making were in line with Friends' distrust of paid ministry, and Penn was glad to find pre-Christian sages who condemned swearing and maintained Friends' testimony against oaths. Penn pointed the contrast on these differences between Gentile Divinity and the practice of professing Christians so sharply that it lent some colour to Keith's charge that he recognized only pagans as fellow-Christians, and disowned all who profess and call themselves Christians other than Friends.[3]

Thus already in the second generation of Friends, when Deism began to occupy the minds of their erudite contemporaries, Quaker Christianity was in danger of becoming a mere name for human goodness wherever it occurred, without regard to the special changes in history, to the upgrading of all human standards, aspirations and hopes, which were brought about by the event of Christ under Pontius Pilate. This danger increased when the thin thread with history which early Friends preserved through their belief in the Second Coming was cut and the orthodox beliefs about Christ's first coming were restored among Friends only for the period of evangelicalism,

[1] Creasey, op. cit., 137.
[2] Works II, 105, here quoted after Creasey, op. cit., 297. Creasey emphasizes that 'inwardness' meant for Penington an 'inward knowing of both inward and outward (historical) events, as against outward knowing, the mere technical knowledge of events describable in lip-service. Creasey calls this Penington's 'spiritual epistomology'.
[3] Herbert G. Wood, 'William Penn's Christian Quaker', in *Children of Light*, ed. by H. H. Brinton, 13 (New York, The Macmillan Company, 1938). I am much indebted to this article.

but otherwise mostly held in abeyance. And yet, neither early nor modern Friends are intelligible if regarded as the product of a historically unmotivated sudden experience of the Inner Light which overtook a group of people out of the blue. The very preoccupation of Friends with their own historical past, right from the first generation who started the tradition of setting great store on exact records, detailed journals and truthful chronicles, seems to belie their negligence of history and God's working through it. But their interest in the history of salvation remained small in most periods. Early Friends, such as Penn, tried at least, if unsuccessfully, to show the relationship of the Inner and the Historic Christ: they were agreed that the Light which was before the world was, was identical with Christ, so that for them it was Christ whose Light shines in everyman. For not a few modern Friends, however, the Light which was before the world was, shines in everyman: hence it also shone in Jesus Christ as a matter of course. These Friends seem to feel no special relationship to Christ, at least no deeper relationship than to other saints and the saints of other faiths. They overlook that if their inner experience may not be Christ-centred, they are still the heirs of what is with justice called our *Christian* civilization because it would be quite unintelligible but for the Christ of history. Concentrating their spiritual life on their ability of direct communication with God, they forget over their mysticism the historical co-ordinates of their existence and indulge without qualms in what Baron von Hügel has called the 'historical ingratitude' of Quakers.

Historical Ingratitude

Nobody would expect from George Fox the scientific understanding of a nineteenth century historian or a twentieth century psychologist. But the sweeping gesture with which he removed all history between 'the Apostles' days' and the Second Coming of Christ as a 'long night of apostasy', a time during which the church existed only underground as 'wilderness church',[1] is symptomatic of the exaggerated view which he has about inner guidance, as entirely divorced from all temporal continuity. While Penn and Barclay used their scholar-

[1] Benson, *loc. cit.*, 156.

ship, not only for critical attack on others, but at least partly also for Quaker apologetics, Fox did not recognize any of the influences which had worked upon him, neither those of the spiritual reformers of the sixteenth and seventeenth centuries nor those of such contemporaries as created for him, and together with him, the historical climate for his ministry. He and his Friends threw over the festivals of the Christian calendar and found something like pride in working on public holidays while meeting for worship in mid-week or any other time they felt guided to it; for they wished to emphasize the independence of the spirit from historical tradition.

Even today some Quaker Meetings avoid taking notice of the great Christian festivals and hardly any assemble on Christmas Day unless it happens to fall on a Sunday, and none on Good Friday. This comes near a betrayal of the very truth they wish to uphold; for Friends share nowadays in the bustle of secular preparation for Bank Holiday outings and Christmas presents: unless they are quite dead to spiritual guidance they cannot help, in the stillness of their Meetings, being led towards a search for the deeper meaning of those festivals, their historical origin and their inspiring message. It would be against the leadings of the spirit not to express such insights even on Easter and Whit-Sunday; and it is a not uncommon practice nowadays that on the Sundays preceding and following Christmas the meaning of the birth of Christ (or Jesus of Nazareth) is the theme of messages.

The most striking example of historical ingratitude may be seen in the attitude of early Friends to the Scriptures. George Fox, whose style luxuriates in paraphrases of Biblical passages and concepts, denied all the same that he might owe his spiritual knowledge to the Scriptures. Where he describes the discovery that every man's salvation depended on the belief in the indwelling light of Christ, he added: 'This I saw in the pure openings of the Light without the help of any man, neither did I then know where to find it in the Scriptures; though afterwards, searching the Scriptures, I found it'.[1] He declared that 'though I read the Scriptures that spoke of Christ and God, yet I knew him not but by revelation'.[2]

[1] *Journal*, 33.
[2] *Journal*, 11.

Such emphasis, partly a reaction to Puritan bibliolatry, overstates his case considerably. Fox had searched the Scriptures not only before his experience; he mentions explicitly that he searched them afterwards, and what reason could he have for this unless to find historical support for his own inner teacher. His use of the word 'open', too, gives him away, for things were not only opened to *him* 'in the pure openings of the Light': he in his turn 'opened the Scriptures' to others 'to lead them into all truth', through the application to the Scriptures of the Light within. There is no denying that in this way his interpretation of the Bible became far deeper than that of his contemporaries, but it was still the Bible on which he relied. Indeed, on occasion he states clearly that 'the Scriptures of Truth . . . were given forth to be believed, read, fulfilled and practised, and the things enjoyed they speak of, that is Christ Jesus the Substance'.[1] Like his contemporaries he exploited the Bible for proof-texts, for instance when he used Daniel 3, 28, to show that that of God dwelt in Nebuchadnezzar, or when he and his Friends refused the taking of oaths or removing their hats.[2] Clearly, early Friends, while denying the preponderant importance of outward knowledge, were far more given to it than they admitted. Their critics often accused them of denying it altogether though, as was said of Dr Schweitzer, they were 'far better Christians than their books'.

The important point for our context is that an emphasis, so valuable in giving the pride of place to the Spirit revealed in the New Testament rather than to the letter of the Scriptural sources, has introduced into later Quaker thinking a difficulty parallel, and nearly identical, with that concerning the relationship of the Inner and the Historic Christ: if we are to be guided by the Spirit rather than by the Biblical records, what is their mutual relationship?

In spite of allegations to the contrary, there is no evidence

---

[1] *Some Principles of the Elect People of God* (1661), 16; here quoted after Creasey, *op. cit.*, 117.
[2] William Dewsbury insisted before the Judge that 'there is not any scripture that expresses any honour to be in putting off the hat'. B.Q., 447. Yet he said: 'I came to my knowledge of eternal life not by the letter of scripture nor from hearing men speak of God, but by the inspiration of the Spirit of Jesus Christ who brought the immortal seed to birth'.

that early Friends ever indulged in Bible-burning.[1] But as just pointed out, they were also suspected of denying altogether the value of the Scriptures. This has never been quite true, at least not before this century when a few Friends seem to think that they can do without reading them, though they may still admit that they contain some good passages—and how do they know?

More characteristic of a sizable body of opinion within the Society of Friends in different periods is the attitude of Elias Hicks, about one hundred and thirty years ago, who insisted in theory on the complete separation of inward guidance and Scriptures and spoke of the dangers resulting from the use of books, but all the same remained himself a faithful reader of the Bible.[2] Already Isaac Penington tried to solve the difficulty of too sharp a separation between Inward Guide and Scriptures by showing that through the Light 'we have seen and received the things that the Scriptures speak of'.[3] Similarly Barclay, though calling the Scriptures 'a secondary rule', points out that we may 'discern the stamp of God's spirit and ways upon them, by the inward acquaintance we have with the same spirit and work in our hearts'.[4]

They would not ask themselves, however, whether they could have had that 'inward acquaintance' with the Spirit in this form had they not been brought up in the knowledge of traditional Christian teaching. It was this knowledge which gave content to their direct mystical experience. But for the Bible they could not have called it the 'Light of *Christ*' nor could they have spoken of his Second Coming; probably they could not even have adopted their Christ-like attitude under attack and persecution. As H. G. Wood puts it: 'The great fabric of religious truth is being woven in history, and if spiritually the Scriptures are a secondary rule, historically they are a primary and indispensable rule'.[5] H. G. Wood elucidates the true relation between inner experience and history with great

[1] Cadbury, 'A Quaker Approach to the Bible', F.Q., 1954, 73.
[2] Herbert G. Wood, *Friends and the Scriptures*, 15 ff.
[3] *Works*, II, 6. See also p. 57, Note 2, for Penington's 'spiritual epistemology'.
[4] *Apology*, III, V. Cf. Thomas a Kempis, *Imitation of Christ*, I, 5: 'Any holy scripture should be read in the same spirit in which it is written'.
[5] *Friends and the Scriptures*, 22.

force: 'The inward light', he says, 'enables us to appreciate history, not to ignore it'.[1]

However hard Friends may have tried, they were unable to ignore it. It is not only their 'frequent reading of the Holy Scriptures and other good books', a practice recommended by Fox particularly in connection with the education of children,[2] and his advice to translate the New Testament 'into everyman's language and mother tongue',[3] which contradicts the antihistorical attitude of Quaker mysticism; it is their very way of looking at the Holy Scriptures and other good books which goes to prove that, however historically ungrateful in theory, they did not escape the historicity of human existence. Immediate guidance, felt deeply as quite personal, prompted them all the same to look for other and earlier evidence of the same Spirit which they met within themselves. The first generation of Friends, living 'in the Kingdom', may not have deemed it necessary to stress this link with past revelations of the Spirit; but with the disappearance of the belief in the actual Second Coming the emphasis shifted quite naturally to all available historical examples, and especially those in the Bible, the book most readily to hand.

In this way not only the Inner Christ but also the Historic Christ who spoke through the Scriptures has nearly always enjoyed the concerned attention of Friends. The Scriptures were seen, perhaps not as a 'rule', but as a case-book full of evidence for the continued, and even progressive, revelation in history of that one unchangeable Spirit. But Quaker interest ranged further, beyond the Biblical canon, because 'the inspiration of the Holy Spirit has not ceased'.[4] Hence, 'for the Scripture to have a Finis is an impiety'.[5] Revelation may happen, in a small way, in each one of us even today if we hold ourselves open for the spiritual experience of Presence. Revelations, though different in expression according to time, place and the human soul in which they happen, allow new glimpses

---

[1] *Ibid.*, 19.
[2] *L.P.Q.*, 666.
[3] Here quoted after Brayshaw, *The Quakers*, 303 (London: George Allen & Unwin Ltd., 1938).
[4] Yearly Meeting Proceedings, 1919.
[5] Rendel Harris in the introduction to H. G. Wood, *Friends and the Scriptures*, 4.

of truth, seen for the first time by the dedicated mind, perhaps in lonely communion with God, perhaps in the communion of an inspired fellowship, and soon shared by him with others in quiet contemplation. Through amassing many such pieces of evidence Friends have actually been engaged on a kind of historiography of the working of the Spirit in time and world; they only overlooked that while they received and recorded their experiences they, too, were men *in history*. Otherwise they have known long before the existentialists that revelation 'does not come as an abstract and universal truth out of history' but 'is always special, for it always comes to particular men in particular situations in history'.[1]

A glance at the *Book of Discipline of the Religious Society of Friends*, published in numerous revisions for over two centuries, will bear this out. It is neither a credal and dogmatic work, a prayer book, nor, despite a section called Advices and Queries, a catechism. For the greatest part it consists, not of expositions and discourses which try to instruct, but of records of what happened to individuals and groups at one time or the other, under divine guidance. Even their resolutions arrived at in their business meetings have not necessarily a directive power but are recordings of what, at a certain point, was revealed as 'in right ordering' to a group of Friends. The *Book of Discipline* is therefore fundamentally historical and fundamentally unpragmatic. So are the Quaker obituary minutes testifying to 'the grace of God in the life' of a deceased Friend. So is the Quaker interpretation of the Scriptures which are for them neither code nor source, but a collection of testimonies of divine-human relationships, culminating in God's revelation in the Historic Christ.

Everything Friends select from the raw-material of happenings in world and time is chosen by them for its transparent witness to the working of the Holy Spirit in and through a man, or a group of men, called to undertake a task or to solve a dilemma or to adopt a form of conduct testifying to the power of the Spirit. Certainly, such case-histories leave out much of the fabric of what is commonly understood by his-

[1] Williams, *Interpreting Theology 1918-1952*, 66 (London: S.C.M. Press, 1953).

tory, and they make sense as history only if they are grasped by the reader as something far more relevant than pious stories, if they are interpreted by the same Spirit within himself. The moment the Spirit fails and becomes an object of mere lip-service, Friends may be far poorer than others because they have not many other links with history: they are then left with no more than some sectarian traditions and behaviour-patterns. This is the revenge of history for having been neglected by mysticism. Once the mystical insight has lost its virtue, and live spiritual experience has gone, no empty traditionalism can provide the power of drawing from the past the inspiration of the Presence which enables us to live towards the future.

Apprehending the Past: Traditionalism and Mythology

Traditionalism is the tragic irony of Quaker history. As already described, early Friends denied their own indebtedness to the past, if with different emphasis. Fox, in particular, appealed again and again to his hearers that they should rely on that which they had 'inwardly from God' and not on even the best historical authorities: 'You will say, Christ saith this, and the apostles say this, but what canst thou say?'[1] Early Friends were equally concerned with preventing later generations from looking back at them as their spiritual fathers. As early as 1657 a group of Friends drafted an epistle containing the clear warning

'that we be not again led back into the errors of those that went before us, who left the power and got into the form . . . that no footsteps may be left for those that shall come after, or to walk by example, but that all they may be directed and left to the truth, in it to live and walk and by it to be guided, that none may look back at us, nor have an eye behind them, but that all may look forward, waiting in the Spirit for the revelation of those glorious things which are to be made manifest to them'.[2]

Unfortunately their hopes were in vain. Their spiritual heirs continued waiting for 'those glorious things', but without finding in themselves a measure of that Spirit that would make them 'manifest' to them. So they 'left the power and got into form', and their peculiarities no longer set them apart for a

---
[1] Margaret Fell's report, here quoted after B.Q., 101.
[2] *Ibid.*, 329.

universal appeal but degenerated into mere oddities. The inspired testimonies of the first generation turned into 'our traditional testimonies' which are often held faithfully, not so much because they are experienced as true as because they have been held for so long. The plain dress which was a witness against the luxurious fashions of the seventeenth century became, in the eighteenth, the token of a sect, but was then often cut from most costly and luxurious material. Conservative Friends in America apply even now the plain speech, the thou and thee, which was introduced as a mark of social equality, but in our days has clearly become one of seclusion and inequality. I still remember Friends who in the forties of this century would not take off their hats in meeting unless for ministry and prayer; though today the taking off of the hat reflects not on social distinctions but on the good manners of the wearer. Quaker silences have often become 'as formalized as masses'.[1]

Perhaps the most telling departure into traditionalism was the introduction of birthright membership, a practice slightly more incompatible with inner guidance than infant baptism. All Friends of the first generation were, of necessity, 'convinced', they joined as adults or adolescents as do today the members of the newly founded Yearly Meetings in Europe and further afield. At a time when being a Quaker implied peculiarity at all events, and often enough bitter persecution for the sake of truth, the early movement would consist of people whose inner experience spoke clearly and irresistibly. At the same time many of the newly convinced Friends would bring with them a dowry of religious and theological education which made their opposition to outer knowledge innocuous. Once the great majority was born into the Society and enjoyed the benefits of a secluded Quaker upbringing, but not the benefits of learning from the wider world, the convergence of anti-historical attitude and the decline of spiritual power would leave them with little more than outward traditions.

It is the more wonderful that, in fact, Quaker traditionalism did not stifle all spiritual energies. Despite the apparently bar-

[1] Richard Niebuhr, *Christ and Culture*, 83 (London: Faber & Faber Ltd., 1952).

ren ground of much of its eighteenth and early nineteenth century life, there was many an admirable fruit and much spiritual beauty. True, even in this period some Friends were newly convinced and brought with them fruit from a different soil. More important, perhaps, was the fact that, with all separation from the world, contemporary influences could never be kept out completely: at all periods Quaker history runs parallel to that of its environment, and thus has shared in rationalist enlightenment, pietism, romanticist pantheism, evangelicalism and the rise of scientific thinking.

Thus it became possible that with the re-awakening of the spirit a movement rose from within the Society which has, for the last hundred years, been breaking up the ground of traditionalism, condemning the 'idolatry of the past' and regretting that 'we stopped thinking in the seventeenth century' (John Wilhelm Rowntree). Let us not assume, however, that the tradition of traditionalism is quite dead: in spite of the spiritual renewal of our Society we meet bits of it in every corner.

On the other hand, the reaction to traditionalism has become almost too strong in some quarters and the tendency to unite with the live forces of history threatens at times to destroy the regained power of the inner guidance, so that politics tries to stifle religion. This may be partly due to the increased number of convincements. The influx of new members, though far from sufficient, must be seen as one of the smaller ironies of Quaker history, for it is to no small extent due to the two world wars and the introduction of conscription: so many conscientious objectors found a spiritual home in the Society of Friends that the Society must be reckoned among the war profiteers. This fact illustrates very well the interrelation of inner guidance and temporal events.[1]

It has already been mentioned that the care which early Friends applied to their own records and the chronicling of their movement belies their anti-historical attitude. But Friends' occupation with history is concentrated largely on their own

---

[1] In the American Civil War such sympathizers, newly found under the strain and stress of war, were branded 'War-Quakers'. Cf. Q.P.W., 440. They should have been called anti-war Quakers, the true war-Quakers having joined up with the 15th Pennsylvania Regiment, the so-called 'Quaker' Regiment, *ibid.*, 424.

past and perhaps on New Testament history. If we think of the galaxy of Quaker scientists, we cannot help regretting the dearth of Quaker historians. This may be due partly to the exclusion of Friends from the universities for a considerable period, partly to our mysticism which is prone to develop a sense for nature rather than man's temporal affairs, and partly to an aversion to, and even fear of, the wicked world of man, in which historic greatness falls often so very short of saintliness and the Quaker scales of value.

Even regarding our own Quaker history, true historical sense was for a long time replaced by interest in minutiae. The carefulness of recording became a fault through exaggerated insistence on truthful wordings. The letter, not the Spirit, seemed to rule supreme. The concern 'that none may look back at us nor have an eye behind them' gave way to antiquarian preoccupation with the past. In recent decades it is probably no longer generally true that the curriculum of Quaker schools is 'overloaded with Quaker history and biography . . . to preserve and transmit "the heritage of the Society",'[1] sometimes rather the opposite may be nearer the truth; but even today the interest for our past history is not always wholesome. If such interest is directed towards finding evidence for the working of the Spirit, it has value and significance. If it is attenuated by a smile about the quaintness of some of our spiritual forebears, coupled with the recognition that we are not as free of traditionalism as we pretend, such interest has at least some reconciling grace. But if it is borne by pride in our Quaker tradition, even worse, if it desires to discover proof texts and lessons for our time, arguing that 'George Fox saith this, the Valliant Sixty say this, so what is left for thee to say?' —then this interest is an attempt at replacing history by hagiography, which is only another form of historical ingratitude because it lacks true responsibility towards past, present and future.

Hagiography, however, is only the negative aspect of a nonhistorical apprehension of the past. Its positive aspects concern our Quaker mythology. A mythology has very important functions which are not always clearly understood, especially not

[1] L.P.Q., 684.

in an age in which 'demythologizing' has become the favourite occupation of some theologians, though admittedly they are trying no more than to replace the mythology of the Second Temple by that of the Nuclear Age.[1] We misunderstand the significance of a myth if we regard it as a mere legend which is probably untrue and must be discarded. A myth may be factually untrue, as for instance the story of the garden of Eden and Adam's fall, and still be the formulation of a truth which cannot easily, or not at all, be grasped in any other way. A myth is one of the human languages for some otherwise indescribable knowledge of faith.

Myth, in its original sense, means word, speech, narration: it narrates religious insights which cannot be reported in straightforward language—though straightforward language is itself anything but straightforward, namely a mixture of symbolic, metaphorical and picturesque usages and conventions. Still, this so-called straightforward language cannot convey religious meanings as profoundly and simply as a myth can. It sticks far more to the surface, to the outward facts. The mythological language, on the other hand, has the power of communicating religious insights without changing them into theory or dogma: it brings together the facts and their deeper meaning in one symbol, the myth; it is therefore the natural link between history and inner experience.

The crucifixion, for instance, is a fact undisputed by serious historians, not excluding Marxists and other anti-Christian or anti-religious writers. For the Christian, however, it has, through inner experience (and not only by pious tradition) a meaning which is not so much plainly historical as mythical: the mere mentioning of the word 'cross' symbolizes to him worlds of experience and insight which he can know from within after having been introduced to the fact from without. The cross is a fact, the mystery behind it as experienced by a man is a myth full of power and glory.

Similarly, the convincement of George Fox or Margaret Fell, which in content may remind us of the story of the baptism of Jesus, is an indisputable historical fact. For a non-Christian

---

[1] Cf. Niebuhr's valid criticism of Bultmann in *The Self and the Dramas of History*, 110 ff. (London: Faber & Faber Ltd., 1956).

psychologist who may take true enthusiasm for mere overexcitement, this fact is the raw-material of a psychological case-history. For an anti-Quaker Christian it is the account of a devil-inspired aberration; and this, of course, is a myth, too. For the non-Quaker Christian it may be a strange incident showing something of God's power in a queer saint: it may fit in with his own mythology and so help him in his faith. For a Quaker, however, even if he be a psychologist and look at it as a scientist at one moment, it is the kind of myth which he understands by a mere hint, which appeals to his emotional consent and which expresses and creates for him and his Friends a sense of deep community. It is then no longer an odd example of the kind of experience a man may have; it is like a word from the family language, a language understood by the members of the family even when used in unfinished sentences, and not too difficult to learn for those who are of the same spiritual stock.

The very story that we must not be 'thieves' and take the words of Christ and the apostles instead of those we have 'inwardly from God' is, paradoxically enough, a myth: how many of us would dare to rely on our first-hand experience rather than traditional myths, how many would clearly know how to understand that we have something inwardly from God, had we not been educated into a tradition which has made the convincement of Margaret Fell into a myth? As in every mythology some of the Quaker myths may not be factually true, such as George Fox's alleged exhortation: 'Let your lives speak', or his apocryphal advice to William Penn when the newly convinced young aristocrat wondered about carrying his sword and was told: 'Wear it as long as thou canst'. May they be historically untrue or inaccurate, they are spiritually true enough, even in an age when swords are no longer worn by aristocrats, and not even by the military except when on parade.

The myth is the link between religious experience and past events, that is, that past which—whether factually true or not —has been apprehended, consciously or subconsciously, as deeply significant for the spiritual self, as expression of something known to the self in his own right.

If this understanding of the word myth is accepted, we can

go on and say that the central myth of Quakerism is the Inner Christ. This myth connects, by its very wording, the historic name with the human ability to communicate directly with God. Hence Inner Christ does not stand in a real contrast to the Historic Christ, as is so often assumed. The intellectual difficulty, the tension between the Light within and the Jesus of history, disappears in the myth, as has always been the case in the experience of the great Quaker saints. The Inner Christ is a mystery which may be analyzed but cannot be solved in thought, yet is, as a myth, quite lucid to the Christian mystic. It is the Historic Christ himself who is apprehended within, however inexplicably, though no more difficult to explain than when he was encountered on the roads to Emmaus and Damascus.

4

THE QUAKER ATTITUDE
IN HISTORY

Hagiography and mythology are two forms of apprehending the past in what, strictly speaking, is a non-historical way. Hagiography distorts the facts beyond the inevitable because it wants to preen itself with its ancestry as though the glories of the past equipped the present with equal splendour. It thus mistakes emotional self-satisfaction for inspiration. The same error may happen with mythology, namely if it treats as factually true the things that are only spiritually and symbolically true and do not come to life unless re-lived in quite different outward shapes. Certainly, such escapist glorification of the past is not remedied by reverting the process and digging up only its ugly remnants; by taking the worm's eyes view or that of the proverbial valet who knows a public hero mainly in his underwear. All the same, we cannot fulfil our own historical task in the way our ancestors have fulfilled theirs unless we look at their mistakes and weaknesses together with their achievements and merits.

Have not modern Friends sometimes found too much satisfaction in praising the greatness of the first generations of Friends for the sake of denouncing our own degeneracy and of finding the pleasure of pseudo-greatness in self-accusations and comparisons to our own disadvantage? True humility humbles itself before God, not before its ancestry. We are neither as good nor as bad as we often pretend, we are fairly ordinary. True, our generation cannot presume to equal the heroic age of Quakerism, and we may be right in improving our 'moral education' by the 'habitual vision of greatness' (Whitehead). On the other hand, beating our breasts and praising the achievements of our forebears as though they had never known any doubts and had never solved them by ambiguities, may result in the opposite of encouragement: it may produce at best a sense of failure, at worst a welcome excuse.

For this reason it is of great importance that we try to understand early Friends in their historicity, with both their creative and their less creative reactions to their time and place. Understanding, however, means far more than reading and knowing about these things: it means absorbing the significance of their weaknesses and failures as fully as we have absorbed the significance of their achievements. Most of the difficulties which beset the minds of modern Friends with regard to action in history, that is with regard to our own political, social, economic and international problems, can be exemplified in the very early days of Quakerism.

The Crisis of 1659

Though early Friends believed that they lived in the Kingdom, their historicity bound them inescapably to the events in England during the Commonwealth and Restoration periods, and indeed their conviction of the Second Coming of Christ forms such a link with their contemporaries. Let us look at the context in which Fox declares, that 'Christ *is* come and *doth* dwell in the hearts of his people'. Where he records his time of incarceration at Launceston in 1656, he says:

'Now while I was in prison here the Baptists and Fifth-Monarchy-Men prophesied that this year Christ should come and reign upon earth a thousand years. And they looked upon this reign to be outward, whenas he was come inwardly in the hearts of his people to reign and rule there, these professors would not receive him there. So they failed in their prophecy and expectation, and had not the possession of him. But Christ is come and doth dwell in the hearts of his people and reigns there. And thousands, at the door of whose hearts he hath been knocking, have opened to him, and he is come in, and doth sup with them and they with him, the heavenly supper with the heavenly and spiritual man. So many of these Baptists and Monarchy people turned the greatest enemies to the possessors of Christ. But he reigns in the hearts of his saints over all their envy'.[1]

The first thing to remember is that this paragraph was written many years after the events; the second that extremist

[1] *Journal*, 261.

IN THE WORLD AND OF THE WORLD 73

groups may be mutually hostile[1] and yet very similar in outlook. Fox denies here clearly any connection between a political and a spiritual Kingdom of God. True, he understands both these interpretations of the Kingdom as happening *on earth*, but in one case it means God's kingship in the hearts of his people, in the other it is clearly a territorial Kingdom in this world, the Kingdom as shown to Jesus by Satan. When reading that passage, we would not think that this temptation could ever have visited George Fox and his Friends; but this is not so, and at one time some of them nearly succumbed to it. While it may be true that in Launceston Fox saw clearly the difference between the inwardness of Christ in the human heart on the one hand, and the external rule of Christ directly or through his saints on the other, early Friends and probably George Fox himself were in their first period not as averse to violent political action for the sake of the Kingdom as we often assume. Like other Christians they distinguished merely between the just and the unjust use of force.[2] Many of them shared the millenarian hopes for radical social changes, a hope very characteristic of left-wing Puritanism in the Commonwealth period.

For instance, Edward Burrough, who called himself A Son of Thunder, prophesied that 'every yoke and burden shall be taken off from the neck of the poor; true judgment and justice, mercy and truth, peace and righteousness shall be exalted; and all the nations shall have judges as at the first and counsellors as at the beginning'.[3] Lest we read this as day-dreams of a religious poet filled with Old Testament reminiscences and describing far-off events at the end of time, let us put this quotation alongside a letter which Burrough wrote in 1659 *To the English Army, to Officers and Soldiers*, indicating something of the methods by which that blissful state of affairs is to come about. Here he says: 'Hew down the tops, strike at the branches, make way that the axe may be laid to the root of

[1] B.Q., 285.
[2] Cf. Cole, *Quakers and Politics*, 1652-1660. Passim, esp. pp. 283 f. Unpublished. Available in Friends House Library.
[3] For this quotation and the following analysis I am greatly indebted to Maclear, "Quakerism and the End of the Interregnum". In *Church History*, 1950, 240-270. For a more detailed narration cf. Cole, *op. cit.*

the tree, that your sword and the sword of the Lord may neither leave root nor branch of idolatry, oppressions and tyranny...'[1]

Modern Christian pacifists may think this is a queer way of addressing an army, particularly if we remember that at that juncture 'tyranny' meant Stuart monarchy and if we put 'idolatry' into the concrete terms used by George Fox, in a letter *To the Council of Officers of the Army . . . and for the Inferior Officers and Soldiers to Read*. Here Fox says: 'To them that do well, the sword is a praise. . . . And if ever you soldiers and true officers come again into the power of God which hath been lost, never set up your standard until you come to Rome, and it be atop of Rome then there let your standard stand'.[2] Fox recommends here no less than a crusade, a religious war against the capital of Popery.

True, even in this period Friends would insist that those who had accepted Christ into their hearts could not fight with carnal weapons because they 'lived in the virtue of that life and power that took away the occasion of all wars'.[3] But while taking that stand for themselves, they felt few scruples about encouraging others who were not yet convinced of the truth, in the use of carnal weapons for the establishment of an outward Kingdom of God. Thus no clear line was drawn in fact between God's kingship given in grace to man through Christ's coming, and man's ability, if and when 'come again into the power of God', of bringing about a utopian Kingdom on earth.

We know that many soldiers of Cromwell's army sympathized with Quakerism, and George Fox no more went out of his way to preach against the vocation of soldiering as such than John the Baptist or, for all we know Jesus himself. Indeed, Fox, Howgill, Burrough and others protested vigorously against the dismissal of Quaker soldiers from Cromwell's army; their egalitarian radicalism, refusing the 'hat-honour' to officers,

[1] Quoted here after Nuttall, *The Holy Spirit in Puritan Faith and Experience*, 132 (Oxford: Basil Blackwell, 1946). Spelling modernized. Cf. B.Q., 358 f.
[2] *Ibid.* Cf. Fox's address to Oliver Cromwell, quoted in B.Q., 440.
[3] *Journal*, 65.

threatened to undermine military discipline.[1] Probably the most balanced expression of the Quaker view comes from Isaac Penington, who grants to governments the power of using weapons and even the necessity of doing so: 'For this the present estate of things may and doth require' . . . 'But yet there is a better state which the Lord has already brought some into, and which nations are to expect and travel towards', and he is quite clear about it that those who have reached that stage cannot fight.[2] His is very nearly the attitude of the early Church and the Christian apologists of the first few centuries.[3] This is not the place to discuss the practical difficulties and the moral ambiguities of such a position: early Friends like early Christians were not so much aware of them as we are today.

Penington's tolerant attitude towards those who have not yet been convinced of the truth and who therefore feel it right to fight is, however, very different from the attitude, mentioned above, of encouraging explicitly, indeed, assisting non-combattantly, those who do the actual fighting. Such encouragement was given spontaneously, not under a system of conscription or outward pressure, and was offered in the clear expectation of enjoying with the soldiers the wages of their unrighteousness. This is a division of labour between vocational pacifist and vocational combattant not altogether dissimilar to that between war-minded priests who do not fight, and the soldiers and weapons blessed by them for the purpose of working death and destruction.[4] It is exactly this which the letters of Burrough and Fox which we have quoted express, it is this, too, which led to the great spiritual crisis of Quakerism in 1659. The word crisis is used here not in that vague sense of modern journalism but in the sense of a true turning point in mortal danger.

When the return of the royalist 'tyranny' was imminent and

[1] Cole, op. cit., 55 ff. and 221. There were similar protests against the dismissal of Quaker magistrates.
[2] 'Weighty Questions . . .' In Works, 293 ff., here quoted after the summary in Q.P.W., 124 ff. Cf. S.P.Q., 610 ff.
[3] Cf. Cadoux, The Early Christian Attitude to War (London: The Swarthmore Press Ltd., 1919).
[4] The most shocking example of such blasphemy in recent time is the prayer offered on the island of Tinian just before the aeroplane went up to drop the first atom bomb on Hiroshima. Quoted in Gollwitzer, Die Christen und die Atomwaffen, 7 (Munich: Chr. Kaiser Verlag, 1957).

with it the possibilities of 'idolatry' and 'oppressions', Friends could not themselves fight with carnal weapons for the salvation of a political system which seemed so much more to the hearts of Quaker and non-Quaker saints alike. In spite of increasing estrangement from Cromwell since about 1656, they could not but sympathize with the Commonwealth rather than the Monarchy. They feared the Restoration as much as they expected it to happen as God's punishment on the republican leaders for their apostasy from the cause of freedom and for the persecution of God's people.

Already the famous letter drafted (possibly by William Dewsbury, later the pattern of political quietism[1]) in the General Meeting of Balby, in 1656, contained a clause recommending 'that if any be called to serve the Commonwealth in any public service which is for the public wealth and good, that with cheerfulness it be undertaken and in faithfulness discharged unto God, that therein patterns and examples in the thing that is righteous ye may be to those that are without'.[2] The question was what service could be considered 'for the public wealth and good'. Dewsbury, for one, did not wish to apply this recommendation to the military defence of the Commonwealth but worked persistently for the withdrawal of Friends from public affairs and their suffering submission to the worldly powers, even without recourse to the law.

But some Friends thought differently, especially when, under Richard Cromwell, The Rump was recalled and new political hopes swayed many of them. They thus helped from their side to produce 'an almost unbearable tension in the community between the tendency toward awaiting the rule of Christ in a quietistic political indifference and the ambition "to rule for God".'[3] These Friends, who would not themselves bear arms, would still support General Lambert in the suppression of the Royalist rebellion under Sir George Booth in Cheshire: they rendered intelligence services and helped with capturing some of the Royalists; though they did not earn much thanks for their help, as Howgill's bitter complaints prove.[4]

[1] B.Q., 312. Cf. S.P.Q., 284.
[2] B.Q., 313.
[3] Maclear, loc. cit., 260. Cf. Cole, op. cit., c. V.
[4] Ibid., 263.

Again, Friends who would not themselves bear arms would not turn down the request of Sir Henry Vane to stabilize the tottering republic by becoming not only magistrates, but also commissioners of the militia: five of them complied in Westminster and seven in Bristol.[1] The French ambassador, adumbrating closer co-operation between the declining Parliament and the Quakers, stated with some irony that 'the spirit of God, by which they are ruled, now permits them to take part in the affairs of this world'.[2] We cannot be surprised, therefore, that after the Restoration political suspicion hovered round Friends for a long time in spite of their frequent declarations of loyalty and repudiation of all violence, even 'for the Kingdom of Christ',[3] and that serious persecution began at once with the abortive rising of the Fifth Monarchists in 1661. Friends had indeed become implicated, if not in 1661, at least in 1659, even though in most cases it may have been no more than 'guilt by association'.[4] But 'as late as November, 1662, Edward Byllinge gave his fellow Quakers cause for considerable embarrassment by refusing to give an undertaking that he would never take up arms against the king'.[5]

George Fox seems to have been uncertain for a time during the critical months of 1659 what to counsel to those who had accepted positions of commissioners of the militia: 'You cannot leave them seeing ye have gone amongst them', is his hesitant advice.[6] Nor was there any decisive repudiation of Anthony Pearson, who had become a commissioner of the militia in the North and who later, after many vacillations, saved his life by making his peace with Monarchy and Church.[7]

[1] B.Q., 461. S.P.Q., 18.
[2] Maclear, loc. cit., 259.
[3] S.P.Q., 13. This telling clause in the submission to Charles II in 1660 is clearly intended to show the distance between themselves and the 'Saints'.
[4] Thus Tolles, Quakerism and Politics, 8 (Ward Lecture, 1956).
[5] Cole, op. cit., 279.
[6] S.P.Q., 18.
[7] B.Q., 462/3, 113/4. Cf. 161 where his very Quakerly conversation with Cromwell of 1654 is recorded. His inconsistencies are only more apparent than those of Dewsbury and Fox. Howgill, so passionate a prophet of social change, was nevertheless more shocked than Fox about Pearson's becoming a commissioner of the militia, a striking example for Quaker inconsistency at that juncture. For Burrough's inconsistency compare the quotations on pp. 73/74 above with S.P.Q., 17.

How much the mind of Fox was occupied with the ever-changing situation may be seen from the fact that in 1659 he wrote his 'most socio-political tract'[1] called *Fifty nine particulars laid down for regulating things*. On the other hand, his *Journal* for that period quotes many warnings to Friends to 'keep out of plots and bustling'[2] and 'of the powers of the earth that run into wars and fightings'.[3] He regrets that 'some foolish rash spirits that came amongst us were going to take up arms', and reports that he refused 'great places and commands',[4] probably a colonelcy offered to him by Sir Henry Vane. As Braithwaite says, just for that period 'the *Journal* becomes strangely confused and fragmentary',[5] and the letters Fox inserts for that time may easily have been misdated by a few months. He admits that he suffered from great weakness, and in the late summer of 1659 he withdrew to Reading where he was 'under great sufferings and exercises, and in great travail in (his) spirit for ten weeks time'.[6] He was 'almost choked' with 'the nations' hypocrisy and treachery and falseness',[7] and only after ten weeks of spiritual darkness was he ready to come forward with his message: now he called clearly for withdrawal from politics and recommended suffering obedience to whatever government may come to power.[8] As he puts it in later years:

'For in my travail and sufferings at Reading when people were at a stand and could not tell what might come in nor who might rule, I told them the Lord's power was over all, for I had travailed through it, and his day shined whosoever should come in; and all would be well whether the King came in or no, to them that loved God and were faithful in him; and so I bid all Friends fear none but the Lord, and keep in his power that is over all'.[9]

[1] Maclear, *loc. cit.*, 254.
[2] *Journal*, 357.
[3] *Journal*, 358.
[4] *Ibid.*
[5] *B.Q.*, 354.
[6] *Journal*, 353. Cf. 356.
[7] *Journal*, 354. Cf. Maclear, *loc. cit.*, 262: 'It is impossible to speak with complete assurance here, but may not this dark night have been due to Fox's wrestling with the problems posed by the attempted inclusion of the Quakers in Vane's kingdom of the saints?'
[8] Maclear, *loc. cit.*, 268.
[9] *Journal*, 361/2.

The Practice of the Paradox of the Kingdom

The travail and sufferings of Fox at Reading are a profound symbol of the unending conflict in the soul of Quakerism, a conflict caused by the necessity, yet impossibility, of harmonizing the life in the Kingdom of God with the historicity of man. At that moment Fox solved it by greater withdrawal from the world. He thus re-established that conservativism inherent in New Testament Christianity. Since 'the Lord's power is over all' including every worldly government, every government is to be obeyed and even appreciated in its righteous functions. But every worldly government is to be disobeyed by spiritual resistance in suffering if it trespasses into the realm of conscience. The important point in distinguishing the New Testament and Quaker attitudes from those of Lutheranism and other Erastian interpretations lies in the fact that this realm of conscience is not circumscribed by individual rights against the government and individual duties towards God: the duties towards God, and his kingship in our hearts, widen the realm of conscience so as to extend to all mankind, not excluding the rulers both tolerant and tyrannical. Hence Christian 'conservativism' as to governments is incomplete if it is not blended with Christian 'radicalism', because even under the best government human brotherhood is never fully realized or realizable. Prophetic exhortation both inside and outside the Church and directed in particular to the powers-that-be is the corollary of the recognition that government, while from God, is still under God, and while claiming obedience, is in need of admonition.

The crisis of 1659 helped to establish in Quakerism that blending of conservatism and radicalism which we find already implied in the New Testament teaching regarding worldly affairs. Before that crisis there was great danger that radicalism alone would hold sway over the Quaker movement and, by trying to bring about a territorial Kingdom or at least a rule of the saints, would destroy, through the use of violence and war, the message of love. This danger was not overcome once for all in 1659. It recurs whenever some Friends, in search of utopia, or even engaged in a righteous cause, help to create situations which lead to violence. Some will stop their horses at the last moment, others will simply be carried away by the passion of their concerns. Such situations arose in America in 1773,[1] and may arise in Africa today.

After the 'traumatic experiences of the Restoration year'[2] the opposite danger began raising its head: that Christian conservativism would rule supreme and would lead from suffering resistance to quiet submission, to the acceptance that 'the setting up and putting down of governments is God's peculiar prerogative',[3] that not prophetic exhortation, but quietist aloofness from the wider world of men is the truly Christian attitude. This danger, too, is still with us, not only among those who hold that 'our citizenship is in heaven',[4] but also among those whose one-sided radicalism has made them hope too long for a utopian territorial Kingdom and who, in their deep disappointment that the world is not progressing visibly towards it, are now withdrawing from the world.

The true Christian and Quaker attitude, blending conservatism and radicalism, shows in ever new varieties our suspense between God and history and causes the many inconsistencies to which 'consistent' Friends are liable. Indeed, consistent Quakerism may never have existed either before or after 1659. Where it seems to appear, it is probably not consistent with the Quaker message but tied up with some legalistic principles. All the same, some people may regret that the events of 1659 seem to have broken the strong spirit of consistency of the Quaker movement and thus opened the so-called 'Second Period of Quakerism', which to them sounds like 'secondary period'. This, I think, is also the view of Maclear, who sums up the meaning of the crisis of 1659 in the following words:

'The earlier millenarian sensitivity was gradually lost, and the once vigorous witness against the evils of society was so quickly altered that analysts of the Restoration period have been able to find little here but an earnest humanitarianism devoid of structural interest. Restoration Quakerism became the norm, and was treated by later historians as coming in an unbroken line from the day the vision burst upon George Fox. When this had been accomplished, the

---

[1] Cf. Q.A.C., 560, on John Dickinson: 'His life was typical of Quaker influence—potent to the very outbreak of war, suddenly and strikingly impotent after it becomes a fact'.
[2] Tolles, *loc. cit.*, 8.
[3] Q.P.W., 109.
[4] Cadbury, 'The Basis of Quaker Political Concern. In *The Friend* (Philadelphia), 1954/5, 71-75 and 86-88.

domestication process was nearly complete, and Quakerism was finding its niche within the pale of respectable English nonconformity'.[1]

All this is perfectly true, but should we really regret that 'domestication'? If we ponder deeply enough over the events of 1659, a few points emerge very clearly: Early Friends, as much concerned for contemporary public issues as most of us are today, were as often of two minds amongst themselves and within themselves as we are. Indeed, the frequent accusation of modern Friends that we have become too 'respectable' for world-shaking action can, with good historical reason, be laid at the doorstep of George Fox himself. But do we not see that his 'domestication' was a Christian choice under divine guidance, namely the portentous final decision for *suffering* evil rather than *inflicting* it? That he chose the cross of persecution rather than the bloody rule of the saints? When he refused to yield to the temptation of becoming another John of Leyden, he opened, in the event, the way for the Holy Experiment, the abolition of slavery and many other forms of constructive Christian action—admittedly most of them full of compromise and ambiguity, but all of them better than another unholy experiment like the Kingdom of God in Münster, which would have been a compromise with historic death.

Granted that the price of non-violence may be apparent impotence at the most crucial moments of history, and that lack of efficacy in matters temporal may create a sense of inefficiency, failure and even damnation: only if we allow this sense (which in Lutheran terminology is no sin, but an *Anfechtung*, a tormenting doubt) to exhaust our spiritual resources, only if we lose faith in the meaning of failure, have we truly failed. 'Domestication' and 'respectability' are adequate verdicts only where 'earnest humanitarianism' (that is radical witness for human brotherhood under the Fatherhood of God) is surrendered, either through withdrawal from the world or through submissive accommodation to the powers-that-be. A truly radical witness for brotherhood is circumscribed not only by the ends for which it testifies but also by the means it chooses for action. It was the decision of 1659 which firmly established our historic peace testimony; it was for Christ's way of love

[1] *Loc. cit.*, 269/70.

that the appearance of 'domestication' was accepted, and revolutionary radicalism changed its method from violent revolution to what appears now as earnest humanitarian concern. Henry J. Cadbury has shown very well why the Quaker method is fundamentally different from simple humanitarianism. He says:

'The Quaker is motivated by what he believes is demanded of him from within, not by what outside him demands something. It is not that war is injurious, but that he should not take part in war. It is not that slavery is abstractly unjust, but that he has no business to own slaves. That is, that he should not willingly join practices of society that he believes are wrong for him to practise. That these practices are injurious or unfair to others is, of course, part of the reason for his non-compliance, his concern for reform, but the proximate (immediate) motivation for the Quaker lies in his own conscience, his sense of duty, his own "noblesse oblige".

'His concern, therefore, is quite different from mere humanitarianism. He wants injustice and suffering for others relieved, but he is perhaps even more anxious to rid himself of any guilt or responsibility for it, and he feels his responsibility acutely'.[1]

In different terms: it is the experience of the presence of the Kingdom and not the utopian hope for a territorial Kingdom on earth which prompts Quaker action. This presence may be understood as already living in the Kingdom, or as God's Kingship in the hearts of his people, as mystical experience of Presence, or as the leadings of love, purity and truth in a more ethical sense: all these forms of understanding have one thing in common, namely that it is the *present* experience which is central in Quaker faith and action. This emphasis on the presence of the Kingdom does not exclude the hope for the Kingdom which is to come. But this is a hope for an action of God and as such outside the reach of man. Man can wait for it, pray for it, seek for it and be ready for it; he cannot work for it in the primitive sense of trying to bring it about. The mustard seed has its growing power from God, and the pearl of great price is an unexpected discovery.

Admittedly, this line has not always been drawn clearly in Quaker and other Christian thinking, and the hope for the coming of the Kingdom has often been whittled down to utopian expectations. The vagaries of our peace testimony may exemplify this. As already pointed out, early Friends saw the

[1] "The Basis of Quaker Political Concern", loc. cit.

peace testimony closely connected with their experience of the Kingdom; it was the corollary of being convinced of the truth. They did not expect the world to accept the ways of peace until it, too, had left the 'mixture'[1] and had attained the 'restoration by Christ'.[2] Modern Friends, on the other hand, insist far more on the necessity of bringing about international peace and justice without much regard to the spiritual state which the world has attained. True, it is merely a change of emphasis since few Friends are unaware of the spiritual conditions of peace. Nevertheless, it shifts our peace testimony in some measure from the religious to the political field. Penn's *Essay towards the Present and Future Peace of Europe* and Bellers' *Reasons for an European State* are the ancestors of many Quaker plans for peace, and not all the planners had proved as clearly as Penn and Bellers that they started from a present experience rather than from a utopian hope based on present disillusionment.[3] The more Friends lost the hope that all or most men would live in the Kingdom before very long, the more have they transferred the hope for peace from its eschatological context to that of utopian political fulfilment on earth through human agency. The less they experienced themselves as *living in* the Kingdom, the more they spoke of *working for* the Kingdom.

However, their continuing experience of the presence of the Kingdom and of the promptings of love, purity and truth within, has prevented them from using un-Christian short-cut methods to bring about utopia. It has kept them nearer a state of love and non-violence and has brought them back, again and again, from utopian hopes to a realistic tackling of the next problem. This is what critics of Quakerism are inclined to overlook. They are rightly apprehensive when they hear Friends speak too often of 'working for the Kingdom' since this phrase is indicative of a utopian attitude. As already pointed out, the Kingdom cannot be 'worked for', but only 'prayed for' and 'sought for'; it is a gift of God, an act of his grace. As the para-

---

[1] Barclay, *Apology*, Prop. XV, XV.
[2] See above, p. 53.
[3] Penn's idea of collective security enforced by the military means of the other States against an aggressor State, would hardly meet the approval of modern Friends.

dox of the Kingdom has it: it is both a gift already received and a gift promised. The seeking and waiting for it, the very readiness for its coming, the attitude of longing hope, consists not only in praying for it to come, but also in actions of love which do not spring from ourselves but are the result of our experience of its real presence, of the promptings of love, purity and truth in our hearts. While we must not pretend that we work for the coming of the Kingdom, we live and work in the experience of its presence and thus live in readiness for its coming. We are workers together with God in spreading his gospel and being his hands and feet on earth—but all this does not create the Kingdom but makes us ready for receiving it more fully in the present while hoping more faithfully for it in the eschatological future. If we presume to try and work for the Kingdom that is to come, we do not work for the Kingdom but for utopia. If, however, we live and work in its presence, we enter the attitude of readiness for its coming.

Our critics assert that because our political hopes may often be utopian, our present attitude of love and suffering resistance is equally utopian. Unless realism has no meaning other than *realpolitik*, our attitude is, however, utterly realistic because it brings to bear on the real conditions in time, an influence flowing through us from our experience of Presence, which helps to shape creatively the next historical moment. Many Friends may be utopians regarding the future of mankind; most of them are nevertheless realistic utopians who start from the given situation, from something that has to be done here and now, and are motivated by an inner knowledge of the presence of the Kingdom. True, there may be less *waiting* for the Kingdom that is to come than *working* for it (which is utopian): but the foundation of their lives is no vain millenarian expectation, it is a present experience which issues in actions of love (which is realistic). The temporal result may have the appearance of many compromises and failures, but the impact of their witness on historical development is as undeniable as is that of many self-appointed realists who, too, achieve nothing better than compromises and failures.

Some of our critics seem to be aware of this; for this is the only explanation of their ambivalent judgment that we were hopeless idealists whose thinking had gone awry, and that it was still good to have us, if only as a 'standing perplexity'.[1] Being a standing perplexity, we seem to fulfil a wholesome function in human society—by the grace of God.

Historic Testimony and Historical Situation

There is, however, another change of emphasis in our peace testimony since its early proclamation, which we should assess carefully for a deeper understanding of the Quaker attitude in history. We must remember that our testimony originated in the conditions of civil war, not of international war. Hence the conflict of loyalties experienced by early Friends was not of the kind modern Friends imply when speaking of war and peace. The central issue of 1659 was not patriotism, but political and religious affiliation. Seen in this light, early Friends solved their inner conflict by declaring, with some notable exceptions, their detachment from party politics. Of course, this is not the whole truth: their detachment was not only a political, but also a spiritual decision, enjoined on them by their obedience to Christ. But their decision against party affiliations did not imply a disloyalty to one of them. Something of the inner conflict of early Friends returned (with many differences, for instance regarding religion and the slavery issue) in the American Civil War, and even in the War of Revolution, in this respect a better name than War of Independence; though the development of American patriotism some time before its outbreak makes the assessment rather complex. The first world war, again, poses quite different issues from a possible third world war, because of the ideological issues involved in the East-West tension.

Beyond dispute, civil wars emphasize the heinousness of bloodshed far more strongly than international wars because they take members of the same family and next-door neighbours to opposite sides of the barricade. No pacifist has described such a situation more powerfully than Shakespeare.[2] To use a sociological term: they are in-group wars rather than out-group wars. We may hold that all men are brothers under

---

[1] Thus in different context the Rev. O. S. Tomkins in an address to the Third World Conference of Friends. *Friends Face Their Fourth Century*, p. 7.
[2] *King Henry VI, Part III*, Act Two, Scene 5.

God, and may strive for making all mankind an in-group, yet the breach of an actual in-group, felt as being one by all its members, is spiritually and psychologically a much more shattering experience than external war. It is not by chance that the peace testimony has become a real issue in Germany for the first time when war threatens to break out between East and West Germans, under the rule of two hostile parties.

In a foreign war, however, even the advocate of non-violence will normally know quite well the side to which his temporal loyalty goes out. This is true even though some pacifists, in the conflict of their souls and the heat of controversy, may make statements apparently abandoning their patriotism. The real conflict within them, however, is not the choosing of sides. but the wrong done by their own side, and the evil means used by their compatriots in the pursuance of perhaps quite legitimate aims and justifiable causes. In brief, the acceptance of the rule of Charles II by early Friends does not mean exactly the same thing as the acceptance of the rule of George III by American Friends in 1773, far less the acceptance of the rule of Hitler or Stalin by the English Quaker of the mid-twentieth century; and it does not help him in his inner conflict when advice is given by pointing to the example of early Friends. It is no example. The peace testimony of 1660 is essentially different from that of 1959; and if we look for its earliest application to inter-State relations in our modern sense, we must refer to Robert Barclay's address to the ambassadors assembled at Nimuegen in 1678.[1] Indeed, the spiritual conflict of the pacifist patriot grows to its full size only with the introduction of universal conscription, though adumbrated earlier by the temporary imposition of militia duties in England and America.

I have chosen the difference between civil and foreign war conditions as an example, though a striking one, of the very different situations which Friends seem to have answered with one testimony.[2] Another example which could be elaborated is the variety of governmental systems allowing for different degrees of popular participation. Obviously, Christian responsi-

[1] Cf. Q.P.W., 147 ff.
[2] The lessons drawn from the Gandhian technique in Africa and India are equally open to criticism if thought of as spiritually and psychologically transferable to international war.

bility demands a different attitude under a system which excludes the people or certain minorities from civic responsibility from that under another system which expects the exertion of full citizenship. It leads to confusion of thought if we treat alike incomparable situations, for instance one in which we are merely *subjects,* which really means subjected objects of governmental control, with another one where we should act as Christian *citizens* in duty bound to help with the control of public affairs.

The introduction of democracy, which is so often assumed to alleviate the problem for the Christian, creates in some respects greater moral and psychological difficulties than absolutism or tyranny: not only is the Christian as citizen far more responsible for governmental action, he is also confronted with the complex issue of the relationship between minority and majority, and with the ambiguity of being called upon to participate in ruling, yet not to obey rulings against his conscience. Indeed, with the emergence of full-fledged Christian citizenship—in contrast to the Christian as mere subject—a profound change has taken place in the consciousness of precisely the most responsible persons: their predicament shows clearly in their deep sense of collective guilt when their own side has gone wrong while struggling desperately against that very concept of collective guilt if it concerns other nations. In brief, our responsibility to Christ remains the same, but its realization in the actual situation is an ever new problem which knows no precedent.

If we read through the various affirmations on war and peace in our *Book of Discipline,*[1] we cannot deny their consistency: they are of one spirit and describe similar attitudes. But if we try to understand them singly, as they arose in their historical settings as expressions of the guidance received at particular junctures, we shall soon discover that, though stated in similar terms, they have different significance and hardly offer concrete advice for the concrete situation. This means in fact that in every new situation our belief in the Kingdom that is to come must be sought anew and that the application of love,

---

[1] *Christian Practice* (1945), 130 ff. Cf. *The Quaker Peace Testimony,* an anthology published by Friends Peace Committee.

purity and truth, resulting from the experience of the presence of the Kingdom, must be found through an original act of creative faithfulness.

True, we speak of Quaker principles as though we could derive from them clear directions for our decisions. There is no denying that at times the attitude of Friends was, and still is, directed by principles and has yielded to legalism enforced by the discipline of tradition. In such moments Friends go far beyond trying to interpret the guidance they have received, in a spirit of humility and search: they predetermine, as it were, what guidance they are going to receive. Altogether I dislike the phrase 'Quaker principles' and think it incompatible with our deepest convictions. We come much closer to what we mean when speaking of historic 'testimonies', a phrase which indicates that in a number of situations a similar spiritual experience has reached groups of people. True, many of them may have brought in the background of a Quaker education and its sensitiveness; but if they have been faithful, they have come to their decision not because 'this is what is habitually done among Quakers', but have testified again to the same spirit out of their own experience. The difference between principle and consistency of the spirit will have to be considered more fully in the second part.

Since the experience is always new and as every situation is unprecedented, our decisions will not be reached without heart-burning and controversy amongst ourselves and inner conflict within each one of us. The example of what Friends did in the past in different situations conveys nothing more, but also nothing less, than a challenge for us to be faithful: it gives no answer to the tormenting question what faithfulness means in the present situation. Little wonder, then, that we find temporal decisions as difficult as Friends did in 1659. Indeed, we may find comfort and strength in reminding ourselves of their predicament: they, too, were not of such calibre as to know all the time where they stood and how they should act. They, too, had their Temptations, their Gethsemanes and Calvaries. In retrospect we are allowed to know that their perplexities opened for them the way to many opportunities—opportunities paid for in advance by suffering and persecution and the acceptance, in faithfulness, of apparent political failure.

May not our own bewilderment and impotence, far from being indubitable signs of decadence, domestication and respectability, be the *via dolorosa* to new opportunities—if only we remain faithful?

Absolutist and Relativist

It is not the task of this study to pursue in detail the attitude of the Society of Friends as it adjusted itself to different historical situations, and how even then individual Friends interpreted that corporate attitude differently according to background and temperament.[1] Nor could we confine ourselves to political, economic and social history: we would have to examine the Quaker attitudes to music, art, the theatre, contemporary thought, hobbies, fashion, in brief: culture in general. We would have to examine their choice of occupations, first under the pressure of outward discrimination (banking, commerce, industry, trades), then under the influence of their mystical and experimental thinking (medicine and science, but not history),[2] finally under the impact of their inward calling (teaching, nursing, social and missionary service').[3] For example, a number of Friends, not coming from farming families, have in recent years been moved to return to the 'simple', 'peaceful', 'natural', 'creative' work on the land, which appears to them more removed from the snares of the world than other occupations and is comparatively safe against military conscription.

For the present purpose we narrow 'history' down to the more conspicuous developments in public affairs and would sum up what we have said so far in the judgment of Tolles that 'there is no one Quaker attitude towards politics',[4] even if we see that there is a palpable coherence of spiritual experience behind the innumerable acts which we can describe as Quaker actions. With Tolles we may possibly discern two

---

[1] The standard works of W. C. Braithwaite and R. M. Jones, and M. E. Hirst's *Quakers in Peace and War* are full of interesting material.
[2] See above, p. 67.
[3] Very good material can be found in Raistrick, *Quakers in Science and Industry* (London: Bannisdale Press, 1950), Lloyd, *Quaker Social History 1669-1738* (London: Longmans, Green & Co., 1950), Tolles, *Meeting House and Counting House* (Chapel Hill: The University of North Carolina Press, 1948).
[4] *Quakerism and Politics*, 20.

basic positions without, however, overlooking the many varieties between them. On the one hand there is the *relativist* who co-operates in public affairs and therefore cannot help compromising the pure testimony in his soul, though he may still wish, like Friends in the American Colonies, to be clearly distinguished from 'the world's people'. On the other hand there is the *absolutist* who endeavours to preserve the testimony in all its purity, who therefore tries to contract out of the world's entanglements even though it may mean in fact the abandonment of his responsibility for it.

I am not so sure as Tolles that George Fox can be counted among the latter before the crisis of 1659, and even his much quoted letter of 1675 to Friends in Nevis, and approved by the Six Weeks Meeting, indicates that his 'perfectionism' is confined to the actual carrying and use of weapons, but does not exclude watch-service against the Spaniards, which would certainly be excluded by modern absolutists.[1] Fox upholds here again the division of labour or functions which he held in the 1650's, namely that it is not Friends who are convinced of the truth, but the magistrates who have to act as 'revengers', yet Friends have to assist in a non-combattant fashion.

It seems necessary, however, to avoid making consistency an idol, and to allow for different attitudes taken up by a Friend at different times of his life and in different situations. Some who went to prison for refusing the payment of tithes would as vigorously support the payment of taxes, even for war purposes, because in their reading of the New Testament the tax money is to be given to Caesar as inevitably as the gospel is to be given freely. Indeed, some Friends who disagreed with paying taxes for war purposes were threatened with disownment.[2] George Fox recommended the payment, using the Biblical argument at different times.[3] This attitude can be contrasted with that of Friends in Norway who in recent years succeeded in obtaining permission to pay the amounts due for defence tax to some agencies pursuing peaceful purposes. Theirs is a fine testimony to the Quaker way of thinking and indeed to the liberal leadership in their State, and

[1] *Epistles*, No. 319. Cf. *S.P.Q.*, 620/1, and *Q.P.W.*, 316/8, 323/5.
[2] See Elizabeth Redford's case in Lloyd, *op. cit.*, 92.
[3] *B.Q.*, 462, and *S.P.Q.*, 601 f.

it will have much relieved the consciences of those who obtained that permission.

Considering, however, the interrelation of all economic activities in modern society, whether for war or peace, is such action more than a 'testimony'? Is it an actual non-participation in military defence, or perhaps only a matter of accountancy in the Treasury and the Ministry of Economics? War and peace purposes hang closely together, so closely that the reduction of armaments may, through a period of increased unemployment, create greater need for governments to export the social tension at home in the form of aggression abroad. The economic and technical interrelation of war and peace is nothing new: the very peaceful occupation of planting sugar beet was much encouraged by the Kings of Prussia because sugar would, in war-time, be an essential raw-material for gun-powder; and peaceful farming was protected, and town-dwellers were forced to pay a high price for home-grown food in peace-time, so that in war-time the country would not be dependent on imports; also the alcohol made from potatoes can be used in many obnoxious ways. There exists no human economic activity which cannot be directed into the channels of Satan.

The distinction between absolutist and relativist positions depends to some extent on a fallacy: we assume that only the relativists are given to making compromises because they do so consciously, whereas the absolutists are inclined not to recognize the extent to which they too are involved.[1] True, it is the relativist who would make money grants 'for the King's use', as did the Quaker politicians in the American colonies, well knowing that the money would be used for waging war; or who as governor or magistrate in Rhode Island would call up soldiers, while not fighting himself, and would organize war relief at the same time to calm his conscience; or would, like Penn, appoint a non-Friend as deputy governor for the 'dirty work' he as a Friend would not do himself. These glaring ambiguities are an easy prey for absolutist criticism, not to

[1] Cf. Richard Niebuhr, *Christ and Culture*, 86: 'The difference between the radicals and the other groups is often only this: that the radicals fail to recognize what they are doing and continue to speak as though they were separated from the world'.

mention the sneers of outsiders who enjoy accusing the Quakers of hypocrisy.

Ambiguities, however, are inherent in the human situation between God and history, and the absolutist is not absolved from them by the fact that his own ambiguities and compromises are of a subtler kind. There has been no finer spirit in Quakerism than John Woolman. He did his utmost to avoid any compromise with evil. He refused to pay taxes which might help warfare or to pay for a substitute in the militia or to have refunded his expenses incurred by compulsory billetings in his house. Even on his death-bed he refused medicine carried by stage-coaches because coach-boys and horses were badly exploited. He reduced his 'cumber and care' in worldly matters so as to be free for Christian service, and refused the accumulation of wealth beyond what was necessary for providing adequately for his wife and child. However, had he lived in a society under the strain and stresses of mass unemployment, he might have found it much harder to forego cumber and care: he could reduce them so easily because, without knowing it, he benefited from the flourishing economy of a slave-holding society. Also, 'adequacy' in providing for one's family is a very elastic concept if held against the low standards of living of some of his contemporaries.

This is not said to reduce the admiration for Woolman's character, to slight the beauty of his saintliness and the purity of his motives and actions. Living at the dawn of modern economics (he died four years before Adam Smith published his *Wealth of Nations*), he cannot be expected to have seen this connection of family security and slavery. It is amazing enough how clearly he pointed at the interrelation of personal possessions and war. Nowadays, however, the interdependence of social, economic and international life has not only greatly increased but also has become common knowledge. We therefore cannot withdraw behind the purity of our motives any longer unless we plead that ignorance is not only bliss but also virtue. The absolutists who do not want to see how inevitably they are involved in society even though they try to live far remote from its sinfulness, take up the moral attitude of George Fox and Francis Howgill who, while living in the Kingdom and therefore not fighting, wished all the same to enjoy the fruits of a victorious war against Popery. We shall have to discuss this 'parasitism on other people's sin' (Reinhold Niebuhr) in the second part; it is the central problem of trying to live the good life in closely knit human society.

For the moment it is sufficient to state that both absolutist and relativist alike live and act in history. The fullest possible withdrawal from the world is, in the act of withdrawal, an action in history and makes its impact, if only as an omission, as a choice of the lesser evil. In spite of all their hopes and endeavours, absolutists cannot escape the historicity of man. Many of them are aware of it as is shown by their gentle tolerance towards the relativist, their understanding of his actions, their own humility and the sense of their own unworthiness and guilt. On the other hand, those who are sure that they are free of compromise are probably more involved, for instance through their possessions and through their feeling 'good' in a tormented world, than the tender spirits who even in their wonderful saintliness suffer under a sense of their own insufficiencies. They are probably more involved even than those among the self-confessed relativists who are wrestling incessantly with their own compromises under the condemnation of their conscience. The error of the strong-minded absolutist lies in the presumption that man can live outside history while alive on this earth. Exactly this claim was made by early Friends at one period: they thought they were made perfect and could not fall again. With this claim, which is not compatible with their ambiguities in history, they proved no more than their earthliness and temporality. Their real worth was tested when they fulfilled the task set to them in their time and place, not shrinking back from suffering any more than from compromise. One cannot die for small things because then one would no longer be alive to die for the great thing.

The Inner Tension of Quakerism

The tension between absolutist and relativist and the complementary function which they have for the life of the Society of Friends have been often described, for instance by Rufus Jones, Harold Loukes and Frederick Tolles. The two positions, as far as they are real and not mere abstractions or dialectical poles of a real tension, are largely a matter of temperament, background and situation. To an even larger extent they may be the externalisation of tensions which we actually feel within ourselves and which are brought into the open during controversy about some vital issue. Most of us will tackle such an issue with a sense of being in two minds about it, not because of the pros and cons, but because of the vision of the desirable and the limitations of the practicable. So each one of us will try, by moving from one side closer to the other and back again, to find a clear position. But unless he surrenders his openness for further guidance, that position will not be final, but will be amenable to new movements and adjustments.

This does not mean that all Friends are at all times worn and torn by the ambiguity of the human situation and the inner and outer conflicts involved. There is much truth and greatness in that steady Quaker personality who is upheld by peace of mind and joy, often attained after prolonged struggle and search, and who lives so close to God that he is certain of continuing Presence and Guidance even in trying circumstances. While re-living and re-expressing the 'ancient' testimonies, he does not stand on principles. Unfortunately this character can easily become a formalized pattern of personality, as happened in the period of traditionalism and quietism: he then sticks to principles, is self-satisfied to the point of self-righteousness, lacks imagination and keeps aloof outwardly from the gay, inwardly from the suffering, world. He is then a Stoic rather than a Christian.

It is probably truer for these very set characters than for the John Woolmans and Elizabeth Frys that, as Henry Cadbury holds, 'Our relation to politics and to government has been most conspicuous when the government seemed to interfere with us rather than when we intervened in government' and that 'we have been at the receiving end of state intervention all our life'.[1] He himself emphasizes, in contrast to this, that 'Quakerism moved from an awareness of our own sufferings to those of others and from self-defence to social reform'.[2] Apart from those over-rigid characters I doubt whether Friends

[1] *The Basis of Quaker Political Concern*, loc. cit.
[2] *Ibid.*

have normally been satisfied merely with having their own grievances rectified; personal imprisonment would lead to their concern for other prisoners; but they would not stop short at that point. On many occasions they have tried to change, through social work, 'lobbying' (which seems to be a Quaker invention[1]) and prophetic protest, conditions which they did not know from inside. Hardly any had been slaves before they began their campaign against slavery; and while Penn's constitution-making was influenced by experiences Friends had had 'at the receiving end of State intervention', it was an act of creative imagination when he concluded his treaties with the Indians.

Of course, all human action can be explained as mere response and reaction to historical conditions, but Quaker action at its best reveals a creativeness and imagination which is not quite met by Henry Cadbury's modest assessment. They were prompted not by their own sufferings when they turned from passivity to activity—though this would in itself not be entirely negligible: they were guided by the spirit, in obedience to which they were exposed to their sufferings in the first place. Then, in the second place, they were led to what Cadbury calls their 'egocentric' concern against getting involved in some public or private wrong which seemed clearly against the will of God as they tried to discern it in their meetings for worship, clearly against the inward promptings of love, purity and truth. That same experience could not be limited to the 'egocentric', merely negative command that they must not get involved, though this was probably their first reaction in many cases: it would soon burden them with the concern to do something towards the removal of that wrong itself. This, I feel, has at all times been the centre of Quaker living and doing: the impingement of the Kingdom, its presence in our hearts.

It is in this experience, too, that we discover how many compromises we have already made; we are thus renewed in the spirit and sent forth to express the same spirit in the world. But we are soon entangled again, not only through our own sinfulness but also through that very act of expression: instead of *waiting* for the Kingdom that is to come, we want to *work*

[1] *Ibid.*; also Tolles, *loc. cit.*, 9/10, 21.

for it and force it down to earth by our determination; or we forget it altogether, being more concerned for the effect of our doing than for the expression of our spiritual experience; or of what other distortions we may become guilty. Aware of the ambiguity of this situation we try, successfully or unsuccessfully, to return into the divine Presence and its absoluteness; we may be renewed again, but again for a life in the world and its relativities. There is no true absolutist or relativist position in Quakerism which is not fundamentally in the heart of each one of us. In the tension between these two extremes we make our continual turns and re-turns—conscious or subconscious, half-hearted or with truculence, driven by the circumstances or in an overbearing attempt at mastering them beyond our human capacity. This is our state between God and history.

While we may appear outwardly divided into 'absolutists' and 'relativists', we are one in that, knowing about the same tension within, we all start from the experience of the presence of the Kingdom and its promptings: we differ only, to a certain extent, in our attitudes towards the Kingdom that is to come. The basis common to most of us, indeed to many Christians and believers in other faiths, is that in listening to God we want to do his will, but in trying to do his will we find ourselves wanting. Have we ever made a pause to think out the full implications of those simple words which we dish out like a cheap prescription? 'Doing the will of God': How can we know it? How, when we know it, can we do it? How can we do anything for a purpose? Indeed, how can we dare to speak of 'doing the will of God'?

PART II

DOING THE WILL OF GOD

5

OUTLINE OF THE MAIN ARGUMENT

Before entering into a detailed examination of our problem, with many illustrations and inevitable digressions, it seems advisable to give here a brief outline of the argument which is to follow.

The great difficulty with which a man wanting to do the will of God is faced, is the question of how the divine will may be distinguished from human volition. The next chapter will start from the proposition that God's will for man is not simply fulfilled by man's will to do good and to be good; and that the discernment of God's will varies with human situations and therefore does not necessarily lead to unanimous judgments. Yet since so much evil has been done in history from the mistaken conviction that this was the will of God, there is a special need to examine anew the character of divine guidance.

It will be argued that with the experience of the unchangeability and consistency of the Spirit of Christ, Friends have developed a theology which avoids alike the dangers of a legalistic implementation of some apparently objectively revealed divine law, of the blind adherence to abstract principles of right and wrong, and of the licence of sheer subjectivity. Through the encounter with the Holy Spirit in our hearts, both the individual self and the inter-subjective consensus of the gathered community are directed always towards the same values: truth, love, purity, goodness. It is thus the Spirit that is consistent, not man or human groups; and every new encounter with the Spirit, if his guidance is accepted, will become manifest as a new testimony to the same Spirit and may therefore appear as the same 'traditional testimony'. But this similarity of attitudes is the result, not of human loyalty to principles or of consistent obedience to the super-natural law revealed once for all, but to the ever same Spirit having once more been experienced and obeyed.

We shall go on to show that the most important commandments of the New Testament give no orders for right action, but directions towards true being, and that they cannot be obeyed except by the existential decision to be what we are meant to be, that is, to be the will of God. We can be our true selves only within the structure of being of which, in the encounter with the Spirit, we become aware as truth, love, purity and goodness. This revelation happens to us not through abstract commandments, but in concrete situations.

In becoming more nearly our true selves, we achieve also a fuller freedom for responsible action. Guidance does not tell us what to do but how to do it; it makes us responsive to God's will and aware of the structure of being; it thus enables us to act responsibly through our own free decisions. Doing the will of God is being his will incarnate in history and therefore meeting situations in accordance with the structure of being.

Responsible action, however, is limited by man's historicity, and the subsequent two chapters will examine the problem of 'doing', namely the conditions of acting in history. They will concentrate on such deliberate action as tries to translate good intentions into good results. Attempts of this kind, however, take too little account of the great variety of situations and are too prone to reduce the failure of well-intended action either to temporary moral shortcomings or the basic depravity of human nature. Such moralist teaching underrates the opaqueness of history and the limitations of human knowledge and power.

A further difficulty arises from the well-nigh inevitable confusion of historical success and spiritual attainment. On occasions the latter may achieve historical success, but it is never a historical means. Good action is action in the full awareness of the structure of being, it is action of the true self in full responsibility. Such responsibility necessitates the calculation of appropriateness and expediency as well as the awareness of the structure of being. The result remains unpredictable since in human experience good intention has produced both good and bad results, and evil intention both bad and good results. Anyway, good and evil in history are very much a matter of selection and interpretation, and it seems illegitimate to trace unexpected results in ordinary historical events to the intervention of Providence.

The unpredictability of results makes all human action risky; it cannot but be risky if man is to be free. This freedom, however, is relative in so far as action starts always from the data of the moment. The agent himself is one of the data, but he has the power of changing himself by the very choice of creative action under the conditions given. Even so the outcome remains unpredictable.

Responsibility, meaning responsiveness to God's Spirit revealing the structure of being, and including careful calculation of potential results, proves the invalidity of the usual distinction between ethics of principle and utilitarian ethics. Neither loyalty to principles nor calculation of effects makes the responsible agent, but being one's true self.

Having discussed the more formal conditions of action between intention and result, our argument turns, in Chapter Eight to the more substantial conditions: man's inescapable involvement in the ambiguities of history. Inescapable involvement, however, must not serve as a ready excuse, it is a challenge: the way in which we react to its inescapability may become a manifestation of grace. Human involvement will be exemplified in three forms, as moral, social and material involvement.

Firstly, our moral involvement is proved by the fact that the choice of the lesser evil is inevitable; for even martyrdom is an evil. In the concrete situation it is often very difficult to judge which of two evils is the lesser; and the conscious choice of not quite so good a means to a hoped-for better end seems as inevitable as it is obligatory never to choose on purpose evil means for supposedly good ends.

Most conflicts in history are not between good and evil but between two relative goods, two justifiable rights. Particularly in situations of this kind the choice of even the best available means to the best potential ends may achieve bad results. Finally, the necessity of having to establish priorities for our actions involves us in the choice of greater good and lesser evil.

Secondly, social involvement is due to the fact that even

spiritual attainments are impossible outside the social nexus. The difference between personal and impersonal (group) relationships is not solved either by trying to reduce all group problems to the personal level or by establishing a double standard of morality. Relationships on all levels have to be tackled in full responsibility, that is in response to God's will, and the responsible self realises that there is no escape from the tension of involvement.

Personal and impersonal factors in human relationships overlap in many ways, and the loyalty which ties a man to his group may lead to a serious spiritual crisis when in response to God's will for him he disagrees with a group decision. Whether he conforms or contracts out, through loyalty and love he is inescapably involved.

Thirdly, material involvement is due to the fact that spiritual ends can be achieved only by the use of material means, that 'being the will of God' depends on 'having' the means for one's own physical subsistence as well as for sharing them with one's fellows. 'Having' means material wealth, also in the forms of education and knowledge; and wealth is the very thing which the true self wants to share. In the modern world no return to primitivity and no simplification of our personal lives can release us from our connections with the machinery of production and distribution, because it alone provides adequate material means for responsible sharing.

In the inevitable tension resulting from his inescapable involvement in the ambiguities of world and time, man could not live responsibly without a deep certitude amidst the uncertainties of his historicity. The concluding chapter shows 'original grace' to be the power by which we live and work courageously amidst all our predicaments. Certitude depends not on beliefs and proofs, but on the, perhaps unconscious, awareness of the structure of being and its ground.

Such a faith neither rests on reason nor attempts to denigrate reason. Faith and reason are complementary in that reason checks faith and faith is the foundation of reason. Their sound correlation is the condition of human wholeness and makes responsible action possible. Even the agnostic can act only by faith, though it is more difficult for him to be reconciled to failure. The experience of grace, however, enables us to live in the Kingdom amidst the great horrors of existence.

This happens because all life is sacramental; for the worst imaginable situation, no less than the most wonderful, may become a channel of spiritual experience. Even though God is not *in* history, he is its ground and he works *through* it: he reveals himself inside history wherever and whenever he is encountered in the heart of a man.

After this summary, let us now turn to the first basic question, namely how it is possible to discern the will of God.

6

GOD'S WILL FOR MAN

Divine Will and Human Action

'Whoever wishes to take up the problem of a Christian ethic must be confronted at once with a demand which is quite without parallel. He must from the outset discard as irrelevant the two questions which alone impel him to concern himself with the problem of ethics, "How can I be good?" and "How can I do good?" and instead of these must ask the utterly and totally different question "What is the will of God?"'

This remarkable statement from Bonhoeffer's *Ethics*[1] is focussing our problem very sharply. Friends have always wished to act on the discernment of the will of God. They firmly believe in guidance through the Spirit both in their personal lives and their corporate life; and in particular their business meetings based, as they ought to be, on worship, are for them the place where God's will for his community is explored, his guidance found and decisions arrived at as from him.

On the other hand, we cannot deny that the revelation of God's will to man depends also on the historicity of the person or groups who receive it, men of a certain character and background who have, in time and place, attained a certain, if varied, relationship to God. Apart from this human element which enters all knowledge of the will of God and can be seen crystallized, for instance, in the Puritan traits of our Quaker heritage, we may have to take note also of all-too-human elements such as our unwillingness to change dear old customs

---

[1] P. 55 (London: S.C.M. Press, 1955). The present chapter owes much to this stimulating book, with all differences of outlook and beliefs. On the other hand Bonhoeffer makes many points of striking similarity with Quakerism.

or to undergo the spiritual discipline necessary for the exploration of God's will.

For these reasons, and probably some more, Friends no less than others tend to slide back into moralism and legalism: they try to be good and to do good rather than to obey the will of God; indeed, without much reflection they identify goodness according to the best present-day standards of the best Western Christian tradition with God's will for man. They thus replace the will of God by their own will, by principles and rules of conduct, all of which may help making them decent and respectable citizens, but not always the faithful doers of the will of God. Consequently the Society of Friends looks more like an association of good people full of good will and doers of good deeds, than like the people of the good will of God, those with whom he is well pleased.[1]

The crux of the matter is this: that precisely religious people, all intent on doing the will of God, presume too readily that they already know it. They talk about human sin with a facility as though they themselves were sure at every instant what they should do or have done and what they should not do or have left undone. But 'in the great majority of cases of moral difficulty what is difficult is not to decide to do what one ought to do but to decide what one ought to do'.[2] Even when Friends admit that they do not actually *know* the will of God, they repeat far too often the somewhat hackneyed phrase that 'there is a way of God in every situation'. Beyond doubt, there is; but can be we certain that it will be revealed to us, that it fits with our traditional testimonies or our interpretation of the Scriptures, and in particular that it is given to us exactly at the moment we pray for guidance most ardently? I cannot quite agree with Kathleen Lonsdale's view that 'surely the essential thing is that we must always believe that in God's world there is a right choice of immediate action which is in accordance with his will'.[3] In my experience there are many moments in our personal and corporate life when immediate

---

[1] In the New Testament sense of *eudokia*, Luke 2, 14; 3, 22.
[2] Nowell-Smith, *Ethics*, 288 (Pelican, 1954). Cf. R. M. Jones, *The Nature and Authority of Conscience*, 41 (London: George Allen & Unwin, 1920).
[3] In her very fine address to London Yearly Meeting, 1955, published as *Peaceful Co-existence*, 5.

action seems incumbent, but not one of the choices available seems really 'right'; moments when we are not in the Light but in the night. In such cases Friends have usually held that we have not yet received clear guidance, though they admit that this may be due to our own shortcomings; and many Friends emerge from such unsuccessful search with a deep sense of failure, realising, as they do, that any postponement of immediate action has the effect of an immediate negative action. May it not be that we have a wrong idea of the nature of God's will for man and our possibility of discerning it?

The burning concerns which obsess us in difficult historical situations such as are in our judgment incompatible with God's will, make us often impatient and hence incapable of exploring it in quiet surrender. We neglect the purification of our human interestedness in such situations; our very concern stimulates us to concentrate on finding the right action instead of God's will, on the *doing* instead of the discerning.

Of course, the dialectical distinction of doing and discerning must not be exaggerated. Not only is discerning itself a doing, but also in the very act of doing we achieve implicitly a better understanding. On the other hand, knowledge of some kind, be it instinctive, intuitive or cognitive, is necessary before we can do. Nothing seems to me less compatible with the will of God than spending so long in quietist contemplation trying to discern it that we forget the doing, or adopting an attitude of faithless resignation that finds that there is nothing we can do or which can be done.

But even if we admit that discerning and doing are inter-connected and that pious inaction may grow to evasion, the predicament of living in extreme situations should not rush us too much. First of all, as I shall argue further on, I do not believe that God's will for us, though becoming clear to us in concrete situations, prompts as much the action which we are to undertake as the attitude which helps us to find what under God we ourselves consider the best possible action. Secondly, we must realise that for God no situation is ever extreme. Thirdly, we must never lose sight of the possibility that God's will for us in such a situation may be inaction, or more puzzling, action for some of us, but inaction for others, or still more puzzling, action which from our conventional idea of goodness we would consider evasive, inadequate or just wrong. The courage to act wrongly may be more in his will than not to act at all; the courage to wait while evil things happen may be more in his will than to act in panic. Bonhoeffer preferred acting wrongly to not acting at all when he joined the conspiracy against Hitler's life, but he held that it *was* wrong all the same, though still in God's will that he acted as he did, and that God's law was honoured by his admission that by his decision for God's will he had actually offended God's law and had become guilty before God.

This reasoning may seem very strange to many Friends who like telling us in Meeting for Worship that 'everything is really very simple, we must simply do the will of God'. They unwittingly betray great inexperience and ignorance; for how could we deny that few contemporary Christians have spoken with greater authority than Bonhoeffer? To understand his attitude a little better, let us look at the story of Abraham sacrificing Isaac, a story thoroughly disliked by modernists as a relic of barbarian customs; yet a story which, since Kierkegaard, has been used by many Christian thinkers to explain how the sovereign will of God may go beyond our human concept of morally good action. It was through unquestioning obedience to an apparently immoral commandment that Abraham was led to the discovery of the truly moral will of God for him. Bonhoeffer's insight that even in fulfilling the will of God we might be driven to sinning in all responsibility, and that even in sinning we might fulfil the will of God—if only we never succumb to the temptation of trying to shift the responsibility for our sins to God or to 'circumstances beyond our control'—seems to me far less blasphemous than the tendency prevailing amongst many Christians to define and cut down the sovereign will of God to the size of sentimental nineteenth century conceptions of love and goodness.

Let me take another example: is it the will of God that a patient should sustain pain, or should the doctor do his best to relieve it by drugs, hypnosis or any other lenitive methods? Few of us would hesitate to emphasize that it is God's will that pain should be relieved because we ought to be merciful, not cruel; but many would also grant that the experience of pain is not necessarily destructive, though it often is; that sometimes it is spiritually strengthening and even illuminating. A group of people I know who are neither obscurantists nor fundamentalists, and doctors amongst them, are of the opinion that 'injecting away' pain is depriving the patient of the opportunity of understanding the meaning of his illness, that is, of the will of God for him. The fallacy of this argument I see in the uncritical assumption that relief from pain is of necessity a less promising way through which God may reveal his will to the patient than his suffering pain. The doctor would have to be like God to know for certain God's will for each patient and to apply or withhold lenitives accordingly; nor will patients themselves know, except in rare cases, whether they should prefer suffering to relief. Most of us would agree that the doctor will normally have to consider the use of palliatives as the will of God for his own medical action—this is the spiritual meaning of the Hippocratic oath. Nevertheless, the effect of the doctor's action may make it difficult or impossible for the patient to discover God's will for himself.

The conclusion we would have to draw from this example is that the will of God, as discerned by men, is not likely to be uniform and may appear even inconsistent, particularly when we think of 'the right choice of immediate action'. The ambiguity involved in all human action will be discussed more fully in the next two chapters. Here it must suffice to understand that the relationship of God's will and 'right' human action may be very complex. What is outwardly one single action may in God's will have many different meanings; in our example, one meaning for the doctor, a different one for the patient, one for the nurse whose self-sacrifice has to be greater when lenitives are withheld, another one for the patient's wife who has to suffer by witnessing 'unnecessary' suffering. And what outwardly is exactly the same kind of action may, if applied to two different persons or to the same person at two different times, have opposite meanings in discerning the will of God.

Altogether we speak of 'the will of God' in either a very personal or a very vague manner and, on closer study, may find that it covers very different things. Let me mention only five: in the first place Friends apply it to the experience of personal guidance; in the second to congregational decisions reached in unanimity after worshipful search. Both personal and congregational guidance lead sometimes to a prophetic pronouncement, a statement as to what in this or that concrete situation the will of God is for *other* people, for the wider society, the nation and its government, and even for mankind. The prophet, like the doctor in our example, assumes the position that he knows the will of God not only for his personal action but also for that of others, and he is little concerned with the question whether others may have explored the will of God on their own and may have been guided differently.

Fourthly, in such prophetic ministry we often rely on more 'objective' revelations of the will of God than our merely personal or congregational explorations which are subjective or (in the congregation) inter-subjective. We refer to the Ten Commandments, the teachings of Jesus, or to the person of Christ as the incarnate God revealing his will. Fifthly, we have again a different concept when thinking of God's providential will not in a concrete situation, but for the whole universe, and in particular for the development of the history of mankind.

Moving rather carelessly from one of these usages to the other, we apply the categories taken from the personal life of prayer and service not only to the congregational life, but also to the organisational and institutional life of the wider society, indeed to the relationships between societies. In this process we change inadvertently the spiritual growth of the individual, exploring the will of God, to the material betterment of societies; the loving service of the saint to the bureaucratic service of public welfare agencies; the concerned action of the dedicated person *against* his self-interest to the prudential action of governments, by our very appeal to their and the world's 'enlightened self-interest'; our own congregational decision in unanimity, attained under the guidance of the Spirit among those who have joined the common search, to the will of God for those who would never think of seeking for the will of God through our Quaker method. Contrariwise we look for world federation or peaceful coexistence as though it was the Kingdom of God, for equality, solidarity or fraternity, as though it was brotherhood, and for physical survival as though it was salvation. In brief, we confuse the outward with the inward attainments.

True enough, 'we must have a conception of God's guidance that is big enough to include all events on all levels and yet keep human freedom'.[1] Human freedom, however, is freedom that is human and that therefore does not receive guidance in the form of unanimous resolutions and actions. Guided decisions may be not solely divergent, but in certain respects even contradictory. Unanimity means basically being of one mind (soul) and spirit rather than having one judgment.[2] We jump too quickly to the conclusion that the former implies the latter or that the appearance of the latter proves the former. It is a very different matter to try to 'include all events on all levels' in our conception of guidance on the one hand, and on the other to transfer in an uncritical manner the experience of personal guidance to the congregational level, and that of congregational guidance to levels and events in which it is even more difficult to discern the will of God.

Guidance True and False

Perhaps we would be less given to this confusion if we had a clearer grasp of the nature of guidance and the exploration of God's will in the personal and the congregational life.[3] When we speak of guidance, we usually think of early Friends who had an extremely strong sense of it. We think of George Fox's visions on Pendle Hill and in the inn the night after, which led him to the Westmorland Seekers;[4] or of the call reaching Marmaduke Stevenson[5] or the voyage of the *Woodhouse*.[6] Such experiences, which we may classify among the psychic phenomena, are not unknown in modern times. But as the fall of

[1] *The Life of the Meeting*, Third Study-Booklet of the Friends World Committee for Consultation, 7.
[2] The German language makes a clear distinction between *einmütig*, of one mind and spirit, and *einstimmig*, with one voice.
[3] For the following cf. W. C. Braithwaite, *Spiritual Guidance in the Experience of the Society of Friends* (London: George Allen & Unwin Ltd., 1909), and J. R. Harris, *The Guiding Hand of God* (London: Thomas Law, 1905).
[4] *Journal*, 104.
[5] *Christian Life, Faith and Thought in the Religious Society of Friends*, 23/24.
[6] *Ibid.*, 18/21.

DOING THE WILL OF GOD

James Nayler and other extravagances of early Friends show, there were great dangers in their extreme subjectivism which, in our view, mixed so obviously the human with the divine will. Nor were they protected from strange behaviour by George Fox's 'working rule' of 1652 that 'guidance which crosses the earthly will is true, but guidance which accords with the will is false'.[1] On the contrary, they felt under constraint to do quite extraordinary things such as walking about stark naked[2] or George Fox's 'woe unto the bloody city of Lichfield'.[3]

All the same, early Friends, like other left-wing Puritans, were confident that they could clearly distinguish the voice of God from their own human promptings like a lamb that knows its mother's voice among many. Hence their belief in their infallibility if they listened to God's voice. Samuel Fisher and other Friends did not think human promptings wrong; they rather made a distinction between 'the good works that proceed from the creature and the good works of which Christ himself, working within the believer, is the author'.[4] The only criterion which they accepted very early, against the laxity of the Ranters, was the clear conviction that the Light of Christ would not lead to immoral conduct; on the contrary, it would bring them to greater purity.

Nowadays we are far less sure in the discernment of God's will, and apart from rare cases of great inner certitude that we have been truly guided, most of us would find good sense in a recent comment on Kierkegaard's interpretation of the story of Abraham: Sartre, the French existentialist, explains Abraham's anguish when he received the divine commandment to sacrifice his son, as inner uncertainty whether the voice he had heard was that of God or of Satan. Like Hamlet we may wonder whether 'the spirit that I have seen may be the devil';[5] but unlike King Claudius, God cannot be caught out by play-acting.

This, I think, is the central question: how can we distinguish the voice of God, or the revelation of his will to man, from our

[1] Braithwaite, *op. cit.*, 55/56.
[2] B.Q., 148/50.
[3] *Journal*, 71.
[4] Creasey, *op. cit.*, 122.
[5] End of Act II, Scene 2.

own human promptings, not to mention the daemonic or Satanic forces which one may see at work for instance in all those developments where human efforts for the good have brought forth destructive features beyond human intention and control? We may believe, with Shaw's Saint Joan, that God can speak to us through our imagination, we may assume that our healthy instincts, our good intuitions and our sound reasonings may be the channels for the communication of God's will, notwithstanding the difficulty in discerning what the adjectives healthy, good and sound imply. But surely, all these channels are at the same time also channels of our own human volition; indeed, the channels of the divine and the human will are likely to be one, and for *our* doing the will of *God* will actually have to be one. How, then, shall we ever be able to discern clearly the will of God from all the other motive forces within us? Even without accepting altogether the pessimistic verdict of neo-Calvinist thinkers like Reinhold Niebuhr that there is never in man a will that is not radically corrupted by self-interest, should we not ponder over the word of Thomas a Kempis that 'often it has the appearance of charity, yet is nothing but carnality, for natural likes and dislikes, self-will, hope for reward and personal interestedness are rarely absent'.[1]

This goes not only for individual but also for congregational action. There is in Quaker history as much evidence for communal as for individual guidance;[2] and communal search for the will of God has proved a valuable safeguard against mistaken individual guidance, provided that the congregation does not exert so strong a discipline that it stifles individual guidance and with it corporate illumination. This danger is part of all congregational effort and reached its height in the quietist period of Quakerism when, in our modern judgment, Friends failed in exploring actively the will of God for them because they frowned too much on individual guidance. But when George Fox first introduced the system of corporate search, it

---

[1] *Imitation of Christ*, I, 15, 2. (My translation.)
[2] For recent examples see *The Life of the Meeting*, loc cit., 7.

DOING THE WILL OF GOD 113

was a healthy attempt at controlling individual extravagance.[1] Inevitably it increased the tension between the extreme subjectivists who would not recognize corporate guidance even though they had their share in searching for it, and those who recognized in it both the will of God for their community and Fox's temporal wisdom. The divisions within English Quakerism in the seventeenth century and the schisms in America in the nineteenth, are not merely regrettable facts about which we should speak as little as possible and with a sigh of relief that by now it is nearly all past and over: they have a profound significance for all attempts at crystallizing what is found to be the will of God, in unanimous decisions and actions for a group of people. Unanimity is bound to break down precisely when each person (or faction) feels most strongly that he takes his own stand by the will of God. While in such situations charity should avoid mutual injury, it can as a matter of course never lead to the discernment of *one* will of God for *all* persons involved in the critical situation, not to one 'right choice of immediate action which is in accordance with his will'.

On the other hand, even unanimity does not warrant the conclusion that the will of God has overruled human wilfulness. Unanimity achieved through the stifling of the Spirit in quietist Quakerism has already been mentioned. It may be equally spurious when attained in emotional excitement in which mutual encouragement and confirmation, and the experience of togetherness and indeed oneness, may easily strengthen the sense that the will of God has been clearly apprehended. Traces of such emotionalism can be found in early Quakerism and many other religious movements. A very interesting example is the beginning of the first crusade which, during the Council of Clermont of 1095, opened with the shout of the crowds that *Dieu le veult*. It is easy enough for us to propound in retrospect how well the crusades served the popes in their urge for temporal supremacy. Not by chance were they

---

[1] This method was originally developed by left-wing Puritanism. Cf. Cromwell's statement: 'At such meeting as this it has been said we should wait upon God and hearken to the voice of God speaking in every one of us. I confess it is our high duty, but when anything is spoken as from God, I think the rule is: let the rest judge'. Quoted after Lindsay, *The Churches and Democracy*, 23.

H

the same popes who were greatly concerned for the moral purification of the Church; and the slogan that 'it is God's will' was equally used when they laboured for the reduction of internecine feuds between Christians by introducing the *treuga Dei*, the peace of God, for at least part of each week—from our point of view a truly Christian endeavour. How far, we wonder, may the work of those great popes have really expressed the will of God for their time? And were all those crusaders who never suspected papal diplomacy of temporal motives, merely deceived or were they truly guided in their act of dedication? Finally, with all the misery the crusades brought to many lands and people, through the 'providential will of God' they brought also great cultural and moral improvements (chivalry) in the encounter of the Christian and Arab civilizations. Few events show more clearly the ambiguity of man's living and acting between God and history.

Again, those who organized the *autodafés* were not all wicked and cruel people or people led astray by hidden self-interest. Some of them at least struggled hard to discern the will of God for themselves and the heretic whom they tried to bring back to God as they saw his will. They prayed ardently to save misguided souls and acted, as they thought, *ad marjorem Dei gloriam*. It is the merit of Huxley's *Grey Eminence* to have shown the closeness, in the same human soul, of profound mystical piety and what in our wisdom we must call political wickedness, even devilry. Another example is Gerson, the 'Most Christian Doctor', who during the Great Schism laboured for the 'reform of the Church in head and members' and who even protected heretics like the Brothers of the Common Life in Holland from their persecutors, but on the other hand recommended the burning of John Hus at the Council of Constance. Rufus Jones has for Gerson this somewhat smug judgment: 'It was the deepest purpose of his life to build up again the invisible Church within the visible, but he was a politician, a reconciler—a man who was ready to put unity above truth, and the result was that in doing much good he also did some evil, and that while toiling with valiant spirit to realize the Kingdom of Christ, he also furnished some material for the kingdom of Anti-Christ'.[1] Instead of condemning such mixtures, should we not ask ourselves whether we, too, may be 'in the mixture'[2] when claiming too loudly God's guidance for some of our decisions and actions? Fortunately Friends have never used the stake for burning their heretics, but they used to disown many of their best young people for 'marrying out', and do we know what mental cruelty and spiritual destruction our ancestors have inflicted on some young men and women, in love, who in the end knuckled under because their elders were so sure that *Dieu le veult*? And a final example: not many people would accept the *Book of Mormon* as true, denying most firmly that it could be a divine revelation to anybody. Yet we cannot deny that for Joseph Smith, Brigham Young and the Latter Day Saints who followed them it has been a guiding influence to much good. What, then, are our criteria for the discernment of the will of God?

The Consistency of the Spirit

Orthodox Christians have claimed at all times that the will of God cannot be distinguished from human volition unless we firmly believe in 'objective' revelation. For them, God's will is laid down in the Law of God as formulated in the law of Moses, the preaching of the prophets and the teachings of the New Testament. Since, however, the understanding of those 'objective' revelations in the Scriptures is difficult, it has often been held that the Church, through the Holy Spirit, has been called to interpret their meaning both in principle and for any concrete situation. This claim for the Church as the authorized vessel of the Holy Spirit is somewhat akin to the Quaker practice of judging individual and corporate concerns by the communal exploration of the will of God.

There has, however, been the admission, though more in Catholic than in orthodox Protestant thought, that apart from the divinely inspired revelation in Jewish-Christian writings and in the Church, there has been a lesser revelation of God's will in his creation, through what Paul calls the law written

---

[1] *Studies in Mystical Religion*, 306.
[2] See above, p. 83 n.l.

into the hearts of the gentiles'.[1] Many Friends have been inclined to accept this as their own view, even to prefer that lesser or 'natural' law to that 'revealed' in the Scriptures, because to them it means much the same thing as the Inner Light. But the terms 'natural theology' and 'natural law' do not describe adequately the spiritual theology of Quakerism. Our faith is not confined to the knowledge of good and evil, right and wrong, as part of our natural, created humanity; nor even to some vague religious awe assumed to be common to every man: it is based on the actual encounter with the Holy Spirit in our hearts. Natural moral and religious inclinations may lead us to God, but they do no more express the full revelation of God's will than does the letter of the Scriptures. Only spiritual experience turns outward knowledge of the law or natural knowledge of morality into an inward dynamic force, a vital and creative power, a passion ruling a whole life.

Against both the strict orthodox and the humanist view Friends should affirm that no literal execution of the biblical revelation of God's law is possible, firstly because biblical revelation is not truly 'objective' but largely a record of the subjective experiences of God's will by inspired men and women of the past, and that we have to seek the same kind of immediate inspiration for ourselves. We should engage on this search both with great eagerness and great scrupulousness lest we confuse too readily human volition with divine guidance. Friends should affirm, secondly, that since no outward fulfilment of the law is true fulfilment without the inward apprehension of divine Truth, the inward encounter with the Spirit is the condition of discerning, obeying and doing God's will. This means that human action under the will of God is neither fulfilment of 'objective' law nor innate human morality but man's action guided by the Holy Spirit.

There is some danger among Friends of identifying the Spirit with Law or Principle. True, the Spirit reveals God's will to different people at different times and places *in consistency*, but as will be shown presently, it is not the consistency of law or principle, but of being. Revelation is, or at least should always be, a *new* revelation and guidance in a *new* situation,

---

[1] Rom. 2, 14/15.

DOING THE WILL OF GOD 117

not the application of pre-formulated laws or principles to a present situation. The consistency of the Spirit cannot be expressed in principles and laws, but only in testimonies which, however, witness to the one and ever same Spirit. Any new revelation in the privacy of a human heart may be testified to publicly in an individual testimony, and subsequently in a corporate testimony, about the newly explored and the newly experienced will of God. Such testimonies may, because of their inner consistency, be formulated in what is called a Quaker testimony, but a Quaker testimony is inherently neither dogma and creed nor law and principle. It merely draws together what has happened to men in history when searching for the will of God, and what testifies to a consistency in such experiences. A testimony is thus the outcome not of deductive but of inductive reflection, but even so it must never become a general rule or a universal because of the untruth which results from translating a truth in history into universally valid truth.[1]

In this respect it is significant that membership in the Society of Friends, far from being based on a common belief in fundamental doctrines, depends to a considerable extent not even on the acceptance of all or the most important Quaker testimonies, but rather on the question whether the life of an applicant proves something of the experience of the Spirit, be it only in incessant search, and a conduct compatible with such search or experience. It must be admitted, though, that this may lead to great inconsistencies not only in the testimonies but even in the spirits.

The best-known statement of that consistency is found in the declaration of loyalty to Charles II, in 1660, where it is said that

'that Spirit of Christ, by which we are guided, is not *changeable*, so as once to command us from a thing as evil and again to move unto it; and we do certainly know and so testify to the world that the Spirit of Christ, which leads us into all truth, will never move us to fight and war against any man with outward weapons, neither for the kingdom of Christ nor for the kingdoms of this world'.[2]

This passage has been understood by many, not excluding

[1] Cf. Jaspers, *Von der Wahrheit*, 495 (Munich: R. Piper & Co., 1947).
[2] *S.P.Q.*, 13. (My italics.) See also above p. 77 n. 3.

some Friends, either as a statement of a moral principle or as the obedience to the law of God formulated in the Bible. I think it expresses neither: it is based neither on human consistency nor on a legalistic interpretation of the divine commandments, even though the word 'commandment' is used. It is clearly the description of actual experience, namely that in his closeness to the Spirit of Christ man just can do no other but reach out to his fellows in love and avoid deliberate infliction of harm on them, no matter what risks to himself.[1] This spiritual constraint is lost, or degenerates into man-made principle or legalistic obedience only together with the loss of that closeness to the constraining Spirit. It is therefore the Spirit that is truly unchangeable and consistent, not man's awareness of it, nor some biblical law the understanding of which is dependent on human interpretations.

The practical difficulty in speaking of the consistency of the Spirit, however, emerges in a letter of William Penn written during the deplorable Wilkinson-Story controversy. When George Fox and the majority of Friends were accused of trying to impose, through Monthly and Quarterly Meetings, a corporate discipline on the free manifestations of the Spirit in individual members, William Penn replied:

'Where doth our apostasy lie? In not suffering loose and libertine spirits to tread down our hedge, under the specious pretence of being left to the Light within? As if the Light were inconsistent with itself, or admitted of unity under not only different but contrary practices in the one family and flock of God'.[2]

The unity here advocated is actually the sameness of practice rather than the consistency of the Spirit. In my opinion this confusion of Penn's is not permissible, though it has happened often enough in Quaker thinking. Varied practices are inconsistent with the Spirit only in so far as they are incompatible with love, truth, purity and similar spiritual values which become visible as fruit of the Spirit. If the attitudes of Story and Wilkinson were inconsistent with the Spirit because motivated in part by personal jealousies, we may duly wonder whether Penn's reactions breathe nothing but the Holy Ghost. It seems very risky to speak of consistency of the Spirit in the

[1] *Journal*, 361/2, quoted above p. 78. Cf. the examples given by Tolles, *Why didn't Gary Cooper fight?* In F.Q. (1958), 95-98.
[2] S.P.Q., 307, in the chapter recording the controversy.

practical expression of those spiritual values unless far greater allowance is made for the multiple possibilities of action.

On the other hand, it is not easy to make quite clear the difference between consistency of the Spirit and the view that Friends hold their testimonies *on principle* or in obedience to the outward commandment of love which is laid down as the will of God through Christ in the New Testament. Granted that in the controversy about our testimonies we often take refuge in the exposition of principles or the exegesis of the Scriptures: it is still the inwardness of the experience through the Spirit which is the core of our faith because it affects man's whole existence. If our experiences are shaped and expressed for ourselves and others in ways which we may have inherited as fundamental principles or biblical commandments, strengthened in authority by parental and other environmental influences, they become the will of God for us only through validation in a spiritual experience which lifts us beyond the obedience to commandments and the loyalty to principles into the realm of free existential decision before God, the decision to be what we are meant to be, what we actually *are* in the will of God. What this means will become clearer if we consider briefly the nature of the biblical commandments.

The Commandment to be What We Are

The biblical commandments are of two kinds: they concern either our doing and then are moral directives, or our being and then are directives of attitudes, directives more by grammatical form than meaning.

Directives for doing begin with interdictions such as most of the Ten Commandments, telling us what we ought *not* to do, right to the golden rule that we should not do to others what we do not want them to do to us. They proceed to the commandments of positive action such as to honour father and mother,[1] to go the second mile, to give the cloke also and to do to others what we would have them do to us. These directions for concrete action can be fulfilled outwardly even

---

[1] In the framework of the decalogue I understand this to mean 'do honour to them' rather than 'have an inward reverence for them'. Else this commandment would better be mentioned among the directions for attitudes.

against our innermost feelings, through a great exercise of will-power. In some cases this may prove very difficult in practice, and probably impossible in the long run unless there is an 'even more innermost' feeling underneath which has not yet been discovered by the conscious will, namely one's true self. But we may say that by and large commandments for doing can be fulfilled outwardly even against one's wish, merely from a sense of duty; they are taken as moral ordinances authorised by a divine exequatur and to be executed in the attitude of obedience, not as an unquestioning inner commitment the surrender of which would mean self-destruction.

Directives for doing seem far less central in our religious life than directives of attitudes which demand no immediate outer actions though they will inevitably result in them. They are no true directives or commandments because they can on no account be fulfilled by a mere exercise of human will-power or an act of outward obedience. They are rather directed towards a change of the will itself, which means a change within the self through a decision affecting the whole life; an 'existential' decision made in the encounter with God, with the Holy Spirit, with the Transcendent or whatever name we may give to the great Other whom, in our highest moments, we meet within ourselves and may discover everywhere and through every thing around ourselves. Commandments of attitudes are for instance to love God, our neighbour and, consistently, our enemy; to 'repent', namely to redirect not only the will, but the whole self so as to be like one born again; to be perfect, namely whole; to be child-like, and so on.

We may be ordered not to do a thing, for instance not to steal our neighbour's apples, and to do another thing, for instance to pay our taxes; but we cannot be ordered to love H.M. Collector of Taxes or to hate the kind neighbour who 'does not really mind' our stealing his apples. Of course, we may love the one and hate the other, or both, or neither of them, but not by order, not even by an act of will. We may be able to love (selflessly in the scriptural meaning of the word), and consequently to be averse to any promptings of hatred as belonging to our lesser or inauthentic self, only by having found a certain attitude through a far more basic decision.

To give another example: I may bind the wounds of the man

who fell among the robbers, from a sheer sense of duty, and certainly, this is no mean moral achievement if I am a Samaritan and the other a persecuting Jew. But I cannot love him or anybody else without—loving; loving at least God and therefore loving that Jewish victim of highway robbery as he is loved by God. How, then, could I love by commandment unless I love already? Again, I cannot be whole from a sheer sense of duty; on the contrary, the stimulus of duty inside me shows clearly that I am not yet whole because I need the whip of 'duty'. How, then, can I be whole by desire to be so and in response to a commandment unless there is already wholeness in me?

And yet, the directives of attitudes are put in the imperative for a very deep reason: some inner action concerning our own being is necessary; perhaps better, some inner event where divine and human wills meet and where something happens that cannot be thought out with the rules of thinking: a transition from the 'ought' to the 'is' and from the 'is' to the 'ought'. We cannot love unless we *are* loving or at least have become loving; we cannot be like those who are born again unless we have discovered, through a turning round of our whole lives, that we are not really what we could or ought to be—which means that we have already turned round. Here, however, it becomes clear that those commandments are, and yet are not, commandments, for we cannot become what is not already a structural part of our being. Phrases like becoming a 'new' or a 'different' man are ambiguous as though a new creation, or worse, a new self-creation, would have to take place. But it is the same man become apparently different because in God's mind and will he has been different all the time, very much like Peer Gynt in the mind of Solveig:

> *Peer:* Can you tell me where Peer Gynt has been
> Since last we met . . .
> With the mark of destiny on his brow,
> The man that he was when a thought of God's
> Created him . . .
>   Where was my real self
> Complete and true—the Peer who bore
> The stamp of God upon his brow?
> *Solveig:* In my faith, in my hope, and in my love.[1]

[1] Ibsen, *Peer Gynt*, Act V, last scene, translated by R. F. Sharp.

Saul of Tarsus was, in his true being, Paul the Apostle from his birth, his conversion being the moment when he discovered his true self encountering Christ. From then onward he lived his true self, both in being what he truly was and in striving to become what he ought to be and therefore was already potentially. Being like one re-born or like a new man means both to be fully what one is, one's true self, and to will all the same to become more fully what one already is.

Directives of attitudes are commandments to be what we are, to attain our authentic self. The true self is the will of God for us, and the more fully we are ourselves, the freer we are and the freer we feel: this is the reason why service to God becomes perfect freedom, and commitment the strength of taking free responsibility. It is God's will for us to be free by accepting in responsibility the true self he has given us, to respond to his will not by doing certain things but by being what he wants us to be.

This, what we really are, our authentic self, happens to us in the spiritual experience of encountering God. The revelation of God's will is not like a moral law to be executed, it is like a structure of being which is real, and which is real not only as God's will for you and me but also, as far as we can discern, as God's own Nature or Being.

It seems obnoxious to speak in an assertive manner about the nature and will of God, thus bringing God, as it were, into the human compass. All we know of and about God is what he wills to reveal to us, what we experience as the structure of our true being and at the same time transcending our own being and that of the world around us. But somehow we feel that the structure of our being must be in harmony with God's own Being, as the ground of all things, even while Being transcends all our conceptions and experiences. We express our limited insight into God's Being through adjectives, attributes and even predicates such as 'the dear Father', 'the goodness of God' and 'God is love'. But God transcends all limitation in anthropomorphic concepts; and Richard Niebuhr warns us rightly that 'though God is love, love is not God'.[1] The experience behind those descriptions of God are often formulated by

---

[1] *Christ and Culture*, p. 32.

us in causal clauses such as: because God loves us, our true being is loving; because God is whole, we, too, are whole in our true selves, or ought to be whole. In this way we see God's Being and his will for us and our being as one, always recognizing that God's Being is infinitely greater than our greatest insights.

But God's Being and will must be discerned by us and accepted in the structure thus discerned; for not accepting the fact of this structure means self-annihilation as there can be no structure outside God's will. Hence there is always an imperative implicit in the indicative, a commandment in the very structure of being. God's will for us is the fulfilment of his commandment through fulfilling our own selfhood, through being what we really are, through willing to be what we really are. The amazing spectacle of Jesus loving his enemies and being indeed whole, even in his very denial that he could be 'good', is not due to the fact that he executed commandments like a law-abiding citizen, but that he *heard* (discerned) and *did* the will of God by being what he was meant to be, thus fulfilling the structure of being. It is this that we express in the sentence that the will of God was revealed in Jesus Christ. Hearing and doing are no intellectual efforts, they are not even necessarily conscious as with Jesus, but they certainly happen in some inner awareness of what the structure of being is.

The True Self in History

The structure of being, the will of the Creator for his human creatures, shows forth in the consistency of the Spirit as encountered and testified to, in life and word, by men at different times and places, men indeed of very different civilizations and religions whose authenticity of living has never been questioned even though their teachings may have been considered erroneous. While we speak here of 'structure' and formulate it in abstractions, it is only in such concrete living that it becomes real, only as a spirit incarnate in situation, attitude and action; that is, only in history. Whenever a man discovers in a concrete situation, often a situation of crisis that challenges his whole life, his own true self in confrontation with God, what he finds is what has been called here the structure of being, underlying not only his own being but that of all human being in any conceivable individuality, variety, mutuality and community. He may then express it as laws or principles, as ideals or values, such as love, freedom, truth, beauty, goodness, brotherhood.

Even though we speak in abstractions like structure of being or some of the values just enumerated, we must never forget the fact already stressed that we become aware of these apparent abstractions only concretely, that is in situations in time and place, in attitudes showing them, and in actions proving them. The structure of being, the ground of our true self, is therefore always intermingled with the stuff of history and incarnate in our own historicity, and unfortunately never appears as unadulterated as in our abstract thinking about it. All the same, the structure of being is the ground and foundation of our human existence, so much so that we cannot even commit the sin against the Holy Spirit without asserting that it is 'good' or 'best' to be evil or to do evil or not to be bothered with such fancy differences; that the only 'truth' is that there is no truth; and that 'ultimate reality' is nothingness. Goodness,[1] truth, reality and so on are so inescapably part of the structure of being, even where one tries to deny or escape them, that their concepts cannot be excluded when trying to signify the opposite. However much we may wish to twist these concepts round, we always come back to truth, goodness, reality. The names are not changeable because the spirit which they express in their true meaning reveals to us consistently God's will as the structure of human being which we may formulate in abstracts, but know only as Spirit incarnate in the actual events of life and the world.

Herewith, however, we reach the crucial difficulty of human existence, a difficulty already adumbrated. We discern God's will in the concreteness of situations, that is in history; and only in history, and not in abstracts, principles, laws, values, which we then, as an after-thought, might apply to all kinds of situations. It is in the situations and events themselves that we become aware of the structure of being, often enough without

[1] Here, of course, not in the sense of the moral demand to be good and to do good but as structural fact of being.

purposeful reflection, but always with an urge to discern God's will in the manifoldness of events. While we are thus directed towards his will, the responsibility for the situation becomes the more fully ours the surer we are of his will for us: to be what we are meant to be. This means that the Spirit will never tell us *what* to do: it prompts us to have an attitude and to act in a way which expresses the structure of being in our authentic selfhood, but this implies exactly our full responsibility. We cannot simply *act* the will of God, we *do* it, namely by deciding ourselves.

Here, I think, we must examine a frequent misunderstanding by Friends regarding the human situation between God and history. On many occasions they seem to identify responsible human action with acting for God, that is, told by him immediately *what* to do. Responsible action, however, is in response not to God's 'order of the day', but to his will which we have called here the structure of being, his commandment for all days: to be what we are meant to be. Many Friends seem to have an exaggerated view of the working of our business method, almost as though the minutes of the clerk were dictated or verbally inspired by God and his Holy Spirit. In fact they are human resolutions achieved perhaps in a more original way than usual. Yet they are the resolution of men and women who are guided. They are guided by God and the Spirit so as to find their true selves and then themselves to act from the true self's awareness of the structure of being. Our business meetings are the place where we seek individually and together after our true selves: to be what we are meant to be. The more fully each worshipper finds his true self, the deeper becomes his relationship to his fellow-worshippers: every true self, responding to God's will, corresponds and communicates with his fellows.[1] The matter under discussion is only the concrete situation through which this happens. The resolution concerning the matter in hand is truly guided and accords with the will of God not simply when we have achieved unanimity,[2] but when this has been achieved by every single Friend responding so fully to God's will for himself that we are able singly to

[1] Cf. my *Friends and Truth*, 62 ff.
[2] See above p. 117 and note 2.

be fully responsible in our decision and yet reach unanimity in the common experience of divine Presence.

For instance, God does not give us the right answer to the question whether a picture should hang on the right or the left wall of our common room, nor is there a 'divine taste' which is preferable to all human taste, at least not to my knowledge. What happens is that in our exploration of his will we find ourselves closer to our true selves so that we shall no longer be able to push aside the rather odd sense of beauty of another Friend which at first seemed incompatible with our own, or the sentimental prejudice of a third Friend who remembers that for the past fifty years there has always been a picture on the right wall and never one on the left. In the slow tuning in to the views of others we are finally united not in our decision so much as in love and understanding. We are 'rightly guided' not into what we decide, but into the spirit in which we should decide, and become thus ready to carry the responsibility of decision in the face of God precisely where we yield to, or persuade, another Friend.

It is not at all surprising that a group of people, engaged in the same concrete situation, on the same problem, and of similar faith and background, should be capable of agreeing unanimously on most matters in hand; but the decision is theirs, not God's. The impact of their human conditions in time and place shows clearly enough in international Quaker gatherings when different national, racial and denominational home-backgrounds come to play their parts. All the same, they will often emerge from their common exercises with a profound feeling of thankfulness and the unspeakable joy of people who have just had together another experience of the divine Presence. This has happened to them not because, as they may well say and even believe, their deliberations and decisions were dictated by the Spirit and written, as it were, in his own hand, but because they have all been through an hour where they faced God individually, but as a gathered group, in true selfhood. They thus became aware of his will in the structure of being, they could not help adopting the attitudes of love, patience, humility, truth: reaching the height of their own responsibility they exercised it in the consistency of the Spirit who once again was, almost visibly, present amongst them.

I think William Penn was seriously wrong in his exacerbated reaction to Story and Wilkinson,[1] not because I would have wished for a different practical solution of the points at issue at that time, but because I cannot agree with his identification of the human decision of the then leaders of the Society of Friends with the consistency of the Spirit. It was exactly the Spirit which was not consistently testified to on that occasion. God's guidance does not relieve us from making our own decisions in our affairs, but we are strengthened by prayer, meditation and common worship so as to comply more closely with God's will for us, that is, to become more fully our true selves who as such are enabled to act freely and responsibly within the structure of being.

This is the paradox we must understand: the will of God is never more clearly revealed to us than when it commits our human will to decide on its own. Doing the will of God never means the execution of another will, but of our own will empowered to act responsibly because it is not merely the will but the whole self of a human being who has become what he is meant to be. Unless we understand the will of God as the structure of being that calls us to freedom in love, truth and those other so-called eternal values, we are turned back to legalistic interpretations of God's will. In the life of Jesus, for instance, very different and even contradictory actions and utterances prove all the same that consistency of the Spirit realized through one authentic self. If we overlook the concrete situations and use *ipsissima verba* as commandments and principles, we would have to ask whether it is better to leave one's family for the sake of Christ or to injure the least of one's children so left behind without care; whether it is better to denounce the evil-doers or to forgive them and to pray for God's forgiveness for them; whether to sell all one's possessions and give the money to the poor or to sit down at festival tables and encourage 'waste'. The answer, however, is quite clear: one should do all these things and none of them, because each depends on the concrete situation in which one has to act. For this no casuistry lays down any directions and no

[1] See above p. 118.

advice is available except one: to act at each moment as one's true self.

We do not live authentic lives if we do the thing adequate for one situation in an entirely different situation where it is misplaced. Consistency cannot lie in actions, which belong to history, but in the spirit in which an action is undertaken, thus revealing the will of God, the structure of being. As Tillich says: 'The final revelation does not give us absolute ethics, absolute doctrines, or an absolute ideal of personal and communal life. It gives us examples which point at that which is absolute; but the examples are not absolute in themselves'.[1]

To put it differently, it is never a category of action as such which can rightly be called Christian, but only an action in a situation undertaken by a fully authentic self. It is for this reason that we cannot depend on any scriptures as on a patternbook which describes this or that action as invariably right or wrong, good or evil. On the other hand, action undertaken in the responsibility of the authentic self depends on the full inner awareness (though not necessarily fully grasped intellectually) of the structure of being. It is for this reason that while some actions may sometimes be right and at other times wrong (for instance, the offer or acceptance of an alcoholic drink may be a 'guided' act, and certainly has been exactly this in millions of moments when offered in the Eucharist), other actions like warfare or cannibalism can never be right in any conceivable situation because they destroy in themselves the structure of being which is the ground of true selfhood, and are therefore self-destructive. So there are no actions which are as such Christian, but there are actions which are never Christian, even if defended by people who have adopted this name for themselves and are proud of it.

Awareness of the structure of being does not mean the same thing as good motives and intentions. We shall see in the next chapter that good motives and intentions cannot be divorced from a consideration of effects and consequences: they belong to each act. Though they should in each case be inspired by the awareness of the structure of being, they are more closely

[1] *Systematic Theology*, I, 168. His whole section on 'The Reality of Revelation' is relevant to this chapter (London: James Nisbet & Co. Ltd., 1953).

connected with human volition than with the will of God. We may say that the field circumscribed by motives, actions and consequences is that of morality, not of religion. The religious life knows only one motive, the will of God; only one action, to decide for one's true self; and only one consequence, the fruit of the spirit.

It is significant that the fruit of the spirit as enumerated, for instance, in Galatians 5, 22, are nearly all concerned with being rather than acting, and that the image of tree and fruit in Matthew 7, 15-21, expresses not the connection of motive and action, but of being and its organic results. This image describes the wholeness of a human life: a man is what he does and he does what he is. In this respect he acts far less from motives than from the fullness of his being, without wondering overmuch what his motives may be. His actions are the overflow of his wholeness and acquire meaning far less by achieving ends and reaching solutions than by witnessing to the Spirit.

Certainly, his whole being is driven forward to action, but the beauty of his being and doing is far greater than what his action may achieve in effect. His very standing in history exemplifies the fact that wholeness of life and temporal success have different meanings in the will of God. He may build up great works of mercy or found new religious societies and orders; but not the survival and extent of his work give him his place but the spirit from which it arose and in which it was done. He may even fail in world and time, but may all the same have become a witness of the Spirit to world and time exactly by the way in which he failed. Doing the will of God is being his will incarnate in history.

7

THE CONDITIONS OF ACTION (I): ACTION BETWEEN INTENTION AND RESULT

When speaking about human action, we must realize that most of our every-day doings consist of routine actions undertaken without our having to render account to ourselves about our motives or pondering over possible effects. We grow into them through imitation and training until they become our second nature. Normally they have the expected results; though when lighting a match I may burn myself, or when pouring out tea I may spill it. These, too, are actions in history; indeed they, too, may have moral implications: I may have spilled the tea not because I am naturally clumsy but because I was absent-minded, or angry that the newspaper was late in arriving and the demand note for rates early. Once the tea is spilled, I may either laugh it off or get annoyed with myself; my family may laugh about it (and I may take their laughter with good or bad humour); or my wife may be upset because I have spoiled the new tablecloth. In the end the children may start late for school because the event of spilling the tea has attained 'historic proportions', and the whole day's work may suffer for each member of the family.

Deliberation is no necessary part of action, not even of action of genuinely historic portent. As Collingwood says, perhaps with a little cynicism but therefore not inappropriately:

'To a very great extent people do not know what they are doing until they have done it, if then. The extent to which people act with a clear idea of their ends, knowing what effects they are aiming at, is easily exaggerated. Most human action is tentative, experimental, directed not by knowledge of what it will lead to but rather by a desire to know what will come of it'.[1]

[1] *The Idea of History*, 42.

Nor should we assume that all our morally good actions are necessarily dependent on deliberate intention and conscious goodwill. On the contrary, it can well be argued that the good action of a true saint is less deliberate than that of a man of smaller moral weight who must make up his mind to do something good. The saint does the will of God from being rather than doing, from living response rather than from deliberate choice.

In the following, however, we shall have to concentrate most of the time on deliberate moral action, often without distinguishing in each case very different kinds of 'good' or the varieties of individual and corporate activity. We shall discuss in particular action which tries to translate good intentions into good results, because it is this kind of action with which Christian ethics is largely concerned. It is this which many Friends mean when they speak of trying to do the will of God.

Morality, Rationality and the Human Situation

Christian ethics is much occupied with the question whether man is good or bad or a mixture of both, whether he is the image of God, fallen irredeemably but for God's one-sided acts of grace, or a sinner forgiven for his repentance and faith and therefore enabled to act creatively together with God. However important such considerations are for our attitude in and to life and our actual living with and treatment of one another, are such moral categories sufficient for the assessment of human nature? Is *human nature* itself an adequate term for the reality of human existence in time and world, or does this expression tend to turn *man*, an abstract singular so useful in discussions like the present one, into a species studied by the social scientist or at best a specimen under detached anthropological observation? For it is not only the moralist who isolates man too often from his actual conditions for the sake of his abstract judgments: the same applies to many sociologists, particularly those who treat man either as an entirely rational being who could achieve his set purposes if he put his mind to it, or as entirely subjected to inexorable historical laws which he accepts if wise and rejects if foolish, but which he cannot alter.

It is characteristic of many religious and ethical activists of our time that their approach to man in history is based on a mixture of moralism and rationalism. But even supposing that we were all good and wise, we still have to act under conditions which cannot be explored except through trial and error because the results are unpredictable. We have to calculate possible results from experience in present and past, but all such calculations are limited by the unwritten clause: 'as far as we can see'.[1]

I doubt whether it can ever be right to look at man in history merely as *man*, a mammal of a specific kind, and not to see men in all their real conditions, in the actualities of their beings and doings and intercommunications. Of course, we cannot survey all these actualities, their number is infinite. But the fact that we can see only some of their conditions at any time is exactly one of the imponderables with which we have to reckon. It does not entitle us to abstract from them altogether and to fit man, in the singular, neatly into any of the optimistic or pessimistic categories regarding his morality.

It is neither sin nor stupidity alone which characterizes human existence, but sin and stupidity will depend on the factors given, and seen as given, at a certain moment under which men may act well or ill, foolishly or wisely. Saint Francis was not stupid when he kissed the leper instead of giving him an injection; it is neither 'better' nor 'worse' if Dr Schweitzer omits kissing lepers when he gives them modern medical treatment. Famine in a far-away country was an 'act of God' until modern forms of communication, transport and food preservation have turned it into a moral issue; so was tuberculosis before the development of bacteriology, hygiene and modern housing, but now it has become a question of social morality; and it is only since the improvement of the technique of blood tests that the death of a patient caused by the transfusion of incompatible blood, may raise the moral question of 'carelessness' at the inquest.

Moralist thinkers treat man far too often as though he were grown up at birth, a sinner from his mother's womb, without regard to the formative and often painful experiences of in-

[1] Cf. for this paragraph Popper, *The Poverty of Historicism* (London: Routledge & Kegan Paul, 1957).

fancy, childhood, adolescence and youth, which become inescapable conditions of action, not for man, but for this particular man. True, there are certain sociological and psychological rules which can be derived from all this, but why do not all maladjusted people become Hitlers? The unique remains the most important factor in history, behind and before all 'trends' and 'tendencies'. Such generalisations are very useful in many respects, for instance for legislation, social welfare and management, but they are rather misleading in others because they neglect the uniqueness of man. This is the truth which religion expresses in the idea of the value of every human soul.

Moralists tend to treat man not only as always adult and always in full psychological and physical vigour (as though human responsibility was in no wise affected by ill-health as is illustrated by certain actions of Woodrow Wilson, Franklin Roosevelt, Dwight Eisenhower and Anthony Eden), but also as citizens of the society to which they themselves happen to belong. In our days they tend to overlook that we do not all live in a modern technical society, that there are still peasants, herdsmen, indeed cannibals left in the world. On the other hand, some of them apply the New Testament as though we were all inhabitants of first century Palestine or as though the Jews of first century Palestine were all twentieth century, atom-conscious post-Christians. Human nature itself depends to a not negligible extent on time and place: for an Indian it is far easier to be a vegetarian than for an Eskimo, and the sayings of Jesus on divorce look different when we realize that in his environment a husband could divorce his wife, but a wife not easily her husband; and that 'adultery' did not include a husband's fornication with an unmarried woman or a prostitute, but any wife's sexual relation with another man. Indeed, in the days of Jesus polygamy, recognized as such, was not yet quite unknown in a few wealthy Jewish households. If we overlook the concrete situations in time and place, we may know much about human nature in the abstract, but not enough about the question why people act as they actually do. It is not merely a moral difference which enabled a Gandhi and a Bhave to rise and to be successful in India, but also one of time, place and historical conditions. Correspondingly it is very 'Western' to turn the abolition of national sovereignty into an issue of international morality, without appreciating the fact that in other parts of the world our cast-off 'self-determination of nations' is still a truly *moral* issue.

Christian moralists are inclined to neglect all this and to speak of human nature in the abstract. Most of them hold that all evil in world and time is due to human failure, disobedience and sinfulness, to the inauthenticity of our existence and our conformity to the 'world'. Friends no less than others are prone to reduce the intractabilities of living in world and time exclusively to human sin. It is unimportant whether they find the main cause for international and social evils in other people's sin (as some sometimes do, for instance, in their denunciation of statesmen), or in our common human sin, or even a little more humbly, in their own sin, because they feel they have not prayed ardently enough nor worked faithfully enough, have lost courage and patience and therefore have become unable to move mountains: they seem convinced that the moving of mountains is to be regarded as a normal effort of human morality. Tracing all evil back to human sin, they commit in my opinion another sin, or should I call it an error? They assume that they have a clear insight into, and knowledge of, what in its very essence is the inscrutable mystery of good and evil and the opaqueness of historical happening.

The full-fledged Christian pessimist goes much further than Friends would: he argues that the very belief in man's ability to be more faithful and hence more instrumental in God's work of salvation is a striking example of his very depravity and pride; for whatever action man may undertake even with all the goodwill of which he might be capable, there is always some self-interest mixed in with it. For the radical pessimist, moral human action is fundamentally an attempt at self-salvation instead of exclusive trust in God's power and grace. Strangely enough, with all his pessimism, he usually finds some reason why all the same it is needful for man to work hard and try to be as good and to act as well as he possibly can as there is still 'the relative possibility of realising the good in history'.[1]

[1] Niebuhr, *Nature and Destiny of Man*, II, 202. Cf. Brunner, *Christianity and Civilisation*, I, 51 (London: James Nisbet & Co. Ltd., 1948).

It is not this inconsistency of thought which we should hold against him—only abstracts can be truly consistent—but rather that he suffers from the same pride of which he accuses those lesser pessimists, those relative optimists, who believe that man, if obedient to God, can take an active share in the work of salvation. Both these moralistic approaches are far too anthropocentric; for both of them it is man, and man alone, who spoils everything, the difference only being that according to the pessimist he cannot do otherwise, for he is the virus in the healthy body of creation, almost the devil. This, of course, is a no less presumptuous image of man than that of the self-saving god.

The pride of moralism consists in neglecting the genuine limitations of human knowledge and power. The pessimist reduces all limitations to original sin, which paradoxically consists for him in the non-recognition of limitations. He thus denies the possibility of man ever being a responsible agent through the grace of God and yet burdens him with a responsibility for all evils of creation which he cannot possibly bear.[1] The optimist, on the other hand, believes that he can work out God's will in the conditions of world and time according to plan; that through his good actions he helps actively in building God's Kingdom on earth in the form of a glorified World Federal Welfare State, where presumably all men have become mongrels of ingenuity and saintliness. This belief takes it for granted that the awareness of the structure of being is comprehended by the 'good' man, or the man who receives the call, in the abstract, as a law or principle, indeed, as a detailed divine blue-print which can be worked out by human morality and

---

[1] Tillich, *Systematic Theology*, II, 43/44 and 63/64, argues forcefully for an abolition of the term 'original sin'. I am not satisfied, however, with his ontological interpretation of Creation and Fall as the estrangement caused by the transition from essence to existence. The ultimate responsibility for all existence and its destiny (as against its freedom) seems to rest with God the Creator, including man's sin! For me this remains an unfathomable mystery no man can plumb, and I have not even tried to tackle the origin of good and evil and of the ambiguity of history. Albert Schweitzer's beautiful metaphor of the warm gulf-stream of the God of Love within the cold ocean of the God of Creation is no answer either, but it gives peace of mind.—It is possible that the third volume of Tillich's work may shed some more light on this problem. Together with my criticism I cannot but record my great indebtedness to him.

which therefore could be, and ought to be, translated by him into the concreteness of real life without any deductions; and that, if we fail in the process of translation, we fail only because we are not faithful and good and sensible enough. But whereas the pessimist sees the error in the optimistic presumption that man could ever be good, faithful and sensible enough for pure action, the error of optimism lies, if I see rightly, in the assumption that pure action is at any time a translation from the abstract concept of the will of God into the concreteness of life by rational methods. As I have tried to show in the last chapter: we know the will of God for us through an actual situation, but not his will *for the situation* itself, let alone his long-term plans for history, apart from that inner direction which we call the Kingdom, that is, God's Kingship. Hence the very idea of translating and applying God's will in the concrete situation is erroneous.

When speaking of God's will, we never have a starting point other than our own experience and awareness: all we know about it is our own human knowledge. The awareness of the structure of being is experienced by us not in the abstract, but through actual situations in time and place of which our own person is not the outside observer and student but an intrinsic part. The perfect we know is experienced and known through the imperfect, the transcendent through the existent, the Spirit through the self, God through me and my historical conditions. For this reason the good life is no concept to be lived out in concrete situations; is no application of the unconditioned, the absolute, the law of love or whatever name we may give to it, in and to the conditions in time and place. Rather the other way round, a human life in the situation of world and time encounters the transcendent will, that is, it becomes increasingly (if sometimes in apparent suddenness) aware of the structure of being behind everything that is and, thus inwardly committed, endeavours to rise nearer to the will of God as discerned through time and world, lifting together with his own upsurge the whole situation of which he is part. But paradoxically enough, with his increasing nearness to God, his sense of inadequacy and limitation increases rather than that it decreases.

This knowledge of the will of God is certainly not rational in the sense a blue-print for a computer is—very complicated, but still comprehensible for the expert. On the contrary, the knowledge of God's will appears quite direct and simple, apparently describable in quite short words such as 'good', 'love' and 'pure'. For this reason it seems so self-evident for the believer that 'it must be rational'. But does he not confuse rational and reasonable?

Though reasonable, the knowledge of the will of God is largely 'subjective', that is, tied to personal spiritual experience of something which transcends the subject-object forms of human cognition.[1] It may be inter-subjective among a group of people, and it may be supported from examples gathered from history. But we can always set other examples against those we choose, which would easily 'prove' the opposite. The reason for this is obvious: our knowledge of the will of God is spiritual knowledge concerning our personal attitude, not scientific omniscience which clearly forsees, as in a well-known chemical chain-reaction, the inevitable effects of one action upon another. It could do so only if there were no freedom, if the person or persons affected by my action could be manipulated in the way in which it is the day-dream of behaviourists, modern tyrants and certain well-meaning social engineers. Most of us are prone to think of actions and consequences in terms of causes and effects, but the latter are predictable within the framework of existent knowledge, the former not, because human creativity intervenes not only in the action, but also in the reactions; and where creative reaction is artificially prevented, we are confronted not with 'human nature', but with some sub-human 'thing'.

Moral Goodness and Historical Success

Once I have discerned that the structure of being implies the setting of good against evil, I adopt the right attitude, which means merely a somewhat better attitude, before God and towards men; better, that is, because I am more fully aware that I am never good enough. I also discover that the setting of good against evil is no scientific method tried so often that it amounts to a 'law', it is only a direction of my own attitude,

[1] Jaspers calls it 'the Comprehensive', Buber calls it the 'Thou', which is no 'object' of the I or of the I's relationships, but the true Other related to and encountered by the I.

whether it works or not. Firstly, it is left entirely to me to find in the concrete situation what in this instance the good and what the evil may be. I have to judge freely, for instance, what the real good for a delinquent boy may be, a firm hand this time or better only next time, and my equally responsible colleague may disagree with me. Secondly, I may be unable, through ignorance and stupidity, or simply through being limited in life-time and lacking omniscience, to discover clearly what the good or the bad in the given situation is. Thirdly, even if I am very good and very wise in my action, another person in his own freedom may misunderstand my action from ill-will, ignorance, stupidity, limitation, or just otherness. This would not only show that I had misunderstood him in the first place and that I was not as intelligent as I had thought; it would also prove that it is very unwise, quite generally, ever to assume that an action must almost inevitably have the consequences or effects which I have been planning.

This means that the slogan, so often repeated amongst Friends and others, that 'good works good and evil works evil', may prove untrue in many cases. The same goes for some other slogans, for instance, that 'war never pays'. Whether war pays or not depends largely on the coin in which payment is expected and what a distance of time we may permit between 'cause' and 'effect', a decade, a generation, a century or half a millenium. Wars have paid handsomely to many nations and individuals. All of us who live in Western countries, warmongers and pacifists alike, live to some extent on the wages of former wars. And many of our acts of goodwill in the form of Christian service and aid have become possible only because of those wages of war and because we belong to a nation whose prestige, acquired equally by the show of force and by cultural and some occasional moral advancement, has opened to us many ways for relief and reconciliation work, which were closed to the members of poorer nations or nations of lesser prestige. It is just not true that war never pays. It may have become true in our nuclear age, but not even that is known for certain. What is true, however, is that war is wrong, evil, sinful, against the will of God, that is, against man's true being.

The same kind of loose thinking I find in the often quoted saying that 'what is morally wrong cannot be politically right'.

It is undeniably true that there is some connection between morality and politics, and that extremes of immorality in public affairs are very often self-defeating, though in some cases it takes a very long time before this mechanism, the mills of God, so-called, do their work. The connection established by belated prophets between some ancient wrong and some recent disaster are dragged into the argument so as to establish the existence of a 'moral law' in history. Schiller's famous saying that world history is the Last Judgment[1] is untenable. If it were true, not only would all wickedness be punished on earth, but also all virtue rewarded. But many morally good actions have failed to be politically successful. On the other hand, even the morally best action in public affairs, if it fails, is likely to cause 'demoralisation' and thus to produce cynicism and other bad consequences. Against this, as I have just tried to show, we must accept the fact that wars, that is, moral evil, may produce some morally good results, often for the aggressor rather than for the defender, and often for the vanquished rather than for the victor—though once again, history can 'prove' anything. The simple truth is that what is morally wrong is and remains morally wrong, however politically right it may prove to be, and what is morally right remains morally right, however dismally it may fail in fact. Moral goodness and historical success, though somehow connected, are in many ways quite incommensurable.

In the actual situation, however, morality and politics are always intermingled since all human action, including the morally purest, happens in history. For this reason the question of success and failure will enter somewhere in most moral actions. But what is a success or a failure in history? Every new generation denounces some of the great moral and intellectual successes of its immediate predecessors as serious aberrations whereas the third or four generation may restore the first estimate. Today colonialism is considered a major evil, but we hear already voices, outside the circle of the colonial powers, who wonder whether in some cases white domination has not proved the most efficient and most progressive form of development of underdeveloped countries. While in no way

[1] *'Die Weltgeschichte ist das Weltgericht'*. From the poem *'Resignation'*.

adopting this as a recommendation, I ask myself whether the day may come when colonialism is seen in the way in which modern Britain looks at the Norman conquest. But no judgment, however distant, is ever final: even in our own time we can read the most contradictory assessments of the 'goodness' or otherwise of the Greek and Hebrew civilizations, over two thousand years after their time. For a valid judgment of success and failure, not only in the short but also in the long term, we would need omniscience or would have to be alive after the last minute of history.

All the same, we cannot act responsibly unless we consider most carefully the possibilities of success and failure of our actions. The means we use must be judged both as to their morality and as to their effectiveness. One cannot be done without the other if we, living in history, act in free responsibility before God. This is the inevitable predicament of all human action, of our existence between God and history.

Martin Buber has emphasised that the religious principle is concerned with the *way* (of life) and the (spiritual) *goal*, the political principle with *means* and *ends*.[1] Friends and other people of burning goodwill have hopelessly confused this difference because they wrongly assume that establishing a difference between the religious and the political principle implies a double standard of morality. This is an error because the two principles work together in every situation. Even where an agent decides consciously, or from instinctive selfishness, for a bad action, the decision is still a 'moral' decision. On the other hand, the best person, when weighing up means and ends as he must, still makes a political decision. Those two principles can never be divorced in practice, but they create in the agent a sense of tension. This tension can be resolved as little by a double standard of morality as by the moralism of the absolutist: whether the agent holds to, or acts on, one or the other theory, he cannot escape that tension imposed on him by the task of deciding. Only the fully amoral person may manage this

---

[1] 'Gandhi, Politics and Us. The Question of Success'. In *Pointing the Way*, 126 ff. (London: Routledge & Kegan Paul, 1957), Buber formulates clearly 'the contradiction between the unconditionality of the spirit and the conditionality of a situation'. Cf. also Jaspers, *Philosophie*, III, 82 (Heidelberg: Springer Verlag, 1932).

to a certain extent, a person who far from recognizing a double standard of morality, professes to recognize no moral standards at all—though in fact he probably does in spite of his words and actions to the contrary.[1]

Beyond doubt, he who accepts any moral standards at all, one single absolutist standard or a twofold one, has to live in the tension between the political and the religious principle. On the other hand, whenever 'means and ends' are confused with 'way and goal', people fail to understand why spiritual reward and historical success do not necessarily co-incide, however ardently they may try to make them co-incide.

In their loose thinking they insist that we are in our present sad condition because 'Christianity has never been tried'. But surely it has been tried often but has not often succeeded. Success is no religious category. Wholeness is, the fruit of the Spirit are; but neither depends on success. Their only 'success' is holiness.

The greatest reward, according to Christian belief, was given for what seemed the most dismal failure, the crucifixion—and precisely because of Christ's act of acceptance. The historic success of Christianity was brought about not by the rejection of violent resistance which led to Calvary, but by the disciples' experience of the resurrection as God's act in history. Of course, we may argue with good reason that the way in which Jesus acted in his life-time and in which he proved to be and do the will of God, had the effect of preparing the disciples for the experience of the resurrection. But those actions and the attitude behind them had no effect on Caiaphas, nor indeed any practical effect on Pilate; and in history it is the practical effect which counts. Success and failure lie entirely outside the spiritual goal which Jesus did in fact attain with the acceptance of the cross. The cross was no political method. It was historically speaking no means to an end unless we accept his uniqueness and inimitability of which we read in the New Testament: that he consciously strove for his crucifixion in order to fulfil the pre-ordained purpose of being the saviour of mankind.

If, on the other hand, we believe that his acceptance of the cross shows that he preferred being sacrificed to being dis-

[1] For a fuller treatment of the concept of two moralities see below pp. 173 ff. and 184.

obedient, the cross proves no more than that good does not necessarily work good. Such action may, or may not, become redemptive for some others, being the concrete event by which they encounter God; but this does not mean that as action it becomes politically successful.[1] That the martyrs have become the seed of the Church, though not exactly the kind of Church they visualized, is a historical *fact*, not a historical *law*, not a means applicable according to plan. There are, however, ardent Christian utopians who hanker after a cross for themselves because they hope to create utopia through their martyrdom. Have they never heard of the martyrs of lost causes about whom we know little because there was no Church or society left who would canonize them? Bonhoeffer puts this very well when he says: 'It was precisely the cross of Christ, the failure of Christ in the world, which led to His success in history, but this is a mystery of the divine cosmic order, and cannot be regarded as a general rule even though it is repeated from time to time in the suffering of His Church'.[2]

The idea heard so often expressed among Friends that 'good works good and evil works evil' may be partly due to a misunderstanding of George Fox's often-quoted appeal to 'answer that of God in every one'. Answering that of God is the way in which a man will act when his true self has become aware of God's will for him. He will try to seek out the true selves of his fellow-men rather than having only superficial contacts with their unauthentic selves. He will try to help towards the actualisation of their true selves: thus himself fulfilling the will of God, he testifies to his deep conviction that God wills that every one become what he is meant to be. But answering that of God is not an infallible, not even a 'working' method in history. Fox thought of it rather as a road out of history, near the end of time.[3] That it cannot be an almost inevitably successful method in history is due to the fact that with the best of goodwill we may choose inappropriate methods of con-

[1] Cf. Nuttall, 'The Church's Ministry of Suffering'. In *Studies in Christian Social Commitment* (ed. Ferguson), 86, n.l. Nuttall does not distinguish clearly enough the meanings of 'success' and 'goal'.
[2] *Op. cit.*, 16. Cf. also Boobyer, 'Christian Pacifism and the Way of Jesus', *Hibbert Journal*, 1957, 350-362.
[3] See above pp. 53 ff.

veying it; that our best intentions may be misunderstood by our fellowmen so that acts of goodwill estrange rather than reconcile; in brief that both we ourselves and the others live and act under the conditions of history.

I will not deny in the least the moral aspects of these conditions, namely that we ourselves, bound by our own background, are not good enough to respond to all the people all the time, and that the others, prejudiced against our background and hence doubting our motives, are equally not good enough to respond. For our present purpose, however, let us neglect moral shortcomings and rather look at the conditions of history in general of which, as I have just admitted, moral shortcomings are a not negligible aspect. Of course, it happens not infrequently that goodwill produces goodwill, and that such understanding as pure imagination can achieve produces a better understanding on the other side. But prudential, calculative, utilitarian considerations of good action like these never guarantee success. As it is, we have to discover in every new situation what action, undertaken in full responsibility and awareness of the will of God, amounts to an answer to that of God in the other. We have to choose the *appropriate* or *expedient* action among several possible *good* ones. In this respect, however, we are limited by lack of omniscience, by the fact that we belong to social groups, understand the world through them and must often act through them, and by all the many other conditions of human life in time and place.

Attempts at Interpreting the Unpredictable

If greatly simplified and brought into a scheme, there are four relationships we have to consider: good working good, good working evil, evil working good and evil working evil.

Firstly, we know from experience that good has often worked good, and each one of us may recall life-long friendships which began with one out-going good action to which response was given. Regarding group relations, the classical example in Quaker history is Penn's Holy Experiment, though it could not have been made if the Crown had not been bought off at a price which absolutists would not think really good. The defencelessness of Friends did 'pay' in their relations with the

Red Indians, for instance during the War of the Spanish Succession.[1] Not the least 'success' of the Holy Experiment was that a number of fine spirits like Woolman grew up in an environment which enabled them to act creatively towards even greater good.

In modern times we may recall the story of Daniel Oliver who in the First World War was captured in the Lebanon, but was subsequently released by a German officer who happened 'by chance' to know something about the English Quaker work for German civilian internees. Hundreds of orphans owe their well-being to this chance which enabled Oliver to continue his work. It is well to remember such facts, not only for Sunday school teaching, but because there can fortunately be no doubt that good has worked good in many situations. It is equally necessary to remember that the action, or reaction, of that officer did not end the war or prevent another one, nor did it make him a conscientious objector. Let us not make the mistake of being selective in the chain of action and consequences.

Secondly, there are many cases where good worked evil. I will not amass many examples of dire ingratitude, such as that of the undernourished children from Austria who, after the First World War, were received into Norwegian homes for rehabilitation, and who as grown-up men were used by Hitler's army to apply their topographical knowledge for guiding the invaders. But would it have been 'better' not to invite them as children and let many of them perish in the way in which they brought misery and death to their benefactors?

Let us choose examples where less ill-will is in the picture: non-violent resistance and even non-violent submission to violence do not always convert the bully; they may instead increase his fury (and with it his damnation) as could be experienced in German concentration camps and during South African *satyagraha* campaigns.[2] Progressive legislation, something which most of us would consider 'good', normally increases the ill-will of the 'reactionaries'; for instance, the response of some groups in the Southern States of the United States to the desegregation legislation. On the other hand, I

[1] Cf. Q.P.W., 336.
[2] Cf. Freda Troup, *In Face of Fear* (London: Faber & Faber Ltd., 1950), c.X., based on Michael Scott's reports.

shall not forget the despair of an old gentleman in Texas, an ardent liberal, who had fought all his life for racial equality and who could not understand why so many coloured Americans had joined the anti-liberal forces of the late Senator McCarthy: in his view 'good' had worked 'evil'. But again, what do we know about good and evil in history before Judgment Day?

We may also observe that the greater equality of the sexes has a direct bearing on the increase of divorce, though certainly marriages are still concluded with good intentions; or that technological advances are used equally for material destruction and material betterment.

An interesting example in the history of the Society of Friends is the development of their mission in Madagascar. Joseph Sewell, the first Quaker who went to Madagascar as a teacher in 1869, laid the foundation of a Quaker community. When Friends Foreign Mission Association took his work under their wings they did not expect that the day might come when Malagasy Quakers would wish to join a common Protestant Church. Some English Friends will regard this as a retrograde step, hence 'evil'; more important, a number of Malagasy Friends dislike such a fusion, which is much desired, though, by the majority. It will be praised as 'good' by all adherers of the ecumenical idea who see in the divided Church the torn body of Christ. As so often in history, a creative action develops in an unexpected direction, which will be called 'good' by some, by others 'evil'. Let us remember Luther, Fox, Wesley and indeed Jesus, none of whom planned the founding of a new religious community; and when it happened they were accused, not necessarily by the worst representatives of the old order, of having done evil. As so often in history it is not a clash between good and evil which produces something at least ambiguous, perhaps even bad, but the clash of two goods, the assertion of two justifiable rights; and evil ensues only because neither side can, in the concrete situation, see that there may be more than one good in history; and neither side is necessarily less faithful in seeking God's will.

This happens even in the small circle of a family where parents may apply exactly the same 'good' education to all their children, but find that the reactions of their children are different: one will blossom under the well-considered educational treatment under which the other will wilt, and yet a differentiation may increase and not alleviate the difference and cause disruption, even hatred. Yet in the end, once the children have left home, the 'failure' may turn out a greater 'success' than the 'success'.

This 'demonism of the unforeseen',[1] 'created by man yet unwilled',[2] has led Mohammedan mystics to the conclusion that Allah is crafty and changes man's good aspirations to evil works.[3] Their pessimistic view stands in sharp contrast to the optimism of Hegel, who thought that 'the cunning of Reason'[4] turns all kinds of human passion towards its own progressive purpose. The devil himself is, in the words of Goethe's Mephisto, 'the power that always wills evil, yet always works good'.

This view is derived from a certain conception of Providence, namely the belief that even if men do evil, or do the wrong thing from stupidity, God in his grace and goodness may intervene and turn it into good. Providence is thus used as an explanation for the third relationship between good and evil, the not uncommon experience that something that is unquestionably evil may sometimes work good. The Old Testament's philosophy of history gives many such examples, one of the best known being the story of Joseph and his brethren.[5] But we find it also in the New Testament, notably in Peter's first sermon.[6] If, however, we see in incarnation and resurrection the mighty act of God, we may well accept the belief that Providence has intervened in this unique event to turn evil to good, without necessarily drawing the conclusion that God acts frequently in history in such a way. At least from the theological angle there is a great difference between that event and the rather facile idea that whenever evil works good, it is due to God's direct intervention.

[1] Jaspers, *Origin and Goal of History*, 124.
[2] *Ibid.*, 122. The term 'demonic' was first used in this way by Tillich in the 1920s. Cf. Tillich, *The Protestant Era*, xxxvi.
[3] Cf. Zaehner, *op. cit.*, 87, also 84/5 and 107.
[4] *Philosophy of History*, Introduction II, 6.
[5] Genesis, 5, 5-8.
[6] Acts 2, 22/23.

I have, from personal experience, a profound aversion to this conception of Providence. If I have escaped from the concentration camp, not only physically unharmed but spiritually enriched, can I forget that for the few of us who were thus blessed there were very great numbers of people as deserving as, or better than, I, and yet they perished, or worse, were spiritually destroyed? When, after a flying-bomb accident during the war, I was healed very quickly and completely from dangerous injuries, why was the family next door wiped out, all and sundry? Where was Providence at work in their cases? We know that in the Trojan War noble Achilles had to die and useless Thersites was spared to continue his unauthentic life. Paradoxically, I may feel thankfulness for my preservation and yet remain unable to think of it as an act of Providence. Calling it 'chance' I just give a name to an inexplicable mystery beyond my ken. The objection will be made that I must look beyond the grave to understand the ways of Providence; but with this we leave the realm of history in which, according to the belief of many, Providence is supposed to intervene.

God's providential actions in history are, in my opinion, confined to what is usually called the history of salvation, whether we connect this with the one mighty act through the life, death and resurrection of Jesus Christ, or with the Inner Christ, God's continual availability. We, who are in history, are able to meet God and his Spirit in personal encounter, since he is ever present to be met and indeed discoverable through all creation and through everything in it, also and particularly through every historical happening, and even through evil. This, the unlimited availability of God, and not the actual goodness of everything that is, stands behind my belief that all life is sacramental.[1]

Consistently with this attitude, I do not believe in the value of such intercession as tries to change the course of events. Prayer is search for a deeper awareness of God; like that of Gethsemane it is a request for greater nearness and strength to deal with the concrete situation by the very submission to God's will either to change or not to change the situation. I

[1] The sacramentality of life will be discussed in the concluding chapter.

do not believe that God, *having created man with the capacity of having history*, intervenes in history directly in the way proclaimed by the prophets of old, or by Friends when they declare that the development of Quakerism in the missionary field of Madagascar must be left to the Lord and his counsel. Most Friends, of course, would see God's intervention only in signs of goodness, mercy and love, whereas the Hebrew prophets recognized it also in his wrath and punishment—and is not 'act of God' still our name for natural catastrophies beyond human control?

But let us concentrate on history: I would see in changes such as those in Madagascar exclusively the work of men, furthered and hindered reactively by other men—in all 'good' respects by men enabled to act creatively and responsibly in concrete situations because they have found and are finding their own true selves in the awareness of the structure of being. What develops in this way through the good and not so good and evil actions of men is history, which as such is beyond man's control, and yet is the computation of human action.

There are two moral dangers in too firm a belief that Providence intervenes directly in history. One is that man may whittle away his own responsibility on the assumption that Providence will take care of things. The other, greater, danger is the temptation that we trust so fully in God's will to turn everything to the best that we are no longer wary enough in the choice of means for good ends. Soon enough we may think it right to 'do evil that good may come'[1] because the evil means we use will or may be changed by God's grace to achieve the good ends all of us have in our minds. I emphatically agree with Paul's 'God forbid' against the idea that we should ever do evil intentionally, though I do believe, and shall argue so in the next chapter, that man is unable to avoid the choice of the lesser evil.

While stressing once again that responsible free action of the authentic self, aware of the structure of being, can never wish to do evil, I think there is no denying that in history evil has worked good on many occasions. Quite apart from the ambiguous progress in the field of other applied sciences, war has

[1] Romans 3, 8, and 6, 1.

DOING THE WILL OF GOD 149

furthered our medical knowledge. Some people would not call this a *moral* good though it is undeniable that healing the sick is a morally good means. But warfare has greatly furthered the understanding of other nations, as our example from the crusales has tried to show.¹ Jakob Burckhardt may have gone too far with his statement that 'because the economy of world history remains dark to us on the whole, we can never know what would have happened if something, and be it the most terrible thing, had not happened'.² Still, his argument that Europe would probably have succumbed to the Osmanic Turks had these not been cruelly slaughtered by Tamerlan, has great force. On the other hand, we shall never know what creative features might have developed in a Europe under Turkish rule —after a time of ruthless oppression. At all events this example shows once more how difficult the application of moral categories to history is because we cannot survey history as a whole, lacking omniscience, and because we have to live and act in the concrete situations of time and place which limit our judgment. 'Man intervenes in history, but does not make it',³ his intervention is active and can, and ought to be, free and responsible, but as man cannot comprehend history as a whole, every action is a risk.⁴

How evil works good, or at least is the matrix of good, may well be seen in the fact that there is no well-run governmental system in our time whose origins have not been tainted by civil war, revolution and all kinds of injustice and violence. Should we deny the real blessings for human dignity and the valuation of the individual soul, which have resulted from the English, American and French revolutions, only because they began under very ambiguous conditions? The difference between these and the Russian and Chinese revolutions are due more to time and place than to morality. Few revolutions can be justified by the means used, but eventually many of their consequences are accepted as good.⁵

As hinted at repeatedly, we must not overlook the fact that

¹ See above pp. 113/114.
² *Weltgeschichtliche Betrachtungen*, Kröner's Pocket Edition, 266.
³ Jaspers, *Philosophie*, III, 100.
⁴ Cf. *ibid.*, 80 and 120/1.
⁵ Cf. Bonhoeffer, *op. cit.*, 52/3.

moral and spiritual goodness on the one hand, and material goodness, public decency, order and social happiness on the other, are not really commensurable. True, what is 'good' in history must in some ways be connected with goodness after the will of God, and yet it seems of a different kind, though very much interwoven with it. These two different aspects of goodness as spiritual and as material give us that sense of tension between doing the will of God, on the one hand, and acting freely and responsibly in history, on the other.

To complete our list of possible consequences, we would fourthly have to add examples that evil often works evil. There is no need to elaborate so obvious a fact, especially since it would not add evidence to our study of the unpredictable. I should refer, however, to the demonic figure of Bishop Nikolas Arnessen in Ibsen's *Pretenders*, a man who in his evil desire to work destruction beyond his death, bursts into the words: 'Is man's wit so wretched that he cannot control the child and grand-child of his own deeds?' (Act III). Bishop Arnessen does find the evil deed which works evil reactions. But, giving him the thought quoted, Ibsen has shown deep insight into the conditions of action: all action springs from, and ends in, the conditions of inter-actions and reactions: the saint may break the evil spell by reacting quite differently from the evil-doer's expectation; the evil-doer or the stupid and limited man may spoil the good action which the saint had planned for his sake. All of us, saints, evil-doers and their various crossbreeds alike, may be instrumental in changing the succession of actions by reacting to other agents, consciously or subconsciously or from sheer unawareness, in a way with which they had not reckoned—if they had reckoned with us at all. This power of changing the succession opens the way to conscious Christian action—but it still leaves the consequences in the realm of the unpredictable, even if all people acted from sheer goodwill.

The Riskiness of Free Responsible Action

We must clearly understand that inner certainty of the rightness of an action under God is not equivalent to certainty about its effects in history. In some rare, but for himself utterly decisive, moments, a man acts 'unconditionally', that is, apparently outside time and world, in fulfilment of his authentic selfhood: 'Here I stand, I can no other. So help me God'. In such moments of 'unconditional' action he himself feels clearly that he acts without regard to motives and consequences other than doing the will of God. Exactly this may make his action one of greatness in history. Clearly enough he has not started from God's will, but has risen to it from the conditions in which he is involved; and the consequences of his action, far from remaining unconditional, issue into the conditions of world and time and help to shape them. All action, even the most independent, and even the purest, is taken from the stuff of world and time and works upon world and time.

In brief, it is wrong to look at man's free responsibility in terms which neglect the conditions under which he has to act, for instance, by arguing that the creative genius shapes his own conditions and that the prophet, listening only to God, neglects them completely in holy obedience. The creative impact of such men is tremendous, but only because it is embedded in the conditions of history: the conditions work upon and with them from the moment of their encounter with their environment through all the creative actions they undertake to the succession of consequences and after-consequences which they evoke. While man becomes aware of the structure of being, of the absolute and unconditional, of the will of God for man, and while in this experience he decides for his true self and for free responsible action, there are conditions at work in the world through which he has to exercise and express his goodwill (or may wish to show his ill-will), through which he can act either responsibly or irresponsibly, either authentically or unauthentically. There are always data which alone make it possible for him to act at all, however changeable some of them may be under the impact of action, but which are data: his own givenness, the givenness of the world, the givenness of time, the givenness of 'human nature'; the givenness also of human creations such as State authority or technology. These creations have acquired a life of their own, not from evil or stupid planning, but because all creative human action is like a risky expedition into unknown territory full of unexpected dangers, not like the running of a train which normally, and therefore almost predictably, arrives at the time laid down in the time-table.

We are far too simple if we denigrate human creations, which threaten to master us, as a mere accumulation of human sin and stupidity, or if we try to reduce them to the action of individual statesmen, civil servants and managers. Many of them are planned and undertaken with a will for the good, indeed with awe before the wonders of God's creation. We are far too simple if we go on to trace their destructive features or their 'degeneration' exclusively to sin or to stupidity or both, instead of realising that any creative action contains risks because it works into an unknown future. The alchemist who seeks to make gold may invent china—or gun-powder. It is not merely guilt and stupidity which make action risky, though they come in as well, but our lack of omniscience and unlimited power.

It is wrong and indeed sinful if the optimist does not recognize our given limitations and acts as though goodwill could create heaven on earth. It is equally wrong and sinful if the pessimist finds man's original sin in the human effort to use his God-given creativity for free responsible action within the limitations of humanity, which make them risky. The creative risk, taken with responsibility and goodwill, is not sinful, however deep the sense of guilt, if a creative risk has led to destruction. On the contrary, if there were no risk, our action would not be free and responsible. On the other hand, we are far too simple when thinking that one or a thousand or a million men of goodwill could restore rational human control over man-made social or technical machineries which were, or were not, rationally planned. Like marriage, every human act is 'for better, for worse'. And it is still for worse if possibly bad consequences, for instance an abnormal child, are accepted with all self-effacing goodness and love and even become the occasion for developing such patience and forbearance as may become an inspiration to others. An event of this kind, so obviously a misfortune though not due to sin, carries with it all the same a sense of guilt; guilt being here the consciousness of unchangeability of what has happened, against my intention yet still through my agency.

Just as the word once spoken never returns, so the act once

ventured is irrevocable: it has become one of the conditions under which new creative and responsible action has to perform. The injury which I have done to a fellow-man cannot be made undone. I can, in free and responsible action, make reparation for it, he can in similar fashion forgive me. Even more important, God can and will forgive me if I turn back, and restore me into a state in which spiritually I can start as from the beginning: all the same, the succession of action, re-action, inter-action, moves on outside in world and time, it has become one of the infinite numbers of conditions under which man lives and acts. The experience my fellow-man has had with my injuring him has changed him, 'for better, for worse'; he will never be and act again as though it had not happened, however hard he may try. What his conscious mind forgives and forgets, his subconscious mind retains 'for better, for worse', for 'repression' or for 'sublimation'. Equally, my injuring another person has changed me, and though forgiven by him and by God, it has become part of my conditions.

To make my point still clearer: the person I have killed intentionally or accidentally, even without any fault on my part, never comes to life again. Whether his disappearance from history has been effaced spiritually through amends, reparations and forgiveness or not, indeed whether his removal has had bad effects or perhaps even good ones, his premature removal is woven irremediably into the course of events, for instance in the repercussions it has on his family.

The same applies to acts of goodwill; they, too, work for better or worse, they do something in the movements of history, but we are never sure of the kind of consequences, the chain of reactions, they set in motion; just as we never know all the conditions behind an action. We seek motives and causes for personal as well as for public action, but any rules which have been established by psychologists, sociologists and anthropologists, however meritorious in their usefulness for a defined purpose, have of necessity to neglect possible effects beyond this purpose. Above all, they seem to fail in one essential respect: if they were more than working methods, if they were 'correct' and could be applied as rationally as they are in theory, they would make the future predictable and put history under the mastery of man. They would turn the Kingdom which is to come into a realisable utopian Kingdom planned and wrought by man. Not only would such a Kingdom show little of God's Kingship: it would thereby deprive man of his free, creative and responsible decisions; for if these were certain to work out with a reliability no greater than that of the time-table of a well-run railway, only real madmen and criminals of extreme wickedness, not common or garden sinners, would fail to act on them without further choice.[1] Man would choose the good because it works, not because it is good. It would no longer be 'good', but just the only reasonable and normal action without any real 'choice' of acting differently. But man, in his awareness of the structure of being and before God, has to act freely and responsibly and, willing the good, can never know whether his action can achieve its purpose as a whole or in part, because he has to decide first, in every concrete situation, what the good is.

I expect two objections. The first is that I cannot speak of man's free creative and responsible action if at the same time I emphasize so strongly the conditions of his action. My answer is that free and responsible action is seen far too often as action in a vacuum. There is never a vacuum, there are always data from which to start. I cannot decide, for instance, whether Columba and Augustine should bring Christianity to England: this has been decided by them, and it may well be that there is no man alive on this earth today who has not been affected in some way by their action and its consequences in the building of Britain and the British Commonwealth. Nor can I decide whether in 1984 the fortieth President of the United States should introduce Communism in his country, though any of my actions, just like those of Columba and Augustine, may possibly have some influence on his decisions without my having the slightest inkling of it.

My freedom and responsibility before God and towards men mean exactly this: that in the place where I find myself this instant I decide in such a way that I do not betray my true self. My freedom consists in my courage to change myself as one of the conditions given to me, in such a way that I grow

[1] The conviction prevailing in the Communist and 'free' countries alike, that the opponents are madmen and criminals, is the corollary of the untenable idea that the future of man in history is not risky but predictable.

closer to the will of God for me; and I change myself by acting in the conditions of my environment in such a way that I change something of them with changing myself, and that with changing them as best I can, I change myself. But I am never a mere 'outsider' because I am always a man in history. What I do as an apparent outsider may be historically my most important contribution to history, and what I do 'against the world' is conditioned by the very world against which I wish to act: it is my free and responsible re-action. What I do for and to myself, I do to and for others; and what I do to and for others, I do to and for myself. What is done by others, be it for and to themselves or for and to me, or to and for the rest of the world, is all done for and to myself. Human action is conditioned also by our limitations, but it is free all the same if it is responsible action before God, with the courage to act from one's true self, in the attitude for which direction has been received in the encounter with God. It is what Tillich calls 'finite freedom' which, if finite, is still true freedom.

The second objection I expect is that on the one hand I deny that my action in history will inevitably have the result I intend, and that on the other hand I speak of responsible action, which implies that in a concrete situation I assume the possibility of discerning what in this instance is the good, wholesome or constructive contribution I should make. Such a contribution would not only show the attitude which I have found as the will of God for me, but would have also the effect of moving other people more closely to the will of God for them.

My reply to this possible criticism is based on the difference between 'correctness' in predictable chains of events, and 'usefulness' in assessing the likelihood of desired results by psychological, sociological and anthropological methods, a difference at which I have already hinted. The results of large-scale and long-term planning are less predictable than those of short-term and partial enterprise, but it is in the realm of the former that the great hopes like 'fraternity' and 'peace on earth' usually move. Observable trends of the moment, conditions of the concrete situation, can be estimated in a more promising way than speculations on the grand scale for the unlimited future. Nor have I tried to prove that all action is *likely* to miss its purpose, but only that all action is risky. I can do the relative best I can see, without priding myself that it is necessarily the best or *the* good. Responsibility means judging what seems good or evil in the concrete situation and endeavouring to strengthen the good against the evil: it is healing wounds rather than making invulnerable, it is building up the body rather than dispensing panaceas which promise to prevent any future disease. Even so, in spite of my best efforts, I may have used the wrong medicine, and woe unto me if I have done so from negligence or a laziness which shirks learning the learnable. I have to consider all available possibilities to the best of my abilities and have to decide what, in my judgment, I must risk to choose as the available best. If I have chosen wrongly without a fault of mine, as likely as not I shall suffer inwardly, accuse myself and ask for God's forgiveness. For in such cases I feel guilty even without having sinned, and a sense of guilt may be more tormenting than a sense of sin: for sin there is forgiveness; guilt is, as said before, the consciousness of the unchangeability of some evil that has happened through my agency, even if against my intention.

The Interrelation of Principle and Expediency

Describing man's position as that of a responsible agent between God's will and the conditions of action, I believe the traditional distinction between utilitarian ethics and ethics of principle falls to the ground. There cannot be a division between morality which judges action according to its good results, and a morality of pure motives, which excuses the agent of all responsibility for results as long as he has acted with integrity.[1] We simply cannot act in purity and from sheer goodwill unless our goodwill brings us to a prudential calculation of the possible effects. If I stick blindly to moral principles, according to the adage that *fiat justitia pereat mundus*,[2] I act as immorally as if over the expediency of an action I surrender altogether all moral considerations. If I want to act rightly, that is, responsibly, I must explore two avenues: firstly,

---

[1] Cf. Bonhoeffer, *op. cit.*, 58 ff.
[2] 'Justice must be done though the world perish', a saying attributed to Emperor Ferdinand I.

what action will, or rather, is more likely to, produce in a concrete situation the good results I desire; and secondly, whether this action, while promising success, is in itself moral, that is compatible with my true self, or an obviously bad or doubtful means to an only presumed good end. I must discover what action may at the same time be wholesome and constructive and what action is more likely to increase the evil I wish to remedy, either because it may not be truly expedient or because it is morally questionable.

This kind of consideration is what responsibility means, and my best intentions do not spare me the trouble of weighing up ends and means until they blend in with my good intentions. Fundamentally it is neither principle nor expediency that makes me a responsible agent, but the fullness of being, the wholeness of personality. Not what I hold on principle nor what I want to achieve, but what I truly am, the will of God for me, makes me act rightly. My whole self is involved. The fact that all action is risky and all results unpredictable does not empower me to 'leave the outcome with God': rather should I feel stirred and take extra pains to make quite sure that I need not blame myself for sheer carelessness if something turns out quite differently from my expectations. True, we can become too morbid when faced with some unintended failure, our sense of guilt may prevent us from accepting further responsibility, that is, from leading an authentic life; but I daresay we are in greater peril of being too light-hearted and of abusing the name of God by pronouncing him the only responsible agent in history. God intervenes in history through me, in the measure in which I am my true self, and act on my own responsibility. Full responsibility is possible only so long as I do not act against the self I am meant to be, that self that does not try to withdraw from the riskiness of action and the calculation of possible success and failure and that is therefore prepared to bear a sense of guilt without succumbing to it. The full self acts by risking himself: the price he pays is the living of his life in escapable tension.

The temptation to escape from this tension is great, and the way out for many good people is to have always the best will in the world, and for the rest to 'trust God' without caring overmuch what the consequences of ill-informed, but emotionally prompted good intentions may be; that is, without caring about the conditions of action in history. Friends are not alone in the one-sided emphasis on purity of motives. Luther, Kant and many other great men can be cited in support of the idea that it is the intention that counts, far more than the action and its results, for the simple reason that consequences are considered so unpredictable. But the supposition that we are surer of our motives than of our results is not much more valid: not alone the future is dark and with it the effects of our action; our motives, too, are never so clear and transparent as our consciousness assumes. Modern psychology has taught us much about 'rationalisations', and long before its discoveries Thomas a Kempis, when stating that in the balance of God motives weigh more than actions, hastens to add the sentence already quoted[1] that many of our apparently loving deeds are not free from carnal motivations.

Once again Ibsen's psychological acuteness has given us a fine illustration by contrasting in the *Wild Duck* one-sided purity of motive and one-sided cynicism of mere expediency. Gregers Werle is the high-minded idealist who suffers from 'the fever of righteousness' and thus acts without regard to forseeable bad consequences. His fatal 'improving of others' cannot be prevented by Dr Relling who, fearing the consequences if people have to face the truth, is bent on preserving the big lie on which their lives are built. Neither of them knows a love that tries to redeem from the lie without working destruction.

Quakers are often complimented for their ability to act with shrewdness and expediency while not losing too much of their disinterestedness and integrity. They have even been honoured with the name 'serpent-doves', in an allusion to Matthew 10, 8. Admittedly, their practice is often better than their thinking, which denies far too summarily the necessity of expediency. This denial is based on two contradictory positions which in some cases are mixed up together in the same person. Either they foster the utopian hope that good works good and evil works evil and that they therefore need not bother with consequences so long as they will and do the good. Or they stress

[1] See above p. 112.

DOING THE WILL OF GOD

principle as against expediency, subconsciously disappointed with the small results Christian action has hitherto produced in history, comforting themselves with the thought that all is well so long as their intentions are good. Consequently, 'whenever they can be brought to argue upon political questions, they reason upon principles and not upon consequences'.[1]

A somewhat different line of argument, however, was taken by Joseph Sturge when, in connection with the slavery issue, he opposed the adoption of a policy of gradual emancipation which was meant to spare the vested interests. In his often quoted words to London Yearly Meeting of 1830 he said:
'When the Christian is convinced that the principle upon which he acts is correct, I believe it does not become him to examine too closely his probability of success, but rather to act in the assurance that, if he faithfully does his part, as much success will attend his efforts as is consistent with the will of that Divine Leader under whose banner he is enlisted'.[2]

This is a very cautious formulation. The consideration of success is not altogether excluded, but only put into the second place, and though the idea of divine providence is introduced, its working seems to be almost conditional on the agent's doing his own part faithfully, and it is not clearly said that it will inevitably lead to the 'good' as defined by man. Joseph Sturge seems to hold here a position nearly equidistant from either extreme of the ethical issue as formulated, for instance, by Max Weber as 'The Christian does rightly and leaves the result with the Lord' and 'You act responsibly and have to take account of the forseeable results'. This, as I have tried to show, is an impermissible distinction because nobody, whether Christian or heathen, can act rightly without concern for the forseeable or imaginable results.

What the Christian can and ought to do, and what may be in his mind when he assumes that he takes his stand on principle, is to recognize that he ought to ignore unpleasant consequences for himself and, at least to a certain extent, for his community, if the rightness of action in a concrete situation depends on this or, put differently, that he should consider

---
[1] Clarkson, *Portraiture of Quakerism*, published in 1807, here quoted after Q.P.W., 205.
[2] L.P.Q., 329.

his own peril the lesser of two evils. This consideration, too, is a judgment of possible consequences, a calculative distinction between better and worse results. The scale of 'better' and 'worse', however, is not a matter of principle, but of spiritual awareness. The final choice is made not on principle, as Joseph Sturge and many others assume, but it is a decision taken by the true self in the awareness of the structure of being, risking his whole person.

The true self does not choose principle rather than expediency, even less does it waver between the two. The agent does *do* the will of God so far as he has *become* the will of God. His action is not a mere link between intention and result, as so often held in books on ethics. It is the expression of a self attaining full responsibility in the encounter with God and the awareness of Presence. The mechanism of conscious or subconscious motivation is merely the channel through which a man's experience of God becomes visible. The deeper a man's awareness of the structure of being, the more consistently will he fuse principle and expediency in the concrete situation, not by applying in practice what he holds on principle, but by his whole being expressing God's will for him. But even so he does not escape the tension between his true self and the conditions of action in which he is involved. Hence he may be and do the will of God and yet fail in history.

8

THE CONDITIONS OF ACTION (II): INVOLVEMENT

So far we have tried to understand the more formal conditions of action, especially as inter-action and as risk. We must now turn to the more substantial conditions of action, conditions through which the agent is involved in ambiguities, in spite of his best intentions and the awareness of God's will for him. Involvement, however, implies no curtailment of human freedom; it implies only that the *exercise* of our freedom is more precarious than we often assume, and that the tensions experienced in its exercise are more painful than expected. Even the desperate feeling that there is practically no freedom of decision left is the painful awareness of its existence and demands, up to the limit of the sacrifice of the self for the sake of its freedom. Unfreedom, on the other hand, consists in the indifference of the unauthentic self regarding its responsibilities, and the shifting of these responsibilities to every imaginable other agency: God, fate, fellow-men, heritage and the devil.

The most sophisticated form of trying to escape one's responsibility lies in the confession, abused as an excuse, that man is a miserable sinner, hence unfree in the bondages of sin ever since Adam's fall. Though I would agree that involvement is inevitable, I want to make it quite clear that in this context it cannot mean something like 'enmeshment' or 'entanglement' in sin to such an extent that the freedom of responsible re-action is denied on the grounds that such re-action, in its turn, is that of a sinner and can therefore only increase the evil. Involvement means here that I am inevitably implicated as man in history but, in the awareness of God's will for me, equally inevitably called to responsible re-action against my implication. Involvement is no excuse, but a challenge. That it

L

is an inevitable part of the human situation is a fact to be recognized and reckoned with; yet inevitability does not mean humble submission to its impact but, in every concrete involvement, courageous resistance against it. While as man in history I cannot escape involvement in the concrete situation, I may equally find, through that very involvement, a deeper awareness of God's will for me which works powerfully against that involvement. Failure in my efforts to escape the inescapable does not lead me to the conclusion that I should never have tried and should have left everything to God's intervening grace—this I hold to be a subterfuge of the unauthentic self—but that God's grace manifests itself in the attitude I take in and to my being involved, not in the escape from the inescapable or the irresponsible submission to it.

Moral Involvement: The Choice of the Lesser Evil

The first form of inescapable involvement which we must discuss is the inevitability of choosing the lesser of two evils. Many Friends and other Christian pacifists deny that such a situation can ever arise in a world in which there must be 'a way of God in every situation'. God's goodness, so they argue, will always show those who earnestly seek a good means to a good end. The difficulties standing against this assumption have already been briefly examined.[1] Though untenable, its recurrence can be somewhat justified because 'the choice of the lesser evil' has been often abused as an excuse for taking the line of least resistance, that is, of least difficulty and cost to oneself. This, of course, is not truly the *lesser* evil, but the evil less inconvenient to myself. As Kathleen Lonsdale puts it succinctly: 'So often the apparent choice between two evils turns out to be a choice between a hypothetical evil that *may* affect us adversely, and a *certain* wrong to other people'.[2] Charles Raven argues similarly:

'The alternative is not between being burned or blasted at Hiroshima and being liquidated or tortured at Belsen but between murdering and martyrdom. . . . Surely a Christian is bound to say, "I would sooner die in Belsen than be guilty of Hiroshima": if not, he tacitly affirms that Christ on the eve of His crucifixion ought

---

[1] See above p. 105/106.
[2] *Security and Responsibility*, 25 (Alex Wood Memorial Lecture, 1954).

DOING THE WILL OF GOD 163

to have authorised His disciples to call down fire from heaven upon Jerusalem or have enlisted the legions of angels in His own defence. . . . We know that martyrdom can be redemptive, and that to suffer is not the ultimate evil . . .'[1]

Martyrdom as alternative to murdering is too easily discarded by non-pacifist theologians. Nathanael Micklem, for instance, argues that had the Good Samaritan arrived on the scene when the robbers made their assault, he would have had either to fight them or to pass by on the other side, like Priest and Levite.[2] Micklem is right in criticizing the facile optimism of such Christian pacifists as claim that they would have tried to convert the robbers in the very act of aggression. If in Raven's words just quoted 'martyrdom *can* be redemptive', not all martyrdom is. What Micklem does not discuss, however, is the possibility of a Christian throwing himself between the aggressors and the victim without fighting and with the probability of being killed, whatever effect this may have in the whole situation—for instance, that the victim might have time to flee, or that two might be killed instead of one, or even that the robbers, faced with this unexpected intervention, might disperse without being converted in any way.

The real weakness of the Christian pacifist argument appears in a different statement of Raven's, where he says: 'There is *never* a choice of two evils because there is *always* the martyr's way, and I may have to take it'.[3] Is then the martyr's way no evil at all but a sheer good? Raven himself is much nearer the truth when in the passage quoted before he holds that 'to suffer is not the *ultimate* evil'. But evil it is all the same; so that if I choose martyrdom rather than murdering, I choose what I consider the *lesser* of two evils.

Once again we are faced with the question of what we mean by good and evil. In my understanding, the crisis of Gethsemane shows that Jesus saw his crucifixion not as a good but as a lesser evil, an evil smaller than doing wrong himself. 'It is not relieved by the expectation of resurrection 'after three days', or by the ecstasy of substitutional self-sacrifice, or even

---

[1] IFOR News Letter, 84, July, 1954 (Special Evanston Number).
[2] *The Theology of Politics*, pp. 137-8 (Oxford University Press, 1941).
[3] 'Is There a Christian Politics?' In *Religion in the Modern World*, 98 (London: George Allen & Unwin Ltd., 1952). (My italics.)

by the ideal of the heroism of wise men such as Socrates'.[1] Pietist emotionalism has distorted this fact by turning the events of Good Friday into an unmixed good because they worked the salvation of mankind. It even praises the glorious wounds of Jesus like any militarist praising the wounds received on the battle-field. Such a view either implies the old Docetic heresy that the sufferings of Christ were not 'real' because as God he lived no really human life and died no real death; or it assumes that his suffering was in fact *good* because of the good results: this is not simply a justification of the means by their end, but an actual revaluation of the means because of their good results. This kind of mistake is made far too often.

The follower of Christ must choose to *suffer* evil rather than to *inflict* it, but the evil thus suffered does not automatically become good, if only because, in the concrete situation, one man's acceptance of martyrdom is the occasion for other men to do evil. Morally speaking, it might have been a far greater good if Jesus could have converted Caiaphas and his servants and Pilate and his soldiers, though theologically speaking God's 'determinate counsel' would not have been fulfilled. In terms of ordinary human beings it would be a far greater good if a Christian, instead of rather dying than doing evil, could have turned the aggressors away from their evil ways before they killed him, that is, before they became still worse evil-doers and in still greater need of forgiveness.[2] It is quite a wrong idea that acceptance of martyrdom is a sure road to the conversion of the evil-doer. As far as we know, Stephen's death led to the conversion of only one of his persecutors, and even in this case it did not happen at once.

I therefore believe that martyrdom is not a good, but just a lesser evil; but I believe, too, that the choice of the lesser evil, far from being an un-Christian practice, is true Christianity and should not be denigrated by Christian moralists. Whenever a man lays down his life rather than do evil, he chooses the lesser evil and the greater good; but it would be still better

[1] Tillich, *Systematic Theology*, II, 150.
[2] In this respect one may say with Kierkegaard that the victim can never be fully absolved of the guilt of the victimizer, though it is guilt, not sin, in which he is involved.

DOING THE WILL OF GOD

if the need for laying down his life had not arisen and he could lead the good life together with his friends and enemies alike. If it were otherwise, the meaning of life, as willed by God to be lived rather than died for, would be denied.

The justifiable accusation to be levelled against theologians who prefer war to other forms of evil is not that in their involvement they choose what they hold to be a *lesser* evil but that they choose what so obviously is the *greater* evil, even though they admit that it is a 'tragic choice' they have to make. Consider the following passage:

'The tragic element in a human situation is constituted of conscious choices of evil for the sake of good. If men or nations do evil in a good cause; if they cover themselves with guilt in order to fulfil some high responsibility or if they sacrifice some high value for the sake of a higher or equal one, they make a tragic choice. Thus the necessity of using the threat of atomic destruction as an instrument for the preservation of peace is a tragic element in our contemporary situation. Tragedy elicits admiration as well as pity because it combines nobility with guilt'.[1]

In my view, this is no 'tragic choice . . . of evil for the sake of good', but an irresponsible choice, because it forgoes consciously the choice of the *lesser*, the smallest available evil all round. Taking the line of lesser difficulty and smaller resistance seems to me neither tragic nor noble; anyway, it is not what Antigone did, the classical example of tragic nobility.

On the other hand, in many cases it is far more difficult to decide which of two evils is really the lesser, and it is only on this, not on the principle of the matter, that discussion is possible. After different views in my younger years, I personally can hardly imagine circumstances where I would judge either war or atomic preparedness to be the lesser evil. But I realise that it is far from easy, and very much a matter of faith, to judge in all circumstances which is the greater and which is the lesser evil. In my conscientious calculations I must not overlook circumstances where martyrdom, far from avoiding the evil of war, may become the occasion of it. I am no isolated individual but a member of groups and of a nation, and while my personal acceptance of martyrdom may set an example to my friends, it may also inflame them so as to counter violence against me

---

[1] Niebuhr, *The Irony of American History*, ix/x (London: James Nisbet & Co. Ltd., 1952).

with violence against my enemies. Gandhi was well aware of this possible repercussion when he called off satyagraha campaigns at once when violence had broken out.

Also, my acceptance of martyrdom may amount to less than the deliberate choice of the lesser evil: it may be a flight from the dilemma of responsibility in the inescapable choice of the lesser evil. Take, for instance, the liberal headmaster of a German school after Hitler's rise to power.[1] Should he try to keep his position in order to protect his pupils from the worst extremes of racialist teaching, or should he resign to save his own soul rather than theirs? If he chose the former course, he would have to compromise with the system, use many prevarications to teach as much or as little racialism as was necessary for retaining his position and so in the end become himself demoralised and incapable of discerning clearly the evil from which he wanted to protect his pupils. If he chose resignation, he would lose his livelihood and be declared an enemy of his people. He would not only expose himself but also his family to persecution, and worse still, might disrupt it; and his successor would be an especially ardent racialist who would indoctrinate his pupils with hatred and thoughts of violence, to counteract the previous 'softness'. In neither case would he escape guilt, in neither could he contract out of his responsibility. Taking either one or the other course, he would still know that he did not do the right thing. The argument often heard that he ought to have tried far earlier to stop the ascendency of Hitler, does not only overlook, without evidence, the possibility that he did try but failed, but that he and like-minded people could have stopped Hitler easily without using evil means in the first place. All such arguments are facile and invalid because none of us can ever start living a Christian life in a good world; we all have to live in history where good and evil are inescapably intertwined.

This may be supported by another example, this time from Quaker history. In the last century many an American Friend helped to send fugitive negro slaves north through the so-called 'underground railway', thereby breaking the law of some

[1] I have used this example before in 'The Christian Faith and the State', in *The Society of Friends, the Church and the State*, 37.

Southern State. When questioned by their persecutors whether he knew something of the whereabouts of a fugitive, should he speak the truth and trust in the extremely remote chance that he could move their hearts, and if he failed, see the fugitive ill-treated and taken back to slavery if not death? Or should he perhaps have followed the advice of some other Friends and have kept away from this whole 'worldly' business of helping slaves in the first place, that is, passing by on the other side? Or should he, as some did, migrate from the slave state to a free state where this dilemma could not arise and he was free to be humanitarian only to those who already had made a successful get-away with the less scrupulous assistance of others?

There is no need to give other examples where Friends as well as other good people had to tell 'white lies', for instance when eliciting travelling papers for members of persecuted minorities, when as relief-workers sharing their army rations with ill-fed Germans after 1945, against orders, and when breaking in other ways the rules of unimaginative bureaucracy. It is a quandary which leaves no opening except *the conscious choice of a not quite so good means to a better end.*

Means and Ends

The conscious choice of not quite good means to better ends is most familiar to us in education and the treatment of refractory criminals and lunatics. It does not necessarily imply physical interference, but only the subjection of another person's ill-will or mistaken intent under a 'better' authority, thus preventing that person for some time, and in his state of immaturity, from harmful action or behaviour. The same right of coercion as a lesser evil to better ends exists also with regard to some races or classes in the fight against cannibalism, witchcraft, human sacrifices and slave trade, that is, in the prevention of some evil involving the wrong use of man by man. In all such cases, however, there is great danger that the justifiable limits of coercion are not observed and that it is exercised not for the good of the individual subjected to it and for that of his group, but for the benefit of the wielder of coercive power and his clique. Both the duty, and the limit, of justifiable coercion depend on the decision of responsible selves who, while applying it in the concrete situation, see in it at best a lesser evil.

Let me repeat with great emphasis what I have said before: we must never choose evil intentionally so that good may come.[1] But this does not relieve us from the inevitability of choosing the lesser of two evils as a means to a better end. Metaphorically speaking, the surgeon who amputates a leg does not do so because he thinks amputation or living with one leg is a good thing, but because he judges that it is better than letting the patient die; and he has no, or only a very limited, right to include in his responsible considerations the possibility of a miracle which might save the man's life against all expert diagnosis. Similarly, telling a white lie is never good; the real moral decay, however, begins when it is not used in responsibility, but light-heartedly, almost unawares, as a habit, and worse still, simply as the easier way for oneself and to one's own advantage: then the white lie turns quickly grey and black. The criterion whether I choose the lesser evil with responsibility is the conscience troubling me afterwards whether there was really no other way and whether, in spite of the good achieved, I did really do the best thing in the given circumstances. In other words, I must feel guilty for what I could not help doing, and must bear this guilt. Bonhoeffer has summed up the solution of this dilemma, if 'solution' it is, in one sentence: 'If . . . I refuse to bear guilt *for charity's sake*, then my action is in contradiction to my responsibility which has its foundation in reality'.[2] The operative words are 'for charity's sake', and they must be upheld against defenders of 'tragic necessity' as much as against extreme moralists. Where moral absolutists refuse bearing guilt for charity's sake, they become all the same guilty through that very act of withholding their love.

The choice of the lesser evil, however, happens not only in 'moments of ethical paradox, when circumstances are such that no available procedure can fully satisfy the conscience'.[3]

---

[1] See above p. 148.
[2] *Ethics*, 214. (My italics.)
[3] Hick, 'The Structure of the War Problem'. In *Studies in Christian Social Commitment*, edited by Ferguson, 29.

It enters in far less extreme moments, namely when we are quite sure that we have chosen the good end and the best means of achieving it. This aspect has already been touched on in our discussion of martyrdom: even martyrdom may not be fully good because it may be a man's decision to suffer rather than to do evil, a decision, however, which increases the sin of those who make him a martyr. Similarly, when working for the end of colonialism, we offend inevitably some of the justifiable, because historically validated, rights of old settlers. When advocating desegregation, we are prone to overlook, over the great wrong done to the negroes, the sense of being wronged of those who, more from their whole background than from ill-will, cannot understand a world of racial equality and who therefore react from a sense of deep injury against our 'wickedness'. The denial that there could be a choice of the lesser evil implies the denial that there could ever be *two* relative goods or *two* relatively good rights. But there is ample evidence that far less wrong is done from evil intention than from asserting one's good right against another equally good right, and be it a wrong only in form of suspecting the claimant opposite of acting from ill-will rather than in assertion of what he considers his own good right.

Much of the East-West conflict consists of such assertions and suspicions. When supporting disarmament, we increase the fear of those, both in East and West, who are afraid (and, of course, pacifists, too, are afraid!) and the inclination to violence of those who, again both in East and West, are by nature violent and ready to exploit any suspected weakness. In this way, what we assume to be working for an indisputable good, becomes only a better, as it has also some less good repercussions among the frightened and the violent. As responsible agents, however, we are settled with the task of calculating the possible evil repercussions of our good actions and include these, too, in our responsibility, yet without yielding to the pressure for lower standards.

In the case of disarmament as in all other cases it is not only Christian charity, but also commonsense, to be deeply concerned for those who do *not* agree with our viewpoint, as we cannot help increasing their aggressiveness by our attempts at reducing it. Nothing reveals more clearly how far we are still from 'being God's will' than that in all our responsible considerations our intelligence is often too much blinded by our good intentions to grasp this basic fact. Reconciliation work is of necessity multi-lateral because in nearly all cases there is something to be said for all sides, and every decision, even the best available means for the best imaginable end, is likely to offend at least one of those involved.

Once we understand that all reconciliation work is multilateral, we may discover the basic reason why action in history is involved with the choice of the lesser evil: we can never take all necessary steps at once, but have to decide for an order of priority. This choice of an order of action is, if we act responsibly, a choice of what in our calculative judgment is the good end which may possibly be achieved at the present moment as a means for a still better end. A few typical dilemmas of priority will make this clear. In 1954 and 1955 German Friends were faced with the question whether they should negotiate with their Government for legislation safeguarding the rights of conscientious objectors, at a time when it was still possible to influence the drafting of the conscription bill; or whether, by doing so, they would implicitly admit the right of the Government to impose general conscription. Both views found their ardent supporters.

Another example is connected with the disarmament issue: if we devote our energies to the abolition of nuclear tests and to nuclear disarmament, do we not admit implicitly that 'conventional' weapons are less objectionable, and thus surrender our testimony against all war, even those fought with bows and arrows? However often we may stress that we regard nuclear disarmament only as a first step, a concentration on the greatest danger will be misunderstood by many.[1] On the other hand, action towards a good end depends on steps, on partial measures for the moment, in brief, on the principle of gradual amelioration. Step-wise amelioration is full of its own dangers as every step taken creates new and unforeseen situations and may thus bring about the very evil the removal of which is our major end. The 'mean-while' is itself a lesser evil.

The necessity of deciding on priorities is not limited to

[1] Cf. Bailey, 'Friends and the United Nations', F.Q., 1956, 115/6.

special situations: the fact is that all action I undertake excludes automatically other possibilities. If I choose one good course, I cannot choose another good course, and I shall never know whether I have chosen the better or the less good course. As Jaspers says: 'Action succeeds only through renouncing other possibilities';[1] this means that every choice of action brings with it something that is negative. In other words, human decision is never for good or evil, but always for a better or a worse, and the choice of the best imaginable leaves open the question whether with a different choice a still better might have been chosen, that is, a still smaller evil. All human decision is a choice of the not absolutely best, hence all choice is at best the choice of a not quite so good, of a somewhat, if lesser, evil—but not of *the* good. This, too, is one of the conditions of our living and acting in history.

Social Involvement: Individual and Group

In the examples given to illustrate the choice of the lesser evil, attention has repeatedly been drawn, for the moral assessment of action, to the part played by other people, for instance, when discussing the choice of martyrdom. Here we touch a major form of involvement: man is not an isolated individual, however lonely he may be in his ultimate decisions. Most of his actions affect other people, just as he is affected by theirs. Man is an individual within society, that is, within a network of groups, the so-called in-groups. In their turn these groups exist among other groups towards which he does not feel a similar, at least a far less strong, sense of belonging, and often one of strangeness and hostility: the out-groups. About the former he is inclined to speak in the first person plural, about the latter in the third person, though he may alternate in his usage with changing situations and issues.

True enough, there may be something like the hermit's goodness, separated from society, but even this goodness develops from a life in the social nexus. In fact, goodness in any *moral* sense, and nearly all fruit of the spirit, depend for their maturing on relationship to others. Man is a being-in-relationship, and as the Great Commandment has crystallized it: a

[1] *Von der Wahrheit*, 526.

being-in-relationship to God, on the one hand, and to his fellow-men on the other. The quality of these two relationships is interdependent: the more a man is aware of God's will for him, the better becomes his attitude to men. Friends often hold that correspondingly a man who establishes right relationships with his fellow-men moves thereby nearer to God's will for him. This I believe to be true, but if he is an agnostic, he may not be aware of it as God's will.

In spite of this interdependence, however, it is just in the relationship with other men that he often feels most strongly the tension between God and history. Just in endeavouring to be what he is meant to be, he feels foiled by his colleagues and employers, his next-door neighbour and even his own family; and whatever the rights and wrongs of the matter, in the very attempt at acting responsibly he becomes most directly aware of how far he remains below the self he is meant to be. Either he cannot help compromising his cause, or he is pressing it over against others to the extent of giving offence. In such conflict he feels he is getting inescapably involved. Certainly, this is, on the personal level, another important aspect of social involvement, but it is not the kind of social involvement I need discuss here.

The relationship of man to God as expressed in the Great Commandment cannot exist in any true sense unless it is, and remains, personal; but relationships between men can either be personal, or they can exist in a very real sense even when no personal contact is possible. Impersonal relationships are an inevitable part of social organization. No doubt, since personal relationships have such an important share in our lives, we cannot be surprised that much religious and moral thinking is concentrated on them. But thinking on personal lines is not adequate to impersonal or group relations.

The mistake we make so often in our consideration of impersonal, that is, of social and international problems, consists in reducing them to a merely personal level. We are, of course, justified in our strong reaction against the depersonalizing usage of universals such as 'labour' and 'capital', 'nation' and 'enemy', and rightly wish to remind ourselves and the world that these universals derive their full meaning from the real human beings, however anonymous for ourselves, for whom

DOING THE WILL OF GOD 173

they stand. But Friends, in their turn, are inclined to go to the other extreme and see the problem between 'bosses' and 'hands' as though five or six honest workers could solve all social tensions of the world in a little chat with a Dickensian owner, and as though the East-West problem could be solved if Dulles and Khrushchev became personal friends. There is, of course, some important truth in the observation that personal sympathies and antipathies have great influence on the form which group negotiations take, and that personalities and characters make their impact on historical developments. All the same, group relatedness in history is not just equivalent to personal relationship.

We may feel great 'friendship' for the Russian people, loving their literature, music, icons, ballet, folk dances and so on, without ever having known a single Russian. We may feel great personal friendship for three or four Russians we happen to know, having met them in a youth camp or an international Quaker Seminar, or on an interdenominational conference of Christians, and yet dislike the character, or better the temperament so strange to us, of the Russian people, as it emerges from their literature and history, their present social system and their leaders who at the same time express and represent it. I may, as a Communist, feel great friendship for the leaders just because of their system, and perhaps even because I like them personally, and yet hate the idea that I would have to live among the 'primitive', 'backward', 'dirty', 'alcohol-infested' Russian people with their very different moods and their own way of life. If, then, we talk, as we do every day, of 'friendship with Russia', using a word which clearly indicates personal relationship, but without implying true personal contact, what do we mean?

Subconsciously we welcome the metaphorical vagueness of a word which helps us to reduce inter-group problems to the personal level. It is convenient to us probably for two main reasons: firstly, because we wrongly assume that the solution of group problems, if reduced to the more familiar personal level, becomes more manageable; and secondly, because we are afraid that, with the distinction between a personal and a group level, we have in fact accepted two different moralities. It is, of course, entirely wrong to be satisfied with, and accommodated to, a lower standard of morality in group problems; though inevitably involved, both within and together with our group, in actions of which we disapprove, we never must make our involvement a standard of morality. Far too often has society been seen as either 'immoral' or at least entitled to a different, that is, a lower, standard of morality. Society is certainly not quite immoral; it is widely recognized that public morality is in many ways the guarantor of a somewhat higher standard of individual conduct, and where public morality is undermined, as for instance in Hitler's Germany, the results speak for themselves. On the other hand, society has never reached as high a standard of morality as its better members demand, in the fullness of their responsibility.

The basic error of the defenders of a two-fold morality is, in my opinion, that they regard involvment in 'duties' imposed on them by their 'station' in public life[1] as a sufficient ground for setting up lower moral standards, indeed, for calling their acceptance 'responsibility'. In this they respond obviously to the demands of their group, not to their awareness of the structure of being. Suffering from the often hardly bearable tension between God and history, they have turned the fact that we are inescapably involved in relativism into a system excusing and defending relativism as the best possible under given circumstances, and then equalizing the best possible with the good, as the standard morality for our station and its duties. Some of them separate carefully the realm of 'justice', as the socially good, from that of 'love', as the personally good, thus surrendering from the outset any chance of ever solving the most normal issue among men: the conflict of two equally justifiable rights. Conflicts of this kind cannot be solved by justice but only by love that sacrifices some of its own justifiable right, be it only under the pretence of 'enlightened self-interest'.

Adherers of a two-fold morality, if they really stick to it and are not in fact much better than their theory, would be inwardly prevented from trying to move their own group to a state of mind where self-sacrifice, even on a small scale,

---

[1] Lindsey (Lord Lindsey of Birker), *The Two Moralities* (London: Eyre & Spottiswood Ltd., 1948), distinguishing a 'morality of the challenge to perfection or morality of grace' from a 'morality of my station and its duties'. This distinction has been emphasized most strongly by Lutheranism.

becomes possible. Their insistence on justice all round as the moral half-way house for society and societies, helps to harden the insistence of each group on its own good right and, of necessity, to question the good right of the others: these will be blackened and their representative leaders will be called evil or satanic. The insistence on justice is, for instance, behind the inter-union struggle for fair wages: one trade-union fights for an egalitarian level, the other for differentials according to skill, all in the name of 'justice'. Justice is open to many interpretations and offers no solution, self-denying love does.

Similarly, the propagandist exploitation of the incidents in Hungary, Suez, China and Algeria, all in the name of justice, blind us to the fact that they were each and all the lamentable results of weakness and fear, not of strength. If we tried to tackle the issues between nations 'in love', not 'in justice', we would not wish to negotiate from strength, trying to exploit the weakness of the other side, but would render aid exactly in its weakness. We would not wish to exploit the difficulties of Soviet agricultural policy, of Chinese and Indian industrialisation, of British inflation and American over-expansion, but would assist one another in solving them. But thinking all the time in terms of justifiable claims and rights and the justice of our case, we lose increasingly the power, and even the will, to see the justice of the case opposite and our own injustices. The ruthless bargaining in international affairs is partly quite immoral, partly, however, due to the overstressing of 'justice' as a viable method. Justice prevents reconciliation because it must, by its nature, weigh up rights. If we acted from true responsibility to God, we would not work for justice but for reconciliation, would *offer* guarantees rather than demand them, take risks upon ourselves rather than try to force them on the opponent, and would not exploit his weakness and his mistakes and sins, but make them into instruments of reconciliation.

This is, I believe, the meaning of 'responsible action' in group relations. What goes by the names of 'duty of one's station' and 'responsibility to one's own group' is not just a somewhat lower than personal morality, but is the exact opposite of responsibility in the sense adopted in this study, namely the response of the true self to the will of God in every situation, against all one's human interestedness on the personal or the impersonal level. However inescapable the involvement in one's own group and its conflicts with others may be as part of the human situation, responsibility means an unending struggle against acquiescence in one's involvement, and the burning desire to replace any lesser evil by a still lesser. Responsibility can never recognize any lesser evil as standard or as a second kind of morality.

On the other hand, this struggle with involvement, unending as it is, cannot be ended by futile attempts at reducing group problems to that of personal relationships in the way it has been done so often by the opponents of a two-fold morality. Understandably resenting the fact that groups and group organisations interfere with that kind of freedom which would offer complete non-involvement, some of them have tried, in radical individualism and theoretical anarchism, to overlook their reality. They deny any connection between person and group other than in the form of a spiritual community, and are driven to quite unrealistic conclusions such as Berdyaev's statement that 'it is to be doubted whether God notices the death of the great kingdoms of the world; but He takes very great notice of the death of an individual man'.[1] Could we ever imagine the death of a great kingdom of the world without the violent death of many men? The writers of the Old Testament saw deeper. It is imposible to sever human life in history from its groupings and organisations.

True, even in group relationships there are personal aspects which must not be neglected. There is, for instance, the spiritual community just mentioned, the sense of inner communion between responsible selves, a present brotherhood experienced, in the face of God, by the I in the togetherness of the We.[2] Community, based on such communion, is not the every-day condition of men in groups, and if it is set up as pattern of normal social existence for which we should work as for the Kingdom on earth, it is a utopian endeavour. This is exemplified by the *Bruderhof* experiment which so far has failed to

[1] *Slavery and Freedom*, 144.
[2] For the importance of the 'We'-experience, against the isolation of the 'I' in existentialist thought, cf. my *Friends and Truth*, 63 ff.

prove its viability. The *Bruderhöfer* depend both economically and technically on the sustenance they receive from or through the wider society, whose social pattern they disparage while benefiting from it.

The more normal pattern of human groupings is *solidarity* rather than *togetherness*, in which the personal aspect is confined to the individual sense of belonging and loyalty towards the group, and the individual participation in its common interests to the exclusion of interests of other groups. This exclusiveness marks also the spiritual community, in the form of separateness and peculiarity as described in Part I. *Togetherness* depends on personal relationship, and as this cannot exist with the whole of mankind, you cannot avoid excluding those outside the community in fact, even while including them in religious search and prayer. Social *solidarity*, on the other hand, depends on common interests and the protection of the individual offered by the group. Interests, however, are varied and contradictory and again exclude one another automatically. For instance, the trade-unions, far from uniting the workers of the world, have set them more efficiently against one another through restrictive legislation against free migration and free movement from one skill to another. The 'community' and 'brotherhood' as well as the 'solidarity' of all men are ideals without roots in the human situation in history. They have produced day-dreams, but no sense of belonging and loyalty. Indeed, the 'world-citizens' form their own little group. With all this I wish to elucidate only the inevitability of groupings, not the necessity of their using violence against one another for ever and ever.

Within the group, the sense of belonging and loyalty is fully personal only on the part of the individual member. True, his interest is protected by the group and he has the experience of solidarity, but his loyalty, that is, a love which is essentially disinterested and self-effacing, is not reciprocated by the group. Mutuality goes as far as mutual aid and mutual interest, but not as far as mutual love: the group can be solidary, but never loving, let alone 'self-effacing' towards me.

There may appear to be another kind of personal relationship, however, when a group functionary is met on a personal level. The long list of Quaker approaches to monarchs and leaders of the people proves that personal, disinterested friendship may open ways where the action of pressure groups fails. Our personal friendship intends and implies a spiritual concern for the functionary in his search for responsible decision. All the same, in such cases our disinterestedness is always only a relative one because our approach to his self is made not exclusively for *his* sake or for the sake of our mutual friendship, but for the sake of our own cause and what we feel to be the will of God for ourselves *and* for him. We, as representatives of our cause, approach him more for what he represents than for what he is in himself. This clearly indicates the involvement on either side, the interpenetration of friendship and interest. The inescapability of such involvement will be clearer to us when we understand some of the implications of living in groups and group organisations.

I can have a very strong sense of belonging to a group without having a personal relation to very many of its members or to any of its representative functionaries; and such personal relationship as I have with those few may be little related to the factors which make that group a group and give me a sense of belonging. Sense of belonging is often far less a personal matter than that of many unconscious influences of environmental norms and habits which are accepted and taken for granted, even though they are, of course, mediated through persons, parents, teachers, school-mates and so on through life. The outcome of all this is that I do not only feel part of the group, but also represented by it and, when outside, representative of it. If I feel wrongly represented, the fact that I resent it rather than shrug it off gives the clearest evidence of my belonging.

Representation is always the beginning of involvement, even when briefing a solicitor in a personal matter. No sooner has he made 'my case his own' than I have lost power over the means and methods used by him. I may not be aware of them at all; but if I know and dislike them and he insists on using them, all I can do is to withdraw my brief; and unless I find a representative more suited to my ideas, I must forgo the attainment of an end which I may have thought valuable and even important. Or else I may consider the solicitor a not quite good means to a better end and let him work in his own way.

Things become more complex where a representative stands for a number of people, a group or an organisation. He will have to concert the views of all, or at least of the holders of power within the group, and may have to take a line from which I dissent even though it be that of the majority. I, in his place, may have to do the same, without accepting, however, that this fact is as such the ultimate moral standard of all corporate action. Instead, I may, and should, try to persuade my clients or whatever they are as group members, to adopt my line. I may fail and may then resign, thus surrendering the matter to a less scrupulous successor; but then I shall be guilty of that surrender. Wherever I stand, in the rank or on top, the group clearly interferes with my free responsible decision, and it is exactly in this situation that I *have* to come to a free and responsible decision and, having considered all imaginable circumstances, that I have to choose in the end a lesser evil. This is what 'being involved' means.

For the moment it is less relevant whether I belong to a group by birth and upbringing or by choice; whether it is fairly easy for me to contract out and perhaps join some similar group, or whether it is very difficult and almost impossible. My personal sense of belonging makes me loyal to the group not as to a collection of human beings, but as to a collective, an anonymous body, a man-made organisation or social organism such as school, club, trade-union, party, church, nation; and every conflict, involving my loyalty, means a spiritual crisis. Some of these man-made creations such as nation and State cannot be explained, as they so often are, as free associations or 'social contracts' of individuals, but must be seen as an inescapable structure of the social existence of man in history. They develop an impersonal character of their own, which has a considerable hold over their members, both outwardly and inwardly, and especially over their responsible leaders, and displays both good and evil, angelic and demonic, features. It is to this kind of structure that I am bound by my sense of belonging and loyalty.

Loyalty
Loyalty, however, is love, and like all love, it is truly tested

not when things run smoothly but when the loved one goes wrong or becomes un-understandable as in Job's relationship to God. In my relationship to the group the test comes whenever I, in my fullest possible responsibility, disapprove of certain group actions. In such situations, should I turn away, if I can, and forsake the group at the very moment when my loyalty tells me that I am most needed? Or should I go to the limits of my loyalty and even to the sacrifice of my integrity, and thus become less capable of exerting an influence towards what I conceive to be the right direction? Whichever way I decide, I become guilty, I am inevitably involved. Deciding *for* the group means that I share in its wrong-doing even while exerting myself to change it from within; deciding *against* it means washing my hands and letting the wrong happen without trying to stop it, thus refusing 'to bear guilt for charity's sake'; and so I am once more guilty.

Among Friends, special attention must be given to involvement in war-time. Not only has the nation protected and supported its citizens from birth, in exchange for their loyalty and services, but precisely the warlike action which I abhor is its chosen way of continuing that protection and support for me. And it is quite true that in the middle of war I still enjoy many advantages through the war-actions of State, Government and the majority, including perhaps the protection of my conscience and its objections against war. I may accept these advantages quite thoughtlessly, may demand them as my unilateral right, and yet insist on contracting out from corporate wrong-doing, without rendering account to myself of the many benefits I receive, and cannot help receiving, through their wrong action. Modern society, in war-time even more than in peace-time, is the necessary basis of every citizen's livelihood and welfare. Even if I managed to provide, through home production, for all my own and my family's needs, I still remain socially involved. Either I refuse, in a self-righteous way, to produce more than my own needs and to surrender a possible surplus; or I do surrender it to my soldier neighbours in need: both my care for them and my lack of care show how inescapably I participate, willy-nilly, through commission or omission, in the life of the group to which I belong by loyalty or by mere presence.

If I am less thoughtless and do not insist on the right of my conscience without considering my involvement as an equally important matter of conscience, it may be only with great reluctance that I contract out from war-service because I cannot deny that I owe my protection to a method, however wrong, of my group to whom I am bound. First, I know in my deepest heart that I have not been much better, if at all, than others in 'taking away occasions' of war. Certainly, I cannot draw from this the conclusion, drawn by non-pacifist theologians, that having sinned with others I must now accept the wages of sin with the others through active participation in war: war is not only a consequence of sin, as they assert, but the commission of a still greater new sin, in which I ought to have no share. But I know nevertheless that my choice lies between being a corporate sinner with the others, or a parasite on other people's sin. Choosing the refusal of war-service as the lesser evil, I still feel that there is great impurity in this very act of trying to become purer: while I refuse to soil my own hands, I participate willy-nilly in all the benefits provided and protected by those who may be less scrupulous—just as, in the case of defeat, in all the punishment.

Anyway, are they less scrupulous? They may be exactly as scrupulous as I am, and even more so, but they have, in full responsibility, decided upon a different form of action. They may wish to be as loyal to Christ as any of us, but they find the sacrifice of their own integrity less reprehensible than the refusal of self-sacrifice in solidarity. Though I do not think that I would decide as they do, I feel much closer to them than to such absolutists as take their stand without qualms.

I am never quite convinced that any pacifist can truthfully say that his pacifism lifts him above the inner conflict of loyalties because his loyalty to Christ resolves for him the tension between God and history. True, most of us argue often as though it did, asserting that loyalty to Christ implies love to all God's children alike. While it is, of course, quite true that the Fatherhood of God implies the brotherhood of men, does this mean that mankind in history forms, or can form, a closed spiritual community of the kind the term brotherhood indicates, that is, a fellowship where everybody has a personal relationship and friendship for everybody else? Far from being a spiritual community, mankind is not even a solidary in-group like a congregation or a nation. The sympathy I have for mankind is devotion to an ideal, but hardly a sense of belonging which does not let me go even when I suffer under its impact, and which, if it ever dismisses me, does so only after a major spiritual crisis.

Seen in this way, loyalty to mankind cannot amount to that higher loyalty that resolves all conflicts of loyalty under which I smart. It does not lift me above my group or groups, but makes me only deeply aware of my involvement: for my loyalty to God demands responsible action in history, not flight into an ideal. I realize more clearly that every action I take towards greater brotherhood among men is likely to be resented by many of my fellows, thus opening new dissensions and creating new group divisions. We cannot push aside the apocalyptic insights expressed by Jesus in various ways, such as that he had not come to bring peace but dissension, and that with the continuation of history divisions would not decrease but increase. He was a far greater realist than many of his modern followers who deny the authenticity of his eschatological sayings, but who are found quoting the next moment the equally apocalyptic passages of the new heaven and the new earth and the Kingdom which is to come on earth.

I do accept, in my loyalty to God and the awareness of his will for me, that there can be no moral or Christian differentiation of attitudes to friend and enemy; I do, therefore, repudiate a division between my 'responsibility' towards the own group which calls on me, for love's sake, to defend them by force, and a merely theoretical 'love' for the enemy, for instance in the form of prayer at a time when I actually join in destructive actions against him. But while I cannot fight, I am still involved: as both friends and enemies destroy one another, my only responsible decision in love is to stop them wronging one another. As I am unable to achieve this, I become guilty, not through participation in their mutual destruction, but through failing both sides in not protecting them from one another. Christianity knows no neutralism, but implies participation on all sides.

In this respect modern Friends feel, on the whole, a wider and more inclusive responsibility than their spiritual forbears.

DOING THE WILL OF GOD

Early Christians and early Friends were satisfied that the actual avoidance of shedding blood was sufficient to save their conscience. They did not reflect much on some other connections they could not avoid having with the 'world', nor on the world's impact on them. Admittedly, it was easier in those days to keep aloof. They lived in spiritual communities so closely knit that the question of what might happen to their nearest and dearest did not arise as a moral problem: they stood unconditionally for one another within their community; and considerations whether in consequence of their own decision some temporal disaster might affect other members of their group need not interfere with their action, because it was self-evident that these others would decide in the same way. We, however, feel far more responsible for those who do not belong to our own spiritual community, we are far less exclusive, just because our own community is far less closely knit. In any individual action we must therefore consider possible adverse temporal consequences, not only for ourselves, but also for other members of the in-group (possibly even members of our own Society) who differ from us. Action in relation to the disarmament question is a very relevant case in point. Such uncertainties increase the sense of tension in our own decisions.

With this we touch the last point we must consider regarding social involvement. So far the assumption has been made that the Christian pacifist is capable of taking a responsible stand equally detached from friend and enemy, though not neutral: as it were, in loyalty to mankind. We have already seen that he is nearly always tied to his group by circumstances, even if not in his aspirations and ideals. But this is only half the truth. Being brought up within his group, living with and within it, impairs his judgment and conditions his whole approach. Though his responsibility may urge him on to the ultimate boundaries of his environmental limitations, the loyalty to his own group continues working as an imponderable bias in its favour. Sometimes this happens in a very perverse way: the wrongs done by his own group which he observes at close quarters, depress him so much that he gives the enemies not only the benefit of the doubt but idealizes their wrong actions, excusing them in exactly the measure in which he condemns the similar or smaller wrongs of his own group. This is anything but responsible calculation: it is the outcry of his offended sense of loyalty. Even in his very protest he shows many characteristics which place him clearly among his own group. An outward sign of such unconscious bias for one's own group can be observed in international gatherings of internationalists: how very national they all are in the forms and ways of devotion to their international ideal, and hence how easily distinguishable according to their origin and background!

Clearly, the hold of the group over its members is not only that of compulsory power or moral pressure, it is a hold through deeply rooted loyalty and the formative influence of early impressions. Their loyalty may involve them in group-selfishness through their most unselfish actions. Unsparing service and dedication to the group, be it nation, trade-union or church, may deceive them about the immorality of the actions of the group as a whole against other groups; and thus the more successfully, the more deeply they are committed to the 'good cause', the less do they think of their individual advantage; the better persons they are. The young idealistic Nazi who gave unsparingly his best self, all his time and energy, to the 'New Order' in which he believed, learnt too late that he had wasted himself in an evil cause. For if good ends do not justify bad means, good intentions do not justify bad ends either. It is exactly here that the limitations of all human morality emerge most clearly: quite unawares, a person can *do* good and *be* good for the evil ends of his group, even those of his religious community, burning heretics in fulfilment of the presumed 'will of God'. If the Church is right in pointing out that subjectivity may lead good people into error, the errors of the 'objective' church, State or society may be exactly as dangerous for good people. This is the deepest reason why a 'morality of my station and its duties' is invalid: it supposes that there is a real morality in the group which is not of my choosing but to which I have to submit. All in-groups, apart from the true community',[1] are erected on principles and laws, not on those directives which concern the true self in wholeness and love. The subject, therefore, rather than the group can have a guide,

---

[1] See above p. 176.

DOING THE WILL OF GOD

if it avails itself of it, in the awareness of the structure of being.

Responsible action means that I must act in every new situation from a renewed search for the will of God for me as I can best discern it, and this in spite of and against the givenness of my place in world and time. I must ask at every juncture: what is, at this moment and for this issue, the responsible action prompted by a full awareness of being loving, being truthful, being pure, being my authentic self, being the will of God? In this search, however, I must not expect to find relief from the tension between God and history. On the contrary, responsible search and action increase heavily the burden of discerning more clearly the will of God in world and time; for I am involved not only through my own limitations and my social conditions, but also through the material means which I must use in my responsible actions. With this we touch still another kind of involvement.

Material Involvement: Having and Being

Friends are best known for their emergency relief and rehabilitation work in war-stricken countries. The purpose of such service is not merely the removal of material distress or the call of Christian charity, nor even the expression of compassion. All these are not unworthy partial motives, but they are not basic. At root Quaker relief work aims at reconciliation among men to the glory of God; it is a sharing with those who are unhappy and therefore feel excluded from love, in an attempt to bring them into the community of love. It is being the will of God by helping others to become the will of God. The material aid given, such as food, clothing, housing, training and so on, is directed not so much to material as to spiritual needs. But the meeting of needs is altogether subservient to the goal of being what we are meant to be by being inwardly with others. The material acts have a sacramental meaning: they seek to reach to that of God in our neighbour by sharing with him not goods but brotherhood. They are means not only for him to *have* a little more, but to *be* a little more, namely to become more truly his real self. For this reason, Quaker aid seeks first to help people to help themselves; and, spiritually speaking, you cannot help yourself unless you help others, too, because the true being of man depends on being for others.

The fact that the meaning of Quaker service is so often misunderstood as a merely philanthropic endeavour is due to a large extent to the unwillingness of Friends to elucidate the meaning of their own actions. Hence their missionary efforts overseas are seen by outsiders either as evangelical work like that of other missions, or as cultural work through agricultural, social, medical and educational services. But their service has a religious purpose: it is meant to proclaim the immediacy of God to every man. Similarly in the 'home field' their basic insights have nearly disappeared behind their manifold activities in the spheres of social welfare, probation, prison reform, temperance, marriage guidance, training of neglectful mothers and so on. But all these activities spring from one conviction: that the Light of Christ, given to every man, cannot shine forth in the individual self, and become operative between human beings to the glory of God, if the self remains undeveloped because of physical and spiritual distress; if the true being of men and women withers under the impact of adversity and evil. The material means used for spiritual outreach are no mere 'comforts', not even mere symbols of friendship and human brotherhood: they are sacramental tools to bring their fellow-men to a greater awareness of the structure of being. For this reason Friends are far less concerned than other Christian or non-Christian missionaries to convert people to their own persuasion: they wish to turn a man to his true self, to the witness of God within, to what God meant him to be.

It is from the same basic motive and for the same religious purpose that nowadays many Friends are particularly concerned for the so-called 'war on want', that is, the different kinds of technical assistance to the economically underdeveloped peoples. True, many other considerations may come in as well: the preservation of world peace, the alleviation of the white man's bad conscience for the way he has treated other races for so long, true compassion for the misery prevailing in distant parts, and last but not least, the avoidance of a huge unemployment problem at home if and when disarmament becomes the adopted policy of Governments. For our context, however, it is sufficient to grasp the underlying religious purpose. Since the fulfilment of this purpose depends on the development of every single human self in its wholeness, that is in the unity of body, mind and spirit, Quaker action, while not seeking material ends, works of necessity through material means.

We must not think, however, as Friends sometimes do, that the ameliorating social activities of other agencies are normally aimed at nothing more than the *material* advancement of people. This is not true even for Marxism, whose declared aim is furtherance, through material advancement, of 'the true happiness of the people' while at the same time decrying religion as an other-worldly, hence 'illusory happiness'. Similarly the American ideal of 'plenty for all' must be seen as part of the 'pursuit of happiness' promised in the Declaration of Independence, and the same intention has promoted the welfare state in England. Material progress of others is rarely seen as an end in itself, but as a means to a spiritual end, namely 'wellbeing', being well in body, mind and spirit, the whole true self.

But the all too obvious fact is that material possessions are in themselves not sufficient to create this wholeness or happiness or, for that matter, the solidarity of all men in a classless society or the brotherhood of men as one community under the fatherhood of God. This obvious fact, neglected by the preachers of the social gospel, has been rubbed in by their opponents, the neo-orthodox pessimists. Yet in spite of being so obvious a fact, material betterment has always been a necessary means. Even Vinoba Bhave's ascetic Bhoodan movement pursues his 'kingdom of kindness' through the surrender of land to the very poor; and the saintliness of the begging friar depends for its fulfilment on a material transaction. In the Hebrew-Christian tradition the material care for the sick, the poor, the orphans and widows has at all times been considered not only the first fruit of righteousness of the donor but, as early Christian communism underlines, as expression of brotherhood and wholeness of all in all.

Happiness, brotherhood and wholeness are a matter of *being*, namely of men and women being more closely the selves they are meant to be. The condition of being, however, is *having*, namely having the minimum livelihood in order to be healthy and happy for oneself and one's nearest and dearest, and indeed having in order to be able to share both by giving and receiving. Far too often do we speak of sharing as though it were a one-sided action, but in fact it means to receive through giving and to give through receiving. For even receiving depends on having, namely having so much that reception is no longer a dog-like acceptance of humiliating charity, nor even a right of human solidarity which can be demanded, but an active contribution to brotherhood, a spiritual giving for what is materially received.

Needing, having and using material things, even in the best way, means of necessity involvement in their production and distribution, that is with wealth. Not only all primary production such as garden and field products, the tools for producing them, the wells to be dug and the spade to dig them, not only the various forms of capital equipment and means of production are wealth, but also the accumulation of knowledge and education, the very know-how, because their availability depends on a short or prolonged existence on material goods provided by others, for instance the parents or the State, for the time during which that knowledge is acquired. Without wealth there would be no freedom to study. The production of wealth, in its turn, demands attention, interest and even concern, and these must be concentrated very largely on the material means rather than the religious end, if the latter is ever to be achieved. In this way we get involved: we must be interested in material things in order to have the means of sharing. If we are not so interested, if we think, in a romantic way, that in the name of simplicity we can go back to primitivity (and primitivity, of course, has its own forms of having), we would have to go back also to greater infant mortality and other kinds of human misery, the overcoming of which seems to be the very method of sharing in our generation.

I hope it is clear, after all this, that material involvement is not a polite expression for sin, namely for the selfish abuse of wealth through avarice, meanness and lust of power. Involvement means that we cannot escape being concerned with the amassing of material things as the necessary means for quite a different end, and that the production and keeping available of these material things have grown to such an extent that they detract our attention from the end pursued.

Let me put it differently: it is no longer possible to show brotherhood by kissing lepers and then let them continue their lives in misery till they die a dreadful death. Being in history, we must accept the knowledge we have been given and use its wealth as material means to the end which we believe is the will of God for us. This wealth, the availability of methods for the modern treatment of leprosy, is the material means to the higher end. Modern treatment, however, depends on generations of education and study, on laboratories for research, on animal experiments,[1] on all the machines and factories necessary to produce every little piece of apparatus and every medicament, also on the production of raw-materials and the various forms of energy to run those factories, and finally on the creative leisure necessary to develop all this knowledge and to increase it through further research on every level from the coal-mine and hydro-electric power station to the syringe and the pill.

In a word, the material means necessary for the pursuit of our religious purpose have become very great; they depend on wealth amassed in past and present, and on the whole machinery of world economics and industry. They absorb thousands of working hours for years and decades before the first injection or the first tablet can be given. Even if I am fortunate enough in that I can give or receive it myself, thus returning to the direct exchange and sharing with people, I depend to a large extent on the work of those who must give their single-minded devotion to the preparation of the wealth which is to be shared, often in most monotonous and arduous labour which, taken for itself, seems without much purpose. Nor can we blame indiscriminately the key-men for errors of judgment and short-sightedness. This machinery, an edifice of human creativity, has become so terrific that responsible action and

[1] This is not the place to enter into the controversy on animal experiments, a very striking example of human involvement, as without them we would have to be cruel to our own kind and to many animals by refusing to prepare ourselves to help them. People who oppose such experiments under safeguards would probably be shocked if they realized to what extent their every-day lives and all the 'good works' they support and advocate, depend in some way on this practice. Nobody has described this dilemma more vividly than Dr. Schweitzer when he calls himself a 'mass-murderer of bacteria.'

the choice of the best order of priorities overtaxes human knowledge and power: man is neither omniscient nor omnipotent.

There is, of course, no denying that a great amount of selfishness is at work in the running of that colossal machinery, much misdirection of raw-materials and of human effort, for instance for armaments and harmful luxuries, and crying injustices in distribution. But with all that, we must not trace back all misery on earth to wrong-doings present and past. Much of it is simply due to the fact that we live and act in history, that different stages of development have been reached by different classes and nations, and that we have not yet mastered fully the fair production and fair distribution of wealth.

For instance, the widening gulf between the living standards in have and have-not countries is very difficult to tackle lest a different distribution (if it were possible without the use of violence and destruction) diminish the wealth of those who *have* without helping those who have *not*, thus merely reducing the human ability to produce and to share with those in need. Nor are the things which one country can produce necessarily usable in another without a long process of adjustment, for instance the consumption of surplus wheat in rice-eating countries, and the use of combine-harvesters for small-holdings in mountainous districts. Men of goodwill, in their eagerness to help, and confronted with much ill-will among men, oversimplify many complex problems and indeed sin by reducing all of them to human sin. Yet how thankful we must be for their single-mindedness which testifies to their sense of responsibility before God.

The best-known example of material involvement is the introduction of modern medical services in overpopulated countries. First we try to save babies; next we have to save the mothers and to teach them proper methods of child-care so that they can look after their infants; then the mothers will have more children, many more, which we save again. Thus our very aid, certainly the most inescapable call for action to every Christian and humanist, is the instrument by which overpopulation increases rapidly, and with it the gap between food production and mouths to be fed and people to be kept in health and happiness. All our present knowledge does not

DOING THE WILL OF GOD

help us to narrow that gap quickly enough: the misery grows with the very effort to reduce it. If contraception is suggested, we must realise that this is not only a matter of education—an education perhaps against deep religious instincts and millennia of tradition—but also again a matter of material means.[1]

We may now understand better the root cause of our material involvement. A man cannot be or do the will of God in history without being alive. Even the act of laying down his life depends on being alive. His true self in history is tied to being alive, that is, to material conditions and the means for fulfilling them. Because life is thus seen as the condition of being one's true self in history, the preservation of, and care for, the lives of others and their protection from all forms of harm and destruction, are understood as the paramount means of pursuing the religious purpose, and this even at the cost of losing one's own life. This leads to the paradoxical attitude that one must preserve one's life possibly to lose it, because our life is a material means to a religious end: to be lived rightly.

Expressed differently: we should act as though death was the ultimate evil and the end of everything for *others*, but not for ourselves. We should work for the physical security and well-being of others as though it were the highest good, and for this we should forgo all concern for our own physical security and well-being. We should act in this way even while realizing that our religious purpose would fail if the others themselves saw their security and life as truly their highest good and not equally as a means to an end. We may even try to convey this to them, especially by our example, but we must never treat them as though, for us, their life and security were not of highest concern to us.

And yet, in order to be able to act in this way, we and they are still dependent on the material means both for our own survival and for sharing our life with them. This dilemma is just another aspect of our living between God and history. It confronts us with ever new responsible decisions from which there is no escape, namely with the decision as to how our life and our wealth are to be used as material means to the

---

[1] This and other burning problems are well treated from the Quaker point of view by Kathleen Lonsdale in *Is Peace Possible?* (Penguin, 1957).

fulfilment of our true being. In all this inescapable, and sometimes hardly bearable, tension, however, we are not left without some deep certitude.

9

GOD THROUGH HISTORY

Certitude Amidst Uncertainties

Many Friends and other Christian and ethical activists are very reluctant to recognize the riskiness of human action, the limitation of human capacity, the uncertainties caused by our inevitable involvement and sometimes even the reality of sin. Even less willing are they to face the mystery of evil. They admittedly fear that such a recognition would lead almost inevitably to inaction and fatalistic pessimism. Their fear, however, betrays them into an unwillingness to take seriously the conditions of human existence, and unconsciously into almost the same kind of scepticism regarding human nature which is displayed by radical pessimism in its one-sided pre-occupation with man's abysmal depravity. Unless they can believe that all existence is fundamentally good *if only* man willed it, they seem unable to have confidence in potential goodness within and amidst ambiguous existence.

In my opinion their anxiety is incompatible with the Quaker testimony to the ever ready availability of grace, that 'original grace' which is the God-given capacity to discern sin and overcome it, at least momentarily; and to accept the existence of evil that in all its mysteriousness can yet never annihilate our ultimate hope.

'Original grace', or 'that of God in every man', in no wise diminishes the ambiguities of human existence in history. But if responded to, it gives us the power to face them, to wrestle with them and not to be dismayed by them; and all this because it is the power that relieves us of the burden of sin and guilt through a clear recognition at the crucial moments of decision that we have once again sinned or been mistaken or short-sighted, that once again we must turn round and that through grace we can do it—if only until next time. Grace is the urge, in our sense of forgivenness, to make amends for the guilt with which we are burdened through sin and involvement. It is the stimulus to work our way back; not for the redemption of others, though in retrospect it may sometimes appear to have this effect, but rather for reparation, for undoing the harm we have done or could not avoid doing, or could not prevent others from doing. It is, if the word may be used, *repentive action*: spiritually speaking it is in some ways a *re*-action or *re*-sponse to the action of grace in the soul of a man, and it is infused with a will to *re*-construction though, as just said, in retrospect it may appear as truly constructive, creative and redemptive.

Grace, too, allows us to live in tension amidst all those perplexities of existence, without perishing in meaninglessness and despair. It is the courage imbuing our whole lives with a burning desire to realize our true selves in history and thus to become readier for receiving the Kingdom; and with this readiness we may suddenly find that it has come amongst us, in the midst of ambiguous and precarious existence. Grace is the persistence which prevents our being defeated in the middle of defeat and continual failure; it is the compulsion towards ever new responsible action. It is given to us as a free gift, just like our freedom, to use or not to use it. Whenever we are called to stand up and declare that with the help of God we hope to do this, that or the other which we experience as the will of God for us, the help of God is not in the hoped-for achievement which may never be attained as intended, but in our strength of having intentions that accord with the structure of being, and of acting in free responsibility.

It is a fact, easily observed, that very few people throw their hands in even after many failures and when prospects are very grim: they go on hoping against all hope, they work on where they fear that little or nothing can be done, they are deeply involved in the forces of destruction and evil in history and universe and still believe in goodness and love. They can do this because they are upheld by their spiritual experience of that inward grace, whether they are conscious of it or not. The more, however, they become aware of God's will for them, the less are they inclined to resign, though at the same time they become the more deeply aware of their insufficiency and involvement.

It is the sign of saintliness, of becoming more closely what he is meant to be, if a man can live in the knowledge of his limitations, his involvement in history, his guilt and his sinfulness, if he can accept all this without the false pride of those who exult in being sinners, or without the false humility of the do-gooders, and yet can take it all upon himself courageously in order to continue his struggle for his authentic self. It is just not true that man, in the awareness of God's will for him, needs the certainty of success and reward, because in all uncertainties about himself and the world in which he has to live and act, he is sustained by a great certitude, a genuine faith, a confidence in being. True, success and reward may well help him to greater awareness, but so may failure and blame. Faith offers no solutions of temporal problems, but it gives the power to tackle them and to live with them and not to be beaten by their insolubility.

It is rather the other way round: certitude which is faith depends on the clear recognition of uncertainty as the condition of living and acting in history; for only if quite unsupported by guarantees, promises and fulfilments, can faith show its true nature, namely that it is more than wishful thinking, self-deceptive illusion and even more than belief in objectively revealed facts. Indeed, the recognition of the uncertainties of existence is our one valid answer to the rationalist: in faith we can gladly surrender everything which can rationally be proven to be illusory. Faithlessness does not consist in the surrender of the untenable, but in the search for proofs for inner certitude, which is unprovable. But even if denied because unprovable, certitude can sometimes emerge in that very act of denial: it is then no true faithlessness, but mere unbelief in what is still behind the courage of denial.

On the other hand, illusion, and this means here especially religious illusion, is marked by the fact that it, too, tends to rationalize like rationalism; that it tries to bring proofs for its illusions, that it does not admit uncertainties, that it thinks it can explain everything or most things and that it knows exactly from where it comes and where it goes. Certitude, on the other hand, which is true faith, 'is not knowable'.¹ It is certain of nothing except itself. It is, for instance, not sure of the human self who has received it, or of the existence in which that self lives and acts. But the self is all the same profoundly certain, not of doctrines, but of its sense of being sustained because it senses in it the ground of being that sustains everything.

Because of certitude the self may become increasingly aware of the structure of being in moments of great spiritual experience; indeed it can live with a continual awareness of it, 'walking with God', as it were. It is exactly because a man sees the limits of human reason that he can have faith, and it is exactly because he has faith that he does not despair of human reason as neo-orthodox theology is inclined to do.

Faith and Reason

Instructed by modern psychology which points at subconscious motivation and rationalisation, and by Marxian sociology which stresses the dependency of our thinking on economic and other environmental conditions, neo-orthodoxy emphasizes the dark self-interested motives of the unconscious mind which harnesses, and dictates to, our reason. It thus condemns reason by most rational arguments. Reinhold Niebuhr says: 'In the field of history it is no pure mind which observes the facts, but an anxious reason, organically related to an anxious ego, reacting with pity or scorn, with fear or pride, to the greatness or the weakness, to the promised support or the threatened peril, of this or that competitive expression of human vitality'.² This is, of course, perfectly true, but it is not the whole story. At another place Niebuhr admits that 'rational discrimination is necessary to weigh the claims made for the self in the name of both faith and reason'.³ Such 'rational discrimination' must be permissible also in assessing Niebuhr's own position.

Neo-orthodoxy no more than rationalism can offer a satisfying answer to man's situation in history. Rationalism, on the

---

¹ Jaspers, *Von der Wahrheit*, 156.
² *Nature and Destiny of Man*, II, 156. Cf. Herberg, 'Faith and Secular Learning'. In *Christian Faith and Social Action*, 199 ff., especially 213 (London: Charles Scribners Sons Ltd., 1953).
³ *The Self and the Dramas of History*, 169.

one hand, derides faith as superstition, partly through mistaking traditional forms of religious expression for the inward faith thus expressed, partly by overlooking the fact that its own ground is of necessity faith disguised as certitude of its own reason. Neo-orthodoxy, on the other hand, denigrates human reason as tainted by original sin and relies for its certainty on 'objective' divine revelation in history. It thus neglects, or at least plays down, the fact that all true revelation depends on inward, 'subjective' apprehension of the revealed and on a reasonable discernment of the manner of spirit that reveals itself. Without reasonable discernment of the spirits, faith is exposed to misdirection, as the case of the young Nazi, mentioned in the last chapter, tried to exemplify. Misdirected faith can be seen also in both success and destructiveness of the witch-doctor's activities. It is not by chance that the greatest spiritualists have always insisted on a reasonable discernment of the spirits, usually considering the fruit of the spirit as the only reliable standard.

Clearly, faith and reason are complementary, not mutually exclusive. Faith must stand to reason, it cannot demand the *sacrificum intellectus* because faith depends on a self's judgment of himself, of his conditions and of the situation in which he has to act in faith. Man must be able to act from 'responsible' judgment, that is judgment enlightened by the awareness of the structure of being and the will of God for him. Reason is the necessary tool for discovering our limitations, our selfish interestedness, our illusions and all the other uncertainties of human existence in history.

On the other hand, reason itself can be trusted only if its own limitations are seen, namely that it, too, is ultimately based on faith. Rationalists like Bertrand Russell build their whole philosophy on values such as truth, but deny or misunderstand their reality. They therefore batter in vain against the unreasonableness of man or history, with which they refuse to reckon reasonably. Just as faith without the control of reason becomes credulity, illusory superstition and fanaticism, so does reason become unreasonable and superstitious in a different sense unless reckoning with faith. Just as faith must stand to reason, so reason must stand to faith. Faith without reason is blind, reason without faith is ungrounded. Reason and faith are like mathematical functions where one approaches zero when the other is pushed near the infinite. Only where they are held in their correlation and neither is allowed to gain on the other, can man attain wholeness.

Faith and reason, then, are different, though complementary forces of human being. The wholeness of man depends on reason checking faith and faith being recognized as the foundation of reasonable judgments. It is therefore erroneous to allocate to them quite different spheres within human being and doing, since they affect them all. Faith and reason co-operate in all fields and cannot be clearly delimited by allocating certain tasks exclusively to one, others exclusively to the other. It is the wholeness of man which holds them together and ensures their co-operation. There is no more sanity in faith over-ruling reason than there is in reason over-ruling faith. There is no sanity in letting each go its own way: only in co-operation can they fulfil their interrelated function in man.

It may therefore be just as confusing to speak of 'a reasonable faith', that latitudinarian phrase occasionally used for Quakerism,[1] as to speak of 'the paradox of faith' if paradox stands for absurdity as it sometimes does since Tertullian's famous *credo quia absurdum*.[2] Reason can serve no more as an adjective to faith than faith as an adjective to reason because they condition each other. Life cannot be lived in wholeness unless faith enlightens my reason and reason purifies my faith, and both fulfil their functions in the wholeness of my being.

To this extent it may be admissible to speak of a reasonable faith. It is, however, an inadequate expression if it implies the subjection of faith to commonsense and tries to exclude anything that cannot be verified by the rules of knowledge or by familiarity. Since faith is not truly knowable, it is not limited by commonsense or scientific knowledge. In this respect faith is indeed paradoxical, namely beyond all rational argument. No test of reason can plant or uproot it in the way it can plant or uproot beliefs, such as theories or hypotheses. Faith persists

---

[1] A Quaker pamphlet published under this title in 1884 caused a great stir. Cf. *L.P.Q.*, 963 ff.
[2] 'I believe because it is absurd'. Cf. Tillich, *Systematic Theology*, II, 104 ff., where in a series of interesting definitions the 'paradox', though used by him entirely christologically, is clearly shown to be reasonable, not absurd.

even where all beliefs and doctrines are proved untenable, because we live by faith and cannot live without it. In so far it is paradoxical, that is, 'beyond reason', but not 'unreasonable', that is, absurd.

The normal way of speaking about faith is the accumulation of numerous paradoxes because the paradoxes of language are the only potential form of expressing the inexpressible. They are neither absurd nor meaningless, they have been used not only by the great founders of religions, but also by other very sane men, and they are understood by those, equally sane, who have a similar certitude of inexpressible faith. Paradoxes of language are understood by reason without their meaning being grasped rationally: they are mere hints at the unspeakable spiritual experience of the ground of being and at the awareness of the structure of being.

Acting as our true selves, in the will of God for us, it is through faith and reason that we can act responsibly. Only where they are held in interdependence shall we neither exaggerate our expectations for human affairs nor lose all our hope. Even in hopelessness we cannot avoid choosing and acting, but only through faith and reason can we act responsibly. Only where faith and reason are held in the balance of sanity by the wholeness of the self, have we the courage to act responsibly in the full knowledge of the precariousness of human action and yet in the awareness of the structure of being. We then need neither condemn God through condemning the insufficiencies of creation and creature, nor depose and deny him by 'improving' his creation in our fancies and thinking it more perfect than it really is: existence is neither good because God created it, nor evil because it is fallen. It is 'in the mixture', and the mystery behind its ambiguity is unfathomable. It must be sufficient for us that we can live and act.

Everybody who endeavours to act morally, acts on far more than mere moral principles: he acts on faith. For there is no way of knowing clearly what action will in the end emerge as constructive or destructive, though there is an awareness that all action should be done in response to God and the consistency of his spirit. The difference between the actions of the agnostic and the Christian is that the former denies this spirit and grace which might reconcile him to failures, errors and sins, but it is still through grace that he finds the strength and courage to act at all and to go on acting. The agnostic moralist must therefore have illusions of some kind: he must reckon with success, with utopia, with unambiguous goodness or with the complete rationality of existence. Many Christian humanists have misunderstood the Christian hope in a similar way.

When Friends call Christianity a revolutionary faith, they may be in exactly this danger. For normally revolution is an act conditioned by history, and achieved in history by human volition. It is far less the will of God for men than at best an effort of men to bring the Kingdom down to earth by political and social action. But Christian action is not political and social action, not action for the Kingdom to come, but it is acting in the Kingdom which is come 'into the heart'. It depends on regeneration, sanctification and indeed transfiguration, on the works of grace within, on the spirit which gives us an ever increasing awareness of the structure of being. It will illuminate all action thus undertaken in response to God's grace and his will, it will indeed be doing the will of God and thus will affect all action in the fields of political and social affairs. But it is not dependent on temporal results, however hard it must try to do the possible best. Rather it discovers the presence of the Kingdom, God's Kingship, through all imaginable situations, in the unlimited 'availability' of God even 'if I make my bed in hell'.[1] It will, for instance, accept conflicts as a call for reconciliation rather than for fighting it out; crime as a call for education and understanding rather than retribution; involvement as a call for responsible re-action rather than weak surrender. But its persistence will never be conquered even though conflict, crime and involvement continue to persist unconquered. We can live in the Kingdom even at the worst moments of history because the Kingdom is amongst us amidst the greatest horrors and leads us into the paradox that we can bear with them while still fighting them as utterly unbearable, in the name and will of God.

The Sacramentality of Life and History

The experience that God can be found through all conditions,

[1] Psalm 139, 8.

DOING THE WILL OF GOD

even the most God-forsaken ones, that his Presence can be experienced even through the deep shock of his Absence is, I think, the only tenable meaning of the phrase, so often used among Friends, that 'all life is sacramental'. As it stands it could mean that God's grace becomes visible in every sin and crime as well as in every saintly and dedicated act of love, in the 'senselessness' of natural catastrophes as well as in the blossoming of young life, and indeed in the inexplicable existence of evil. Few Friends would accept this generalizing interpretation, but as it is one of their favourite quotations we must start with finding out first what, taken literally, it asserts and which meaning it would convey to outsiders. It offers a good example of the rake's progress of some Quaker idioms.

Early Friends held that every moment of their lives was filled with, and expressed, that divine grace which the churches try to symbolize in a visible sacramental act. For Friends a special act of this kind would tend to devalue all other human actions which in their view should all and sundry bear witness, as outward signs, to the same inward grace. Since soon enough the Quaker conviction that 'all my life is sacramental because Christ has come into my heart' has proved unfounded in their own self-judgment, the 'is' was turned into an 'ought', and it was held that 'all my life ought to be sacramental': every minute of it ought to express that inner spiritual grace. The word 'life' means here clearly the personal way of life, and to this day that 'ought' has retained much of its educational power. As the Yearly Meeting Epistle of 1857 puts it: 'The life of saintliness . . . is itself the true sacrament'.[1]

But sometimes the meaning of 'life' as my own way of living has been further loosened so as to include everything that exists, and thus the commandment of direction was turned back into a statement of fact. In this conception the phrase that 'all life is sacramental' expresses a vague pantheism which ends of necessity in amoralism, or an equally vague optimism for which everything is indiscriminately good or very far advanced on the road to becoming good. Little regard is paid

[1] *Christian Practice.* Second part of the *Christian Discipline of the Religious Society of Friends in England*, 3.

to the fact of sin, the mystery of evil and the ambiguity of existence.

Nevertheless, this sentence, just as it stands, may well describe a central experience of man suspended between God and history: that nothing that happens is ever so terrible that it cannot, as by an act of revelation, become the channel of experiencing the Presence of God and his loving will. This does not mean that what appeared evil at first becomes now good, in fact that all the time it has been a hidden good. This is a frequent error after the event, shared by great saints such as Fox and Woolman, who in retrospect find in their spiritual and physical suffering the reason for calling evil good for the good results it had in their own development. In the previous chapter it has been argued that the good results of the crucifixion and of any martyrdom in no wise vindicates those acts and the suffering involved. Evil and sin, incompatible with the structure of being, but very much part of existence, remain evil and sin even though they may suddenly become transparent and thus instrumental towards the discovery of God's grace, both for the martyr himself and for one or a few bystanders who may thus be opened to God's will for themselves. But the revaluation of sin and evil because they have unlocked, like a key, profound spiritual experiences and insights, seems to whittle away the reality of temporal life, the many less inspiring consequences of evil-doing, and the persisting existence of the mystery of evil.

Evil and sin are not really comparable to a key, rather to spade and hoe loosening up a man's soul and preparing his inner receptiveness for the 'seed'. Even so most people, whether they are victims or onlookers, are hardened under the impact of sin and evil and become not more but less receptive of grace. There is not even the rule, sometimes propounded, that under that impact 'good' people normally become better, while 'bad' people normally become worse: 'the wind bloweth where it listeth'. All one may say for certain is that grace has become visible through most unpromising situations in history just as through many inspiring ones, and that therefore such situations are sacramental whatever the moral judgment on them must be.

An example of such revelation of grace through history was

the sudden recognition of a prisoner in a concentration camp that he could never take adequate revenge for the torments suffered unless he was willing to act exactly like his tormentors; and as he could not see himself in that role, nothing was left to him but the insight that evil was no answer to evil. This insight was no vindication of the treatment he received — no concentration camp could at any time have been a 'hidden good' or 'God's providential guidance'. But while as a prisoner he was prevented from doing anything in the way of responsible action, he had begun doing the will of God in the increasing awareness of the structure of being.[1]

This example may also serve as an illustration for the contention that the sacramentality of history does not mean the same thing as the belief that the sequence of historical events is itself God's handiwork and ruled, at least in all its beneficial aspects, by divine Providence; but rather that all features of history and every situation may become quite indiscriminately the channel of his grace: the catastrophic physical disaster as well as the beauties of nature, the wickedness of man as well as his goodness. The wind bloweth where it listeth and may reach one man in a situation of shame and misery and another in a situation of uplift and thankfulness. It would therefore be better to speak of God *through* history than of God *in* history. God is encountered *through* history as an inward experience; he is *in* history because it is in history that the encounter happens, and that we reflect on it.

In this sense God is in history as *the Father*, Creator and Sustainer of heaven and earth, that is as Being and the ground of being. This means that he is not in history as continual interloper who distributes reward with his right hand and punishment with his left, as some of the Hebrew prophets saw it and as some neo-Calvinists seem to think. Judgment in history is not God's interfering act, but is inherent in the structure of being: what runs counter to this structure is ultimately self-destructive and hence 'condemned'; and what fits into the

---

[1] The depressing and at the same time exhilarating book *Dying We Live* (London: Harrill Press, 1956), which contains 'the final messages and records of some Germans who defied Hitler', brings many other striking examples of the experience of divine grace through evil. They are, of course, selected for this purpose and can prove no general rule.

structure of being is ultimately creative and hence 'saved'.

God in history appears most concretely as *the Son*, in the life, death and resurrection of Jesus Christ. From whatever personal convictions we look at these events, we cannot deny that they express something most relevant for the understanding of the human situation. Firstly, the doctrine of incarnation symbolizes a relationship between the Supranatural or Transcendent on the one hand, and creation or nature and history on the other, which is far profounder and far more realistic than any other religious or philosophical teaching. Quite apart from the christological interpretation of the historical person of Jesus called the Christ and our individual beliefs about him: Christ is the one religious symbol that keeps God and world in close relationship and mutuality without any need of denying either the reality of the world or the ambiguity of this reality.

Secondly, the doctrine of the cross shows that love, truth and goodness and all the great values which we receive as directions in our spiritual experience when becoming aware of the structure of being, are attacked and possibly destroyed by the ambiguities of history. But even in spite of complete temporal failure, the cross is the sign which 'draws many' to God; for in the cross history has become more real and at the same time more transparent than anywhere else. Thirdly, the doctrine of the resurrection confirms that the glory of God, however consistently denied, neglected, removed and buried, appears again in history unconquered and unconquerable and is recognized by the saints in spite of, and through all temporal disaster.

God in history is most accessible for us as *the Spirit* which works in his saints, the grace which opens them to his will and brings them closer to their true selves; the comforter which leaves them undismayed whether they are sent into arena and prison, or honoured and worshipped by the multitude for their humble self-dedication. Even when involved in ambiguities while they try to serve, and when faced with their own shortcomings and inadequacies, grace has been given to them once more to avail themselves of it as forgiven-ness, so that through every new situation they can find a renewed vision of God's will for them. Their real cross, whatever the events of their outward lives, is a sense of tension between God and history, between their visions and their achievements. But in that tension they are upheld again and again by grace, and with the increasing awareness of God's will for them they become his will ever more, showing forth the abiding fruit of the spirit amidst the ambiguities of human existence.

INDEX

Absolutism, see Moral Ambiguity.
Act of God, 132, 146, 148.
Action in History, 40, 47, 72, 81 ff., 89 ff., 93, 95, 100, 106 ff., 114, 125, 128, 130 ff., 149, 151, 155, 159 f., 182, 185.
Agnostic, Agnosticism, 20, 102, 172, 199 f.
Ambiguity, see Moral Ambiguity, Action in History, Historicity.
Anabaptism, 36, 52.
Angelus Silesius, 39.
Animal Experiments, 189 n.
Anti-historical Attitude, 22 f., 47, 56 ff., 65.
Autodafés, 114.
Availability (of God's Grace), see Grace, God Through History.
Awareness (of God's Will, of the Structure of Being, etc.), 100, 118, 123 ff., 128, 135 f. 147 f., 151, 160 f., 172, 182, 185 f., 194 ff., 199 f., 203 ff.

Baptists, 72.
Barclay, 35, 51 n., 58, 61, 83, 86.
Being (of God, Ground of Being), 15, 21 ff., 27, 122 f., 196, 199, 203.
Being, see Self, Structure of Being.
Being and Doing, 119 f., 129.
Being and Having, 185, 187 f.
Bellers, 83.
Belonging (sense of belonging), see Loyalty.
Benson, 52 n., 58 n.
Berdyaev, 33, 176.
Bible (Quaker attitude to it), 59 ff., 105, 119.
Bonhoeffer, 104, 106, 142, 156 n., 168.
Book of Discipline, 63, 87.
Booth, 76.
Braithwaite, 78.
Brotherhood, see Community.
Bruderhof, 176 f.
Buber, 137.
Buddhism, 24 ff.
Bultmann, 14 n., 20 n., 68 n.
Burckhardt, 149.
Burrough, 73 ff., 77 n.
Byllinge, 77.

Cadbury, 61 n., 80 n., 82, 94 f.
Calvinism, see Puritanism.
Catholicism, 115.
Certitude, see Faith.
Christ, 24 ff., 33, 48, 50 ff., 109,

119, 122 f., 164, 181, 204. Inner Christ and Historic Christ, 48 f., 56 ff., 60 ff., 68, 70. *See* Second Coming.
Christianity, 24 ff.
Church, 35, 52, 58, 113 ff.
Citizenship, *see* Responsibility (civic).
Collingwood, 130.
Colonialism, 139 f., 169.
Commandments, 99 f., 109, 115 ff., 127, 171 f.
Commitment, 41, 120, 122, 136.
Commonwealth Period, 72 ff., 85.
Community (spiritual community), 69, 99, 104, 109, 112 f., 126, 176 f., 181 ff., 187.
Compromise, *see* Moral Ambiguity.
Conditions, *see* Data, Situation, Unconditional Action.
Conscience, 79, 82, 93, 168.
Conscientious Objectors, 66. 90 f., 144, 170, 180 f.
Conscription, 86.
Consequences (of action), *see* Results.
Consistency (of Quakers), 77 n., 80, 87 ff.
Consistency of the Spirit of Christ, 62, 67, 87 f., 99 f., 115 ff., 199.
Creasey, 48, 55, 111 n.
Creative Action, 20, 33, 72, 84, 88, 95, 101, 131, 137, 145, 148, 151 f., 190, 194.
Cromwell, O., 51, 74, 76, 77 n., 113 n.
Cromwell, R., 76.
Crusades, 113 f.
Cullmann, 28 f.

Cynicism, 13, 23, 139.

Daemonism of History, 112, 146, 151 f., 179, 190.
Data of History, 20, 101, 151, 153 f., 185.
Day of the Lord, 53 ff., 78.
Death, Dying, 18, 191.
Decision (existential), 119 f., 125.
Deism, 57.
Democracy, 87, 179.
Descartes, 14.
Determinism, 20.
Dewsbury, 54 n., 60 n., 76, 77 n.
Dialectical method, 13 ff., 106.
Dickinson, 80.
Discerning and Doing, 99, 106.
Discernment of Spirits, 197.
Docetism, 164.
Dodd, 21 n., 33.
Doncaster, 51 n., 53 n.
Duty, 120 f., 131.

East-West Problem, 85 f., 169, 173.
Erastianism, 79.
Eschatology, 28 f., 53 f., 55, 83 f., 142, 182.
Eternity, *see* Time.
Evangelicalism, 57.
Evil, 23, 34, 44. *See* Good and Evil.
Evil, its mystery, 134 f., 193, 199, 201 f.
Evil, choice of the lesser, 93, 101, 159 ff., 176.
Evolution, 22.
Existentialism, 39, 63.
Expediency, 100, 134, 143, 156 ff.
Experience of God, *see* Spiritual Experience.

INDEX

Failure, see Success.
Faith, 21, 22, 102, 193 ff. The Paradox of Faith, 198 f.
Fallenness (of man and world), 27, 37 f., 131, 134 f., 161, 199.
Fell, 64 n., 68.
Feuerbach, 20 n.
Fifth Monarchists, 51, 72, 77.
Fisher, 54, 111.
Fothergill, 36.
Fox, G., 46 n., 48, 49 ff., 68 f., 72 ff., 90, 92, 110 f., 118, 142, 145, 202.
Freedom, 19 f., 100 f., 110, 122, 127, 137, 149 ff., 161, 176.
Freud, 21.
Friendship, see Personal Relationship.
Fruit of the Spirit, 38, 40, 66, 92, 118, 129, 131, 141, 171, 197, 205.
Fry, E., 36, 94.

Gandhi, 86 n., 133, 166.
Gautama, 24 ff.
Gerson, 114.
God Through History, 16, 58, 103, 124, 142, 147, 200 ff.
God's Will and Human Volition, 96, 99, 104 ff., 116, 122, 127, 129, 154 f.
Goethe, 18, 146.
Good and Evil, 99 ff., 124, 131, 134 ff., 154, 156, 158, 163 f., 169, 174, 193, 199, 202.
Goodness, 57, 99, 104 f., 113 ff., 123 f., 131, 136 ff., 150, 153 f., 162, 171, 193, 200.
Grace, 29, 101 ff., 131, 134 f., 162, 193 f., 199 ff.
Group Relationships, 85, 102, 109, 165 f., 171 ff., 176, 182 ff.
Group Selfishness, 184.
Guidance (divine, spiritual), 41, 42 f., 59, 63 ff., 81 ff., 87 f., 94 f., 99 f., 104 ff., 116 ff., 125, 203.
Guilt, 82, 84, 87, 93, 106, 152, 156 f., 164, 166, 168, 179 f., 182, 193 ff.

Hagiography, 67 f., 71.
Harris, 62 n., 110 n.
Hegel, 146.
Heidegger, 18.
Hicks, 61.
Historical Religions, 24 ff.
Historicity (of man), 16, 17 ff., 53, 62 f., 72, 79, 85 ff., 93, 100 ff., 104 ff., 124, 143, 151, 155, 161 f., 189 f., 193 ff., 200, 204 f.
Historiography, 9, 58, 63, 66 f.
History (its meaning), 21, 26, 148 f.
History of Salvation, 24 ff., 53, 56, 58, 141, 146 f., 164.
Holy Spirit, 51, 52, 63, 99, 120, 124 ff., 204. See also Guidance, Inward Light, Spiritual Experience.
Howgill, 42 f., 47, 50 f., 55, 74, 77 n., 92.
Hügel, von, 43, 46, 58.
Human Nature, 56, 100, 131 ff., 137, 193.
Humanism, 22, 200.
Humanitarianism, 80 ff., 185 f.
Huxley, A., 45, 114.

Ibsen, 121, 150, 158.
Idealism, 19, 32.
Immortality, 31, 33, 44.
Incarnation, 13, 33, 34, 39, 53.

Inner Light, see Inward Light.
Intention, 128 f., 152 f., 156 ff., 169, 184, 194.
Involvement, 38 f., 87 ff., 95, 101 f., 151, 161 ff. passim (esp. 174, 176, 185, 188), 193 ff., 200.
Inward Light, 35 ff., 40, 48, 54, 56 ff., 69, 73, 116, 118, 147, 186, 193, 201.

Jaspers, 16 n., 24, 32, 34, 46, 117, 137, 146, 149, 171, 196 n.
Jesus, 39, 48, 50, 53, 68 f., 73 f., 109, 123, 127, 133, 141, 145, 147, 162 ff., 182, 204.
John, Johannine, 13, 34, 51.
John of Leyden, 81.
Jones, C., 49 f., 53, 55.
Jones, R. M., 93, 114.
Judaism, 24 f., 27.
Just War, 73 ff.
Justice and Love, 174 f.
Justin Martyr, 57.

Kant, 158.
Keith, 57.
Kelly, 41.
Kierkegaard, 107, 111, 164 n.
Kingdom of God, 27 ff., 32 f., 41, 42 f., 48 ff., 62, 72 ff., 82 ff., 87 f., 92, 95 f., 103, 109, 135 f., 154 f., 176, 182, 194, 200. The Paradox of the Kingdom, esp. 28 ff., 54.
Koran, 57.

Lambert, 76.
Law, see Commandment, Principle.
Lessing, Th., 23.
Light of Christ, see Inward Light, Christ.

Limitations of Man, 38, 100, 132 f., 135 f., 138, 140, 145 f., 149 f., 152, 155, 185, 189 f., 193, 195 ff.
Lindsey, 174 n.
Line of Least Resistance, 162, 165, 168.
Lonsdale, 105, 162, 191 n.
Loukes, 93.
Loyalty, 177 ff. Conflict of Loyalties, 85 f., 102, 129, 181 f.
Luther, Lutheranism, 79, 81, 145, 158, 174.

Maclear, 73 n., 76, 78, 80.
Marcel, 13.
Marsh, 29.
Martyrdom, 49, 65, 81, 93, 101, 129, 141 f., 162 ff., 169, 171, 202.
Marx, Marxism, 22, 33 n., 68, 187, 196.
Materialism, 14.
Means and Ends, 81, 86, 100 f., 140, 148 f., 157, 162, 165 ff., 178, 184, 187 ff.
Micklem, 163.
Mohammed, Mohammedanism, 24 f., 146.
Monasticism, 36, 37.
Monistic Mysticism, 43 ff., 48.
Moral Ambiguity, 73 ff., 81, 84, 87, 90 ff., 101, 162 ff.
Moralism, 105, 131 ff., 142, 164, 168.
Morality, Double Standard, 79, 102, 140 f., 173 ff., 176, 179.
Mormons, 115.
Motive. Purity of Motive, 156 ff.
Mystic and History, 16, 22, 34, 43, 58, 64, 67, 146.
Mysticism, 22 f., 43 ff., 47 f.

Myth, Mythology, 46 f., 67 ff., 71.

Natural Theology, 38, 116.
Nayler, 110.
Neo-Orthodoxy, 15, 34, 187, 196 f.
Newbigin, 35.
Niebuhr, Reinhold, 19, 28 ff., 68 n., 93, 102, 134, 165, 196.
Niebuhr, Richard, 65 n., 91 n., 122.
Non-Violence, 141, 144, 166. See also War.
Nuttall, 49 n., 74 n.

Oliver, 144.
Omniscience, see Limitations of Man.
Optimism, 132, 135 f., 152, 163, 201.
Original Sin, 28, 135, 161, 197.
Otherwordliness, 25, 34 f., 36 f., 48, 89. See also Quietism.
Overpopulation, 190 f.

Pacifism, Pacifist, see Peace Testimony.
Pain, 107 f.
Pan-en-henism, 43 n.
Pantheism, 43 f., 201.
Pascal, 45.
Patriotism, 85 ff.
Paul, Pauline, 13, 48, 51, 115 f., 122, 129, 164.
Peace of God (mediaeval), 114.
Peace Testimony, 66, 74 ff., 81 ff., 165, 170, 186.
Pearson, 77.
Peculiarity, 49, 65.
Penington, 52, 57, 61, 75.
Penn, 40, 57 f., 69, 81, 83, 91, 95, 118, 127, 143.
Perfection, 93.

Personal and Impersonal Relationships, 171 ff., 176, 178, 181 ff.
Pessimism, 29, 112, 132, 134 f., 152, 193.
Plato, Platonism, 23, 32 f., 57.
Politics, 25, 66, 78, 83, 85. See War, Social Testimonies.
Prayer, 65, 75 n., 105, 147, 182.
Predictability, 101, 132, 137, 143 ff., 150 ff.
Presence, 19, 32 f., 41, 42 f., 51, 55 f., 62, 82, 94 ff., 126, 160, 201 f.
Primitivism, 102, 188.
Principle (law) versus Testimony, 80, 88, 94, 99 ff., 105, 116 ff., 127, 156 ff., 184, 199.
Priority, 170 f., 190.
Promptings, see Guidance.
Prophet, Prophetic, see State.
Providence, 101, 109, 146 ff., 159, 203.
Prudential, see Expediency.
Puritanism, 23, 50, 60, 104, 111, 113 n.

Quaker Business Method, see Unanimity.
Quaker Service, its meaning, 185 ff.
Quakerism, 23, 32, 36, 46-96 passim, 99, 104 ff. passim (esp. 116), 145 f., 148, 166 f., 198.
Quietism, 47, 76, 80, 94, 106, 122.

Ranke, 30.
Raven, 162 f.
Reason, 102, 137. Faith and Reason, 196 ff.
Relativism, see Moral Ambiguity.

Repentive Action, 194.
Representatives, 178 f.
Responsibility (civic), 82, 86 f., 90, 107, 138, 165 f., 174 f., 182, 200.
Responsibility, Response to God, Responsible Action, 87, 100 ff., 107, 122, 125, 131, 143, 148 ff., 156 ff., 161, 165 f., 168 f., 174 ff., 179 f., 182, 185, 190, 194, 197, 199.
Restoration Period, 51, 72, 75 ff., 80.
Results (effects of action), 128 f., 132, 137 ff., 164, 194, 200, 202.
Revelation, 62 ff., 105, 108 f., 111 f., 115 ff., 128, 195, 197, 202. *See* Spiritual Experience.
Riskiness of Action, 101, 149 ff., 193.
Rosenstock-Huessy, 52 n.
Rowntree, 66.
Russell, 197.

Sacramentality of Life, *see* God Through History.
Saintliness, 93, 114, 131, 141, 187, 195, 201. *See* Fruit of the Spirit.
Salvation, 110, 204.
Sartre, 20 n., 111.
Schiller, 139.
Schweitzer, 28, 48, 60, 132, 135 n., 191 n.
Scott, 144 n.
Second Coming of Christ, 28 f., 55 ff., 61 f., 72.
Selfhood, True Self, 20, 44, 47, 69, 100, 102, 119 ff., 142, 147, 151, 154, 157, 160 f., 172, 184 f., 191, 194 ff., 204.
Separation from the World, 35 ff., 50, 65, 67, 76, 78 f., 89 ff.
Sewell, 145.
Shakespeare, 23, 85, 111.
Sharing, 188 ff.
Shaw, 111.
Simplification of Life, *see* Primitivism.
Sin, 105 f., 134 f., 138, 152, 154, 156, 161, 181, 188, 190, 193 ff., 202. See also *Original Sin*.
Situation in Time and World, 38 f., 63, 85 ff., 90, 96, 100 f., 105 ff., 123 ff., 131 ff., 161 ff., 179, 185, 200, 202.
Slavery, 81 f., 85, 92, 95, 159, 166 f.
Smith, A., 92.
Social Morality, 174 f.
Social Testimonies, 73, 81, 92, 95, 109, 186 f.
Society, *see* Group, Personal and Impersonal Relationships.
Socrates, 57, 164.
Solidarity, 109, 177, 182.
Spengler, 22.
Spinoza, 43.
Spiritual Experience, 16, 20, 21, 33, 41, 42 f., 45 f., 51, 68 f., 82, 88, 96, 99, 103, 108, 116 ff., 126, 136 f., 160, 194, 196, 199, 202 ff. *See also* Guidance.
State, Quaker attitude to it, 73 ff., 79, 85 ff., 94 f., 109.
Stevenson, 110.
Story, 118, 127.
Structure of Being, 100 f., 121 ff., 154, 194, 196, 202 ff. *See also* Awareness.
Sturge, 159 f.
Subjectivity (also Inter-sub-

jective), 33, 99, 109, 111, 113, 116, 137, 184, 197.
Success, 81, 84, 88, 100, 129, 137 ff., 146, 157, 159, 194 f., 200, 204.
Suffering Obedience, Suffering Resistance, 76, 78 ff.
Suspense, see Tension.

Temporality, see Historicity.
Tension, as human experience, 13 ff., 20, 21, 31, 34, 38, 41, 42, 49 f., 54, 56, 79 f., 92 ff., 125, 140 f., 150, 156 f., 160 f., 172, 174, 181, 183, 185, 191 f., 194, 202, 205.
Tertullian, 198.
Testimony, Testimonies, 40, 49, 57, 59 f., 63, 65, 74, 80 ff., 88, 90 ff., 94, 99, 105, 117 ff., 193. See also Peace Testimony, Social Testimonies.
That of God, see Inward Light.
Thomas a Kempis, 61, 112, 158.
Tillich, 20 n., 128, 135 n., 146 n., 155, 163 f.
Time, 18 ff., 31 ff., 53 f.
Togetherness, 177.
Tolles, 77 n., 80 n., 89 f., 93, 118 n.
Toynbee, 37.
Traditionalism, 58, 64 ff., 88, 94, 104, 115.
Unanimity, 109 f., 113, 118, 125 f.
Unconditional Action, 150 f.
Universalism, 40, 48 ff., 57 f., 65.
Utilitarianism, see Expediency.
Utopianism, 30, 55 f., 72 ff., 79 f., 82 ff., 109, 135, 142, 152, 154, 158, 176, 187, 200.

Values, spiritual, 99 f., 118 f., 124, 127, 197.
Vane, 77 f.
Villon, 18.

War, Quaker attitude to it, 73 ff., 84 ff., 165, 170, 180 ff.
War on Want, 186, 190 f.
Wealth, 102, 185, 187 ff.
Wheatherhead, 54.
Whitehead, 71.
Wholeness, see Selfhood.
Wilkinson, 118, 127.
Williams, 63 n.
Wood, 57, 61.
Woolman, 36, 92, 94, 144, 202.
World, Worldliness, 25 ff., 34 ff., 72 ff., 89, 183.

Zaehner, 43 n., 45 n., 146 n.
Zarathustra, Zoroastrianism, 25, 27.

For Product Safety Concerns and Information please contact our EU representative GPSR@taylorandfrancis.com
Taylor & Francis Verlag GmbH, Kaufingerstraße 24, 80331 München, Germany

www.ingramcontent.com/pod-product-compliance
Lightning Source LLC
Chambersburg PA
CBHW061445300426
44114CB00014B/1843